SELF-FIDELITY

CASSANDRA GOODMAN

SELF-FIDELITY

HOW BEING TRUE TO YOURSELF UPLIFTS YOUR WORKING LIFE

'The self-examination and awareness that is so deftly encouraged in *Self-Fidelity* leads to the discovery of your true, authentic self. This book provides the keys to unlocking a more engaged and fulfilling life.'

Dr Stuart Brown, Founder, the National Institute for Play

'*Self-Fidelity* guides us through challenges to be true to ourselves. Cassandra does not claim that the journey will be easy, but if we are prepared to do the work – our efforts will be rewarded. You will get to live in your own skin very comfortably. If you choose one book this year – choose one for yourself, that may well be *Self-Fidelity*.'

Naomi Simson, Founder, RedBalloon

'*Self-Fidelity* is a must read for anyone seeking to not only succeed, but also to thrive.'

Professor Alex Christou, Managing Director, Thrive Global Asia Pacific

'This is the book I'd been waiting for! Cassandra delivers a timely and insightful guide for navigating modern working life that is affirming and uplifting, yet also practical and grounded. 'Know thyself' said the ancients. *Self-Fidelity* guides us to a place where we might just love thyself. Find the courage to read this book; you will not regret it.'

Richard Miller, Chief Executive, The Ethical Money Company

'While the world drowns in a sea of self-help and professional development books, *Self-Fidelity* leaps out as something profound, fresh, and fundamental. Cassandra provides an outstanding set of compass points to help you find your own unique ways of thriving in a challenging world.'

Audrey McGibbon, Psychologist, Wellbeing Researcher and author of the GLWS

'*Self-Fidelity* invites us on a pilgrimage to be true to ourselves and to not only develop an authentic relationship with our work – but also to cultivate a secure and meaningful relationship with ourselves. This book is a wonderful life resource.'

Dr Carrie Hayward, Clinical Psychologist, author of the Being Human series

'True organisational transformation only becomes possible when leaders find the courage to embark on the work of personal transformation. Learning how to be our genuine, true selves at work is not just helpful – it's essential. *Self-Fidelity* supports both individual and team resilience, performance and transformation. This book is a must-read for all business leaders.'

Mark Cameron, Chief Executive, W3.Digital

'A beautiful read, inspiring the unshackling bravery to be true to one's self. *Self-Fidelity* is the perfect marriage of waking up to yourself, and faithfulness to your truth, to enable your full potential.'

Karen Davies, Global Executive Director Digital Strategy & Innovation, Microsoft

'*Self-Fidelity* offers a raw and powerful insight on how to get out of your own way – to overcome all that is within you that is innately holding you back. Read this book – and break out of your own artificial mould.'

Adam Jadresic, Environmental Health & Safety Lead, GSK

'*Self-Fidelity* grants permission to show up at work in a different way – what a relief! This book is an important contribution to future ways of working offering a whole new way of perceiving work – and ourselves.'

Penny Rush, Diversity & Inclusion Manager, Aurecon

'*Self-Fidelity* is an incredible guide to help you experience the world differently. It has opened up my mind to live beyond who I "should" be towards authoring my own unique story of success. Cassandra's knowledge, experience and care can be felt on every page. This is a book you will not be able to put down.'

Tu Tihirahi, Portfolio Change Manager, NAB and Performance Coach

'As the business world struggles to balance automation with humanity, *Self-Fidelity* show us that by being true to our essential nature, we can uplift ourselves, those around us, and the systems we are a part of. *Self-Fidelity* is a guidebook to becoming a better boss, co-worker, friend, spouse, and parent. It has helped me to become the best version of myself – for those I lead and for those I love.'

Dylan Whitehead, CEO, Alloy Claims Inc

'Cassandra's power comes from her extensive real-world leadership experience, the depth and breadth of her toolkit, and her refusal to be bound by the dogma of any one discipline. *Self-Fidelity* is a comprehensive and profound guide towards living and maintaining an authentic life.'

Bill Sheffield, Chief People Officer, Westfund

'This book is a masterpiece in remembering who we really are and why we really do what we do. *Self-Fidelity* opens the door to play into your freedom and bring forth the essence of your potential.'

Marianne Walker, Group Executive Experience, Australian super fund

'*Self-Fidelity* gave me the permission, tools and confidence to continue living whole-heartedly. A must read for anyone that aspires to authentically show up as their best self.'

Lucy Broadbent, Senior Manager, RACV

'*Self-Fidelity* is the purest form of high performance and Cassandra's knowledge on the topic shines in this book. It is beautifully articulated and supported by wonderful personal stories that bring vibrance and warmth to this important topic.'

Mark Dobson, High Performance Specialist

'*Self-Fidelity* beautifully expresses what it means to embrace both work and life, both head and heart. This book is the perfect guide for anyone who is questioning the status quo.'

Ariane Taylor, Director, Evergreen Careers

'*Self-Fidelity* is not just a book – it is a life-cleanse! Cassandra is a master at creating and holding a space that is free of ego, striving or hustle. Her book invites you into this space to discover your best self.'

Jasmine Malki, Head of People and Development, Grattan Institute

'A professional life being true to ourselves is a right belonging to all of us. *Self-Fidelity* paves this path with a clear process of enablement. I only wish I'd had this book years ago!'

Peta Sitcheff, Sales Leader & Coach

'As soon as I finished reading *Self-Fidelity*, I found myself going back to the start to read it all over again! *Self-Fidelity* is a fantastic guide-book on how to engage your team and most importantly yourself at work.'

Michael Paredes, Head of Corporate Sales & Strategic Partnerships, Grow Finance

'I actually started reading *Self-Fidelity* with a sense of responsibility to my friend – to provide her feedback and support. A few hours later, I was sure this was my new favorite book in the world. This is a book I will buy by the dozen and give to as many people as I can.'

Renata Bernarde, Career Strategist, Job Hunting Expert, & Host of The Job Hunting Podcast.

'*Self-Fidelity* helped me see that I wasn't alone in my experiences at work. Cassandra offers us practical ways to explore growing our own fulfillment to uplift our lives. Immerse yourself in *Self-Fidelity*.'

Cherie Logan, General Manager People, Safety and Performance, EnviroNZ

'*Self-Fidelity* helped me to discover that the keys to unlocking the working life I wanted were inside me all along, waiting patiently for me uncover them.'

Blair Newman, People and Culture Project Lead, Westfund

'*Self-Fidelity* has taken me on a journey of self-awareness, self-understanding and most importantly self-love. It has empowered me to steer my career in the direction of my choosing.'

Pip Macdonald, Client Engagement Manager, Monash University

'*Self-Fidelity* is a book that's time has come.'

Nicky Wilson-Kelly, Continuous Improvement Specialist & Life Designer

ABOUT THE AUTHOR

Cassandra Goodman is guided by an aspiration to generously serve in order to uplift life. Cassandra loves working with courageous pioneers to reimagine work and redefine success. She can be spotted on the streets of Melbourne cruising between lively conversations on her bright red pushbike.

She has three decades of business experience across multiple industries and has held many different senior leadership roles, including Global Director of Employee Experience at a healthcare company where she activated the organisation's purpose 'Longer, Healthier, Happier Lives' for their 86,000 employees across the world.

Cassandra's work is ever-evolving and spans a portfolio of coaching, facilitation, co-creation, writing and speaking.

In addition to growing her own business, Cassandra is a Thrive Global facilitator and executive coach. Thrive Global is an organisation founded and led by Arianna Huffington with the mission to end the global epidemic of stress and burnout. Cassandra is passionate about contributing to this mission.

I respectfully acknowledge the First Nations people of
Country throughout Australia.

I acknowledge the cultural and spiritual connection
that Aboriginal and Torres Strait Islander peoples have
with the land and sea.

I pay my respects to the Traditional Owners
of the land where I live and do most of my work,
the Wurundjeri peoples of the Kulin Nation.

I also pay my respects to all Elders past and present,
as well as existing and emerging leaders.

I dedicate this book to
my two beautiful sons and greatest teachers,
Elliot and Zachary.

To borrow the words attributed to A A Milne,

Promise me you'll always remember:
You're braver than you believe,
and stronger than you seem,
and smarter than you think.[1]

First published in 2020 by Cassandra Goodman

This book uses real-life stories to reinforce and enrich meaning. Names and identifying details have been changed to protect the privacy of individuals.

All inquiries should be made to the author.

self-fidelity.com
cassandragoodman.com

A catalogue entry for this book is available from the National Library of Australia.

ISBN: 978-1-922391-76-6

Printed in Australia by McPherson's Printing
Project management and text design by Michael Hanrahan Publishing
Cover design by Cassandra Goodman

The four-core process image ID: 48281713
Copyright Arbuzu | Dreamstime.com
dreamstime.com/arbuzu_info

The paper this book is printed on is certified as environmentally friendly.

Contents

Put down the weight of your aloneness,
and ease into the conversation.

David Whyte[2]

self-fidelity noun
self-fi.del.i.ty

The practice of being true to one's essential nature

Prologue

I walk into the meeting room that has been booked for my mid-year performance review. This will be my first performance review with my new boss, Megan. Megan is savvy, smart and straight-talking. I'm a few minutes early. I want to make sure I am 'on' and ready to start at exactly 2pm. A large table sits at the centre of the room. I hesitate. Where should I sit? Should I choose a chair next to one of the corners of the table in the hope that Megan might sit next to me? Or should I sit at the head of the table to try to create the impression of confidence? I decide to play it safe and sit down in the middle chair on one of the long sides of the table.

As I arrange my pen and notepad, I suddenly realise how exhausted I am. It is Friday afternoon. I have been in New York all week, thousands of kilometres away from home. The week has been a blur of giving presentations, attending meetings, eating crappy food, drinking too much wine and staring at the ceiling of my tiny hotel room in the wee hours of the morning.

This trip has come off the back of one of my most exhilarating and gruelling career chapters to date. I have recently taken on a new, extremely challenging leadership role. I am not only bone-tired – I am also nervous. The moment I first read the job description for this role, I knew it was the perfect job for me. However, only a few months into the role I am already exhausted. I'm haunted by a feeling that I'm just pretending – at work and at home. Life has a strange surreal quality about it, like I'm having a very long out-of-body experience.

Megan walks in and sits on the chair directly opposite mine on the other side of the table. Almost two metres of table separates us. She does not look happy. Oh-oh. I do my best not to look scared.

Her opening line hits me like a blow to the stomach. 'Cassie, if this was 1980, I would be telling you to put on shoulder pads and red lipstick. You are so small you lack any sort of gravitas.'

Wow. Okay, then. I think this is what they call 'radical candour'. Ouch.

My head spins, but I manage to hold it together for the rest of my performance review, by doing all the right things, asking for specific examples, nodding, pretending to take good notes, thanking her for the feedback. Not crying.

It would have been really easy to tell myself that Megan was just talking about my stature – at five-foot-nothing, I have never been described as an imposing figure. However, I knew she was not referring to my height. She was talking about how I had been showing up. She had been paying attention. Damn it.

When the meeting ends, I noisily wheel my suitcase across the car park and fall into the back of the taxi that has been booked to take me to JFK Airport. I burst into tears. I am pissed. I feel betrayed. I had worked so hard and sacrificed so much – where the hell was my gold star? Later, midway through my second, very generously poured glass of wine in the airport lounge, I admit the truth to myself.

Megan is right. I am small. So much smaller than I want to be.

My agency is being diluted by subtle, all-too-familiar patterns of unhealthy striving and trying to prove myself. I have been lured into chasing a ladder-climbing-at-all-costs version of success that does not actually work for me or my family. I have clambered to one of the highest rungs in my organisation, but I am so petrified of slipping that I have completely lost touch with my sense of lightness and play. My clear-thinking has been clouded by frantic busyness. The 'elephant in the room' conversations I know I need to have remain well-rehearsed but unspoken. I've failed to earn the respect of my peers. I've only been harnessing a narrow sliver of myself at work – and that sliver is completely and utterly depleted.

However, I also realise that Megan is wrong. She is wrong about the shoulder pads and red lipstick.

If I could travel back to 1980 and give myself a good talking to, this is what I would say to the five-year-old version of myself:

The world you are growing up in is a masterclass on how you *should* be. But you don't have to be a good student. You will be very, very tempted to join the hustle and to strive relentlessly to collect gold stars – first in the form of good grades and later in the form of fancy job titles, 'top-talent' accolades and big salary packages. However, clambering your way to the top won't fulfill you. It will never get you anywhere *close* to feeling like you are enough.

Instead, you can learn what it means to be true to yourself in life – and at work.

This will not be easy. The world of work will try to twist your kindness into weakness, and your desire to take care of people into a liability. Your playfulness and sense of humour will be made to feel inappropriate. Those single-mindedly clawing their way to the top will take advantage of your openness to gain personal leverage. Those in power will try to diminish your high ethical standards, labelling you naïve.

You will face many challenges, but keep on practising being you – short, kind, open, caring, playful, idealistic, imperfect and at times inappropriate. Be brave. Learn to trust in the importance of your uniqueness, the truth of your worthiness, and the vastness of your potential.

Do this, and you won't need to wear masks or armour – or red lipstick and shoulder pads. Do this, and your enough-ness is off the table.

...

Many years later, Megan would tell me that she had also been fighting her own secret battle over the period we worked together. She was experiencing a serious health crisis and was 'soldiering on' at work against the advice of her doctors.

That conversation that day in New York took place because two good humans had lost touch with the truth of who they were. We were both striving to fit in and prove ourselves at work, when what we were both yearning for was to be seen and to know that we were enough.

Megan's feedback was incredibly difficult for me to hear. Her powerful words pierced my armour and penetrated my heart, awakening me to my conditioning and the many ways it had diminished me.

It was not until many years later that I realised that this awakening was the greatest gift any leader has ever given me.

We get lost in the weather of our minds.
Yet above the thick cloud, clear sky always awaits.

We get pushed around by constant winds.
Yet we can all learn how to find shelter.

We are held down by an invisible heaviness.
Yet we can gently let go of this burden.

We all contain a powerful lifeforce.
And by learning how to feed it, we are buoyed.

Remembering the truth of who we are,
we lift.

INTRODUCTION

Welcome

Welcome. I'm so grateful you're here.

Our working lives are a pilgrimage of discovery. A pilgrimage that shapes who we are and the way we think and feel about ourselves and all others. A pilgrimage that can illuminate how we might best serve the troubled world we inhabit.

Self-fidelity is an invitation to create an uplifting working life. A working life that honours our humanity and nourishes our hearts, minds, bodies and souls. A working life that supports us to better serve our colleagues, customers, friends and family. A working life that works in harmony with our other big loves and the delicate ecosystems we inhabit. A working life that tumbles and brings forth the brilliant jewels buried deep inside of us.

Together, we will…

Wake up to the reality we find ourselves in

Let be our essential nature as human beings

Let go of the things that weigh us down

Let in the nourishment we need to lift.

We will discover that what we have been desperately seeking has been available to us all along – waiting patiently inside of us.

John Mellencamp sang, 'Oh yeah, life goes on, long after the thrill of living is gone.'[1] So many of us feel we have no choice but to settle for a kind of half-dead existence. But life does not have to be this way. Through the practice of self-fidelity, we can rediscover the thrill of living – through our work. This is what I offer through this book and the community of thrill-seeking pioneers it is bringing together.

WHY DOES THE WORLD NEED ANOTHER BOOK?

Despite the thousands of personal development, self-help and leadership books that exist, we continue to suffer, settle and conform. Research shows that when we don't use our gifts to engage in meaningful work we feel disconnected and suffer from heavy feelings of emptiness, frustration, resentment, disappointment, shame and even grief.[2] Yet, so many of us are still striving to *fit in* at work, when what we truly yearn for is to *be seen*. At a time when we so desperately need to activate and share the very best of ourselves, human potential continues to be overlooked, suppressed or diminished in most workplaces across the world. We acquire the belief that who we are is inconvenient, not enough or somehow broken – or all of the above. As a consequence, so many of us have lost faith in ourselves and each other.

On top of all of that, we are also navigating times of enormous change and opportunity. We find ourselves in the tumultuous winds of a paradigm shift. The dominant 'machine paradigm' of work – one that treats humans as resources to be consumed in organisations designed for the relentless pursuit of value-extraction and profit growth at all costs – is falling away. Alternative paradigms of work are emerging in its stead – paradigms that honour our humanity, uniqueness and connectedness.

This shift brings with it the possibility to rise above stale, narrow conversations about how to 'optimise headcount', increase productivity, and balance work and good-enough human lives. This shift opens a window to fresh conversations about how to inspire heartcount, activate our brilliance and work in a way that honours all life on this planet. As we rise above our legacy of rigid, restricted thinking and limiting assumptions, we can begin to consider a broad spectrum of new perspectives and possibilities. We can reconnect with our essential nature and each other. We can explore the highest aspirations we hold for our one short, exhilarating, working life. This book contributes to this fresh conversation.

There are so many conflicting 'expert' opinions, so many people on social media and in-real-life pretending to have perfect lives. It is easy to feel overwhelmed, inadequate and disheartened by the reality of our own working lives. It can sometimes feel like these other people are floating way up high in the sky in their fancy hot air balloons calling down to us, 'Come on up – the view is amazing!' Yet we remain stuck on the ground, looking up at them, feeling helpless and exasperated. I have written this book as a fellow pioneer and have endeavoured to make it *honest*, *real* and *practical*.

This book will support us to reconnect with our essential nature and lift ourselves and others up. Self-fidelity restores our faith in ourselves – and each other.

What is self-fidelity?

This above all:
to thine own self be true.

William Shakespeare[1]

It took me many years to locate a term that accurately encapsulated the essence, the core aspiration I hold for my own working life and the work I do to serve others. After much searching and reflection, I have come to the realisation that what I practise and share with the world is self-fidelity.

The word fidelity is derived from the Latin word *fidēlis*, meaning faithful. Self-fidelity is essentially *being faithful to one's self.*

The term self-fidelity appears in the interpretation of the work of Albert Schweitzer, the French-German writer, humanitarian and philosopher. Albert's quest was to discover a universal ethical philosophy as a means to raise human development 'to its highest value and offer it to the world'.[2] In 1952 Albert was awarded the Nobel Peace Prize for his philosophy, *Reverence for Life.*

In his interpretation of *Reverence for Life*, Mike W Martin wrote:

> *Self-fidelity – being true to ourselves – implies commitment to self-realization, to 'the completest possible development' of our faculties by exercising 'the widest possible freedom'.*[3]

I define self-fidelity as:

> *the practice of being true to one's essential nature.*

I use the term 'essential nature' in my working definition of self-fidelity to describe the shared aspects of our humanity that are both irrefutable and good. Our essential nature concentrates into a one-of-a-kind blend in each of us – this is our essence. Our essential nature is shared, yet its expression through each of us is as unique as our fingerprints. If our essential nature is water, our essence is a single gloriously unique snowflake. We will explore the concepts of our essential nature and our essence in more detail in the *Foundations* section.

In this book, I have chosen to focus on five truths of our essential nature that are often forgotten in the context of our work. These five truths are:

We are all worthy

We are all vulnerable

We are all caring

We are all creative

We are all playful

This is in no way a complete catalogue of all the aspects of our essential nature, but rather the aspects that we could all greatly benefit from honouring – especially while we are working.

Suppressing our essential nature is like trying to hold a beachball underwater – it's wobbly and exhausting. As the pressure builds, the suppressed parts of ourselves can make surprise appearances in ways that are exaggerated, unhelpful and sometimes hurtful. Over time, we can become sick and jaded.

WHOLEHEARTEDLY INHABITING OUR ESSENTIAL NATURE

Self-fidelity is a faithfulness not only to the vibrant expression of our essential nature but also to its wholehearted inhabitation. It is about the expansion of our working lives to allow space for all we have the potential to become. It's a rejection of the belief that we need to change who we are to succeed at work. Instead, self-fidelity is based on an understanding that vitality and success flow from freeing ourselves to be who we are and honouring the aspirations we hold deep in our hearts. Self-fidelity emboldens us to activate the true potential that exists within each of us, activating our true collective potential.

We are the only creatures on this planet that suffer from a learnt tendency to deny the essence of our being-ness. Humans are really good at learning how to deny our human-ness. Many of us lock ourselves into artificially lit concrete and metal structures every day to do our work. Within those structures we sit in small cubicles and further deny our human-ness by treating ourselves and each other like robots. Over time, we forget the essence of our own humanity – as it exists in its natural state. When we think about it, it's all a little bit nutso. When we deny our human-ness we deny ourselves the thrill of living. The root of the word 'health' is wholeness. Denying any part of ourselves while we work is corrosive to our vitality.

Self-fidelity is a practice of remembrance and reconnection. It's a refusal to internalise the machine paradigm by remembering that we are unique, interconnected, vital, vulnerable beings – not resource pools of interchangeable, controllable, separate components to be optimised, re-arranged and depleted. Being true to ourselves is about understanding the value of our uniqueness and being wide-awake to the dangers of fitting in. It is the decision not to disown the aspects of ourselves that are deemed to be 'inconvenient' by the 'system'. Joseph Campbell said, 'The privilege of a lifetime is being who you are.'[4] Self-fidelity supports us to exercise this basic privilege through a focused, powerful practice.

Self-fidelity is not simply the desire to live our #bestlife. Authenticity is part of self-fidelity, but it is not the full story. This book does not espouse what psychologists would call *magical thinking* – a belief that somehow we can cure our suffering through the magical protection bestowed on us on account of our special knowledge or attitude. Self-fidelity is not about the accumulation of more knowledge. It is not purely cognitive. It emerges through committed, regular play and practice. It is a heightened way of being.

Self-fidelity is also a form of freedom. For me, freedom in this context means gratefully exercising the right I have the good fortune to be able to exercise in my privileged life. The right to experience a dynamic, uplifting working life that gives back in meaningful ways. Freedom is rising above the restrictions of narrow roles and limiting assumptions to explore the broad spectrum of opportunities that emerge from an awareness of my essential nature and the highest aspirations I hold for my one short, precious working life.

Self-fidelity is the opposite of self-betrayal. Self-betrayal undermines our vitality, our sanity and our relationships. Betraying ourselves at work can begin to feel like a cheese-grater on our soul. There have been times in my working life when I have experienced this. I know how it can drain the energy and joy from of all facets of our lives, lead us to numb ourselves, close our hearts and turn away from the people we care about the most.

HONOURING OUR INTERCONNECTEDNESS

Self-fidelity is not the narrowly focused pursuit of our own individual needs. At the heart of the practice of self-fidelity lies the acceptance that the ethical embodiment of our potential is inextricably intertwined with the desire of others to do the same. This acceptance stems from an understanding of our interconnectedness and the awareness that our actions create a ripple effect of both intended and unintended consequences. This is essentially about cultivating a new mindset and understanding that organisations are complex, dynamic systems that connect groups of complex, dynamic human systems nested within fragile, complex communities and ecosystems.

This sort of mindset – known as a Benefit Mindset – is an evolution of Carol Dweck's 'Growth Mindset'[5] and is being pioneered by Ash Buchanan. Growth Mindset is primarily concerned with learning, achievement and improvement, Benefit Mindset focuses on how we can 'recognise our interdependence, turn towards our individual and collective shadows, and realise our unique potential in a way that serves the wellbeing of all'.[6] We will cover Benefit Mindset in more detail in the *Foundations* section.

HONOURING OURSELVES

The central metaphor of this book – the hot air balloon that naturally wants to rise – was inspired by Michael A Singer's book *The Untethered Soul*.[7] The practice of self-fidelity invites us to rediscover ourselves and to remember over and over again that everything we need is already inside of us, that our main task is to let go of the things that weigh us down. The practice of self-fidelity continuously rekindles, celebrates and honours a commitment to our most important and only truly enduring relationship – the relationship we have with ourselves.

If there was a vow of self-fidelity, it would go something like this:

I promise to love and honour myself
in good times and in bad,
for better and for worse,
for richer or poorer.

I promise to trust in my worthiness,
understand the brilliance of my uniqueness,
keep my heart open,
and give my creativity space
with lightness and play.

I promise to serve with love,
nourish my vitality
and allow myself to rest.

But above all else,
I promise to keep remembering all of this
every time I forget.

As we cultivate a deep sense of faithfulness to our essential nature, we restore our faith in all of humanity.

Elements of the practice

> Work is not a static endpoint or a mere exercise in providing, but a journey and a pilgrimage in which the core elements of our being are tested in the world.
>
> David Whyte[1]

We all love the idea of a quick fix and there are plenty of books that will promise one. The truth is however, that there are not 'ten easy-to-follow steps' when it comes to the work of being true to ourselves. There is no one key that 'unlocks us' because we are not fixed mechanisms with pre-fabricated components. Self-fidelity is a pilgrimage of discovery. There are no clear pathways to follow, because we are exploring uncharted territory. The practice requires us to venture beyond our current boundaries, illuminating each next best action as we go. Our next best action cannot be predetermined or pre-planned – it will reveal itself as we move forward and sense, learn and respond to what we encounter. Our pilgrimage will require us to be in continuous conversation with the elements and guiding stars. Things might be a little bumpy at times, but the further we go, the more self-trust we build, and the more exhilarating things become.

Self-Fidelity blends findings from the latest science and research with the wisdom of contemplative traditions. It also draws on the biggest lessons gleaned from my experience of working within dozens of small, medium and large organisations activating, understanding, protecting and salvaging my uniqueness and my potential. All of the ideas, practices and reflection tools share the same aspiration – to assist us to illuminate our next best step in our own unique pilgrimage. My invitation is to play around with these concepts, adapt them and make them our own.

FAITH

> Faith is a place of mystery, where one can find the courage to believe in what we cannot see and the strength to let go of our fear of uncertainty.
>
> Brené Brown[2]

Having faith sits at the core of how I define self-fidelity.

Cultivating self-love is essential to experiencing love. Cultivating self-respect is essential to feeling respected. Cultivating self-fidelity is essential to having faith. As we cultivate a deep sense of faithfulness to our essential nature, we restore our faith in all of humanity.

I love how Brené Brown defines faith, based on her research into people who are living wholeheartedly, as a source of 'strength to let go of our fear of uncertainty'. Rekindling our faith in ourselves and in the goodness of others is a tremendous source of strength and courage.

WAKING UP, LETTING BE, LETTING GO AND LETTING IN

Our self-fidelity practice involves a continuous flow of waking up, letting be, letting go and letting in. We will learn how to **wake up** to our inner and outer reality. We will learn how to **let be** our essential nature and trust that everything we need is inside of us. We will learn how to **let go** of the things that weigh us down. Finally, we will learn how to **let in** the nourishment and strength we need to keep moving onwards and upwards.

We can think of these four continual and intertwined practices as an ongoing learning loop. The core practices – waking up, letting be, letting go and letting in – combine to create a powerful adaptive cycle that is the practice of being true to ourselves at work – and in life.

Self-fidelity: The Four Core Practices

The challenges we are navigating

This is the current evolutionary challenge
that most people don't yet grasp:
the desired outer changes cannot come about
without the inner change.

Scilla Elworthy[1]

This book has been created to address three core challenges that are being experienced by so many of us.

CHALLENGE #1

Our current ways of working are making us sick, sad and lonely

The world conditions us to conform, comply and compete. Our individuality is often an inconvenience to the systems we work within. We believe that fitting in is more important than being ourselves. We chase a flawed model of success – one based on status and money – and rob ourselves of true happiness. We are terrified of losing jobs we don't really like for reasons we can't fully explain. We struggle with feelings of frustration and sadness. We precariously hold it together at work, but lose it with the people we love the most. We act like petulant five-year-olds. Deep down, we just feel so lonely. True prosperity continues to elude us – because we are just aiming to survive. At a time when care, courage and creativity are so desperately needed, we fail to see that all of these qualities – and more – already exist inside of us.

CHALLENGE #2
Our current coping strategies are making things worse

In order to survive and function, we numb ourselves with over-working, busyness, wine, food, social media, shopping and Netflix. We work hard to fit in, to prove ourselves, and hustle for our worthiness, enough-ness and belonging. None of these strategies work. Over time we feel more and more overwhelmed. More and more alone. We no longer trust ourselves. We begin to lose faith in ourselves and in others. Turning away from life becomes our default. Work begins to feel like an out-of-body experience. The people we love the most bear the brunt of our pain. Our ways of working are not working for us, our families, our organisations or our planet. We grossly underestimate the full cost of maintaining our status-quo. Over time, our dis-ease at work morphs into ill health.

CHALLENGE #3
We can't help ourselves until we wake up

Because of our conditioning, we are blind to the reality that while we remain out of touch with our essential nature, and our thinking remains anchored to a redundant paradigm and the associated limiting beliefs, no amount of hard work will help us. We must wake up to see clearly. With this new awareness, we can reconnect to our essential nature and break free from the things that weigh us down. We restore faith in ourselves and others and begin to understand that the gifts we each have to offer the world flow from our uniqueness, not from our compliance. We see new possibilities to redefine success, to experience true belonging and prosperity. We awaken to the truth that the things we yearn for require us to *be* who we are, not *change* who we are.

Johann Hari's ground-breaking research identified a range of disconnections that form the underlying causes of depression. In his words 'they are all ways in which we have been cut off from something we innately need but seem to have lost along the way'.[2] In the book *Lost Connections* Johann explores the implications of our disconnection from meaningful work, meaningful values, nature, a secure future and status and respect. All of these lost connections are lurking causes of poor mental and physical health. I believe that disconnection from our essential nature is another form of disconnection that is slowly but surely draining our life force.

This book is a catalyst for awakening and reconnection. We will play with a diverse and powerful collection of practices. We can all begin to take inspired, empowered action today. We don't need to seek someone else's permission or wait until we are more qualified or experienced. We don't have to hope for mere chance to somehow change the story of our working lives.

Beneath all the layers of conditioning, under the masks and armour, we all want the same things. We want to understand and harness our potential. We want to live and work in a way that honours the truth of who we are. We want to be part of something bigger than ourselves. We want to feel seen, *really* seen.

Being true to our essential nature supports the emergence of true prosperity, for ourselves, our loved ones, our colleagues, as well as the organisations and ecosystems to which we belong.

Why I care so deeply

There are tremendous forces at work upon us,
trying to make us like everyone else,
and therefore we must remember something intensely personal
about the way we were made for this world
in order to keep our integrity.

David Whyte[1]

I care deeply about the emergence of more uplifting ways of working because our current ways of working have hurt and diminished me, and so many of the people I care about.

I grew up in a home that existed under the ever-present storm clouds of work-related stress. My father's experiences of work and the suffering those experiences created for him had a big impact on me as a child. I can still vividly recall the feeling of dread that would clench my little stomach in the evenings when our hallway home phone would ring three times – the signal that my dad's train had arrived from the city and he was at the local train station waiting for Mum to pick him up in the car. I could not fathom the traumas Dad carried in his weary soul when he walked through our front door every night, briefcase in hand, nor could I take away his suffering. But I knew for sure that it was not right.

Right from the very start of my working life, work also began to shape me. I landed my first ever job as a 'cake shop girl' at a small local bakery when I was 15. The first thing I learnt at the start of my first shift was that I was inconvenient – or more specifically, my name was inconvenient. I had not even finished tying on my apron when the bakery manager Mrs Donaldson (a matronly, no-nonsense woman in her 50s) matter-of-factly informed me that my name would be changed to Sandy because there was already another cake shop girl called Cassie. It was very clear that I did not have any say in this decision – nor about my allocated new name. I remember feeling slightly upset by the unexpected realisation that my much-anticipated enrolment into the world of work required me to change my name. But, without even a hint of quibble, I diligently complied. And so, my sometimes bewildering, often secretly disappointing, exhilarating and ever-shaping pilgrimage of work began.

Later, when I was 21, I contributed this quote to my university graduation yearbook:

> *Do what you love and love what you do, and you'll never work a day in your life.*

At the time, I had no real understanding of the sorts of challenges I would face at work. I have since discovered that the secret to true success is not to love what we do, but to love who we are *being* while we do it. An even more important discovery is that it's impossible to love who we are being at work when we are not *being ourselves.*

I have spent three decades working for dozens of organisations ranging from that small family-run cake shop to multinational behemoths. I have held dozens of different leadership roles, progressing from looking after a small team of cake shop girls to being responsible for improving the health and happiness of an 86,000-person global workforce. Today I have a deep appreciation of the reality of working life and the perils of trying to reach a mirage – the shimmering, ever-elusive version of 'happiness and success' based on amassing more money, more status and more gold stars.

My life to date has also been a quest of self-discovery. I have chanted in incense-filled ashrams, done yoga headstands at dawn, skydived, bungee-jumped, karate-chopped through thick wooden planks, completed marathons and triathlons. I have attended dazzling no-expense-spared leadership development events in Dubai, Prague,

London, Barcelona, Arizona, Hong Kong, Cape Cod, Melbourne and Sydney. I have had the privilege of soaking in the radiance of many gifted speakers and teachers at live events, including the Dalai Lama, Malala Yousafzai, Dr Brené Brown, Sir Richard Branson, Ellen Langer, Simon Sinek, Dr Kristin Neff, Martin Seligman, Johann Hari, Susan David and Marcus Buckingham. I have completed in-person training with great teachers including Dr Stuart Brown, Dr Rick Hanson and Tal Ben-Shahar. I have completed extensive training in mindfulness, positive neuroplasticity, design thinking, lean thinking, six sigma, systems thinking, and neuro-linguistics. In addition to the support I have received from mainstream psychologists and psychotherapists, I have also spent many hours in many small rooms being counselled, coached, guided, mentored. I have experienced many forms of healing, including reiki, art therapy, dance therapy, singing therapy and hypno-therapy. Along the way, I have navigated multiple real-life challenges including international and interstate relocations, huge mortgages, domestic violence, workplace bullying, toxic workplaces and the raising of a young family.

To say it has been an exhilarating ride would be an understatement.

Throughout it all, my zest for work and for life has continued to burn. There has not been a single working day when I have not experienced feelings of anticipation upon firing up my computer, checking my calendar and email and discovering what the working day has in store for me. Sure, there have been days when the feeling was more one of nervous anticipation than one of excited anticipation, but I can honestly say that I have never, ever lost touch with my sense of anticipation and adventure.

To give myself the space I needed to create *Self-Fidelity* and serve the community it is bringing together, in late 2018 I made the decision to step away from a full-time job. At the time of writing, I work for several different organisations, including Thrive Global as an activator, co-creator, coach and facilitator.

WHY I WROTE *SELF-FIDELITY*

Toni Morrison said, 'I only wrote the first book because I thought it wasn't there, and I wanted to read it when I got through.'[2] In many ways I also created this, my first book, for myself. This book represents my most powerful learnings I have collected over my pilgrimage to date. The form of a book offered me the perfect constraint to distil and make sense of what I understand to be important and true. I really wanted to own this book, to hold it in my hands, to keep it on my bedside table to bring me back to what is true, to what is important. Even after doing this work for so many years, I often find myself forgetting.

I have no doubt that when I read this book in years to come, my understanding of what it means to be true to ourselves at work will have evolved. I would be disappointed if it doesn't. This is the shadow-side of a Growth Mindset. The awareness that I am always getting better at understanding and practising self-fidelity could have easily prevented me from writing this book. I have chosen not to allow this shadow to stop me from sharing what I understand to be true right now – at the age of 45. The voices in my head often tried to convince me that I didn't know enough and that I wasn't committed enough to my own self-fidelity practice to put these ideas out into the world. Sometimes I have been able to gently tell them to hush – other times they have stopped my writing for weeks on end. We can all continue to practise, and discover within ourselves the next level of understanding and presence *and* we can serve just as we are now, with whatever we can share in this moment.

I have also reminded myself on many occasions that we don't need another 'expert opinion'. We need to know that we are not alone in our experiences at work. We need to know that the struggle is real and that we are not crazy. We need to hear stories from people we can relate to. We need to get clear on the most powerful practices we can embed in our daily working lives to reduce our suffering and experience greater meaning, fulfillment and peace.

On the days when the voices in my head were particularly loud, I would visualise myself at age 85, finally granting myself permission to share my voice with the world. I would imagine myself dictating my long-awaited book from my recliner chair, my crooked, arthritic fingers having lost the ability to type. My opening line would be: 'Okay, listen up world – I've got something I want to say!'

How to use this book

Your lifelong task is to grow, deepen, and evolve yourself as a member of this living world... We all need a practice to recall to ourselves, moment to moment, and remind us of the person we want to be.

Carol Sanford[1]

I do not like to think of myself as an expert on any of the concepts I share in this book. Please consider me as a fellow pioneer whose struggle and liberation is bound up with my readers. This book serves as our guidebook.

Many of the practices we will learn about (or be reminded of) are simple yet powerful. Of course, simple truths are not necessarily easy to embody. While we may intellectually understand many of the practices and ideas that support self-fidelity, converting this intellectual understanding to a deep knowing and a day-to-day embodiment requires dedicated practice. Putting the ideas in this book into practice is vital because this is what converts understanding into deep knowing. I recommend using a dedicated journal to capture the questions, insights, outsights and understandings that emerge as we play with the practices I offer in this book.

I have tested, evolved, adapted and synthesised all the practices through my real-world working life and my real-life struggles. I am wholeheartedly convinced of their power in my own working life. But of course, I am not you. Only you can figure out what is helpful and relevant to you, at this time. I ask that you do not blindly adopt any of the practices I offer you in *Self-Fidelity*. And, I ask that you don't blindly reject any of them. Dig deep with an open heart and mind. Sometimes we resist what we need the most and feelings of discomfort may be a signal that this is something you may benefit from further exploring. I invite you to play around with the practices and provocations I offer, to test their helpfulness and relevance for you. Figure out for yourself if and how they might serve you during these times of tremendous change, challenge and opportunity. Use your creativity to discover new and better ways to cultivate self-fidelity – make the practices your own.

The practices of self-fidelity are an invitation to explore vast territory. I have designed the book in a way that creates a sense of spaciousness and dwelling time. We can avoid feeling overwhelmed by pacing ourselves and following the recommendations I share. The last thing we want is for the vital work of being true to ourselves at work to be dumped into the too-hard basket.

Prepare for our pilgrimage by getting an overview of the potential experiences that await you. We can get this overview by reading the book once all the way through from start to finish. This will provide us with a high-level map of the territory. From there, I suggest that we go back and take another look at the *Foundations* section of the book. As the title of this section suggests, getting a firm grasp of these foundational elements will help to set us up for success. We can then build on these strong foundations by really taking our time with the *Waking up* section and playing around with the practices and burning questions included in this section. Becoming familiar with what it means to wake up and having some firsthand experiences of reconnecting with our essential nature takes us across the threshold of self-fidelity.

Once across this threshold, the full possibilities of Letting be, Letting go and Letting in will begin to lift you up. Once you are on your way, and have a sense of momentum, you can begin to play in a less structured way. You can dip in and out of the practices of Letting be, Letting go and Letting in and call on them as you need, in a just-in-time way.

At the end of each of the main sections of the book, I provide a short summary, detailed prompts to take action and 'burning questions' to ignite new perspectives. I love how David Whyte describes poetry – 'language against which we have no defences'.[2] Throughout the book I will also offer morsels of poetry to contemplate. I have included poems that have touched my heart and have caused me to experience insight, awakening and uplift.

Given the very real headwinds and high-pressure systems that exist, progress can be slow at times. The systems in which we work are prone to self-protection and inertia. As we restore our faith in our essential nature, we will encounter tension, pushing and pulling. Even within ourselves we may experience tension between a yearning to experience change and a desire for things to stay the same. We may take one step forwards and two steps back and there will be moments when we feel like hanging up our dancing shoes for good. No matter how slow our progress, we can remain oriented towards our highest aspirations and continue to move forward, course-correcting and taking shelter when needed and resting often.

Our aspirations serve as our guiding stars. And, just like the stars in the sky, our aspirations may not always be in sight during our daylight struggles at work. I recommend creating a new evening ritual of dedicating a few quiet moments at the end of each working day to lift our sights to recalibrate with our guiding aspirations. In these vulnerable moments as the sun sets on another day of work, our stars become clear once again. And as we prepare to rest and rejuvenate, we can orient ourselves once again and resolve to course-correct as needed when the sun rises on the working day ahead of us.

In *Untamed*, Glennon Doyle shares her motto – 'life is hard, but we can do hard things'.[3] At times, the practice of self-fidelity may feel hard. This is to be expected, because we will be playing outside the boundaries of our comfort zone, where personal growth happens. Please never forget – self-betrayal is also really hard and really painful. However, unlike self-betrayal, self-fidelity is 'the right sort of hard' – it is the discomfort of becoming. After getting to the other side of the 'right kind of hard' we say to ourselves: *Wow. That was really hard. But, gosh was it worth it.* Above all else – we must remember to be kind to ourselves, ask for help when we need it and stay playful.

There have been moments in my journey of personal development when I have felt I lifted the lid on a deep, festering can of worms. My desire to put the lid back on and shove the entire disgusting matter into a small, locked cupboard in the back of my consciousness has been at times very, very strong. When I have found the support and courage to open those cans of worms and clean out the stinky muck, it has been so very worth it.

While this book is informed by the latest research, my understanding of what it means to be true to ourselves at work has been primarily enriched by philosophy, poetry and the contemplative traditions. David Whyte once said in an interview, 'I always felt that scientific language wasn't precise enough… Science, rightly, is always trying to remove the "I" but I was really interested in the way the "I" deepened the more you paid attention.'[4] I also feel that even the best research can only illuminate the smallest patches of our human experience.

We know that not everything that matters can be measured. Yet in the workplace, it is easy to forget this important truth. We become hardened, closed and sceptical. We are quick to attack even the faintest whiff of 'woo-woo'. We will get more out of this book if we choose to suspend any conditioned scepticism – even if just for a few breaths.

My hope is that my readers find this book to be both comforting and challenging in equal measure. As we illuminate and navigate our way towards greater fulfillment, meaning and freedom at work, more than anything, I hope we will learn that we are never alone.

Supporting ourselves

The world doesn't change one person at a time.
It changes when networks of relationships form
among people who share a common cause
and vision of what's possible.

Margaret Wheatley[1]

The practice of being true to our essential nature is not an individualistic pursuit. We don't have to – nor should we – go it alone. *Self-Fidelity* is not just a book – it is an invitation to shape the conversation about how we work in ways that enable the best in us.

One way we can do this is by visiting **self-fidelity.com** where there is a whole bunch of helpful, growing resources including real-life stories from fellow pioneers, articles from me, additional reading and resource recommendations and information about how to be part of a much deeper conversation.

STAYING WELL

Finally, it would be irresponsible for me not to mention that some of the concepts I will share in *Self-Fidelity* may cause feelings of disorientation. The process of exploring the beliefs associated with our current paradigm may challenge the core of our conditioned identity. It's okay to feel overwhelmed. Also, some of the breathing practices I share are not for everyone, and in some cases, may be triggering, especially if you have trauma in your past. If any of the suggested practices really do not feel right – please don't do them.

This book is not a substitute for professional support and I implore my readers to talk to someone should we even suspect we need help. I know for sure I would not be where I am today without getting the help I needed over the years from psychologists, psychotherapists, counsellors and coaches.

FOUNDATIONS

May you have a strong foundation
when the winds of change shift.

Bob Dylan[1]

Understanding our essential nature

Don't ask what the world needs.
Ask what makes you come alive, and go do it.
Because what the world needs is people who have come alive.

Howard Thurman[1]

In the Indian spiritual tradition, everyone has a dharma – an essential way of being in the world that exists in harmony with the dharma of nonviolence that applies to all forms of life. A person's swadharma (swa meaning own, and dharma) is their own unique way of being in the world – a set of capacities that when fully developed allows us to take our place in the world. It is believed that dharma is that which holds the mind, intellect, memory and our inner soul together in harmony and that our growth comes from following our swadharma. The Bhagavad Gita describes the discovery of our swadharma and its use in the spirit of service as the goal of human life. In his translation of the Bhagavad Gita, Eknath Easwaran reminds us, 'we are not cabin dwellers, born to a life cramped and confined; we are meant to explore, to seek, to push the limits of our potential as human beings'.[2]

Our essential nature is the language I will use to describe that which is shared and good in all of us – our natural, innate warmth and goodness. At the heart of our essential nature is our essence – our own unique way of being.

Like our essential nature, our unique essence is a way of being – a way of being that makes us uniquely us. When we are working from

When we are working from our essence, the work we do cannot be replicated and we feel uplifted and alive.

our essence, the work we do cannot be replicated and we feel uplifted and alive. When we connect with our essence and live into it while working, it can transform our experiences of work. It becomes possible to do our best work while nourishing our vitality. By aligning our essence with the aspirations of the organisation we work within, it becomes possible to serve in ways that are unique, energising and powerful. Here is how Carol Sanford describes essence – why it is important and how we can lose touch with it:

> *Essence is what makes every living system and being unique and it is THE source for ongoing and life-giving creativity in your life. When we lose sight of it, we can more easily feel lost in who we are and what we are doing with our lives … When people are persuaded to conform, their essences are overtaken by personality traits, and the characters they play take center stage, nudging out their true selves. In order to develop the capability to recognize and engage with essence – our own and others' – we must hold it in mind and pursue its living expression in all of our efforts.*[3]

Self-fidelity is the practice of being *aware of* and *faithful to* our shared essential nature, which encapsulates our unique essence. When we are connected to our essential nature, we feel at home within ourselves – and when we feel at home within ourselves it becomes possible to feel at home anywhere.

It is very easy to tie ourselves in knots trying to discern which of the voices in our head is the 'real us' – which one represents our essential nature. Like a dog running in frantic circles trying to catch its own tail, trying to catch a glimpse of the 'real us' by listening to the voices in our head is dizzying and futile. The 'real us' is not represented by any of the voices in our head. Our essential nature transcends all these voices. It is the vast, sky-like presence that these voices so often cloud. Our essential nature is something we *feel* – not think about. We will learn how to lift above the clouds and get to know our true nature in the *Waking Up* section of this book.

My essence is a blend of being a change activator and being full of zest – which I experience as a combination of courage, agency and vitality. To begin to get a sense for our essence, we must ask ourselves:

Who am I when I am *being most myself?*

The answer to this question will become much clearer through the practice of self-fidelity.

Connecting to our essential nature

Reconnection is a possibility that lives with us
as long as we live.

Gabor Maté[1]

Self-fidelity is not something we can ever permanently 'achieve' – it is a moment by moment practice. It's an ongoing cycle of remembrance and reconnection. The practice of being true to ourselves invites us to continuously remember who we really are and to keep connecting back into that truth. Over time, this process of reconnection becomes easier.

When we are connected with our essential nature, we are unconstrained and our potential is vast. We are able to see clearly and we are present. When we are *not* connected to our essential nature we are constrained and heavy. Our perspective is narrow and clouded and our potential is limited.

So, what does it means to be connected to our essential nature? On the next page I offer my understanding of the experience of being connected to the truth of who we are. Don't worry if it does not make complete sense just yet. It will become much clearer as we move through the book and we begin our practice.

When we are connected with our essential nature

We are present.

We have the capacity to respond to the world around us, rather than react to it.

Our thinking is spacious, clear and inspired.

Our self-worth is not in question.

Our hearts are open yet discerning.

We are inhabiting our vulnerability.

We can work in ways that are creative and playful.

We are open to alternative perspectives.

Life is vivid.

Our potential is vast.

Redefining work and success

Success is liking yourself, liking what you do,
and liking how you do it.

Maya Angelou[1]

Work is a necessity for most of us; however, even when our livelihood and our current lifestyle depends on our salary, work is about so much more than money. What new possibilities might emerge if instead of seeing work as a means to earn a living, we came to see our work as an opportunity to serve and to experience the thrill of living?

Research suggests that experiencing more meaning from our work, instead of feeling like we are 'just doing a job to pay the bills' largely comes down to changing our perspective.[2] We all have the opportunity to be more intentional about how we think about work and how we define success. The nature of work is changing rapidly, offering us the opportunity to think about work in entirely new ways. Technological advancements mean that for many, work has become an activity and not a location. Our modern-day workplaces are lounge-rooms, cafes and co-working spaces – as well as traditional office buildings. Many of our children will never work for a single organisation, instead choosing to share their talents with multiple organisations in the gig economy.

Glorious new possibilities emerge when we let go of inherited definitions to create a new way of thinking about our work that works for us. Changing the way we think about work and success can change the way we *feel* about our work. And changing the way we feel about our work can have a profound impact on us and the people we care most about. It leads to significant shifts in the way we show up at work – and at home.

It has been said that success is the key to happiness and happiness is the key to success. This philosophy comes with a huge caveat – that the definition of success has been designed by us, not imposed on us. When we conform to a version of success that has been defined by others – often including wealth, status and power – chasing it can make us sick and miserable. Making the decision to let go of an imposed, narrow definition of success is a key step in our journey.

In the machine paradigm, we define work and success in terms of a value exchange – I give something to my job and my job gives something to me in return. One of the foundational assumptions that heavily influenced the machine paradigm is the belief that as humans we are both inherently lazy and materially motivated and, if we want someone to do something, then we have to make it worth their while. The belief that money is our primary motivator to work has led to the creation of complex systems of carrots and sticks to attempt incentives and control humans at work. The origin of these beliefs can be traced back to the late 1700s when Adam Smith wrote about humankind's tendency to perform work in 'as carelessly and slovenly a manner that authority will permit'.[3] Later Frederick Winslow Taylor built on the work of Adam Smith using time and motion studies to perfect the 'scientific management'[4] movement. This movement espoused the productivity benefits of reducing humans to the equivalent of small cogs in big machines. This period saw the emergence of elaborate systems of rewards and punishments that corralled people to work quickly and accurately on tightly controlled tasks. As these systems of work drained meaning and satisfaction from work, Adam's perspective became a self-fulfilling prophecy. The only thing that our work gave us was money, and so money became the only thing we expected to be given.

It is possible to elevate the way we think about work to consider how we are contributing to the creation of something bigger than ourselves – something that supports life in broad and important ways.

My own thinking about work has evolved significantly over the years. In my 20s, work was the means to earn enough money to pay rent in a share house, buy food, clothes and petrol, pay for my gym membership, Friday and Saturday night drinks and travel overseas. Being unskilled, I was not in a position to be fussy about how I earned my spending money. I tried working the night-shift in a service station for a while but could not cope with the way it messed with my sleep rhythms. For a while I was a mobile DJ and played music at 18th and 21st birthday parties. My DJ uniform consisted of black 'slacks', a white collared shirt, a thick red satin cummerbund and matching red bow-tie. I sucked at being a DJ. I shook with nerves every time I had to make an announcement on the microphone and spent the night standing stiffly behind my 'decks', feeling jealous of everyone else who was dancing and having fun. I decided to hang up my red bow-tie for good after I was walking into a club one Saturday evening to set up, with my huge bank of flashing disco lights under my arm. Upon seeing me, a young party-goer elbowed his mate wide-eyed and loudly exclaimed, 'Awesome! They've hired a stripper!'

After graduating from university, I began to see my work as a career. I worked in a wide range of organisations and industries in many different roles all focused on how to improve processes and technology in order to improve performance and deliver great customer experiences. Over time, I began to notice something really interesting. I noticed that while process and technology were contributing factors to great customer experiences – the most critical factors were almost always the human factors within the organisation. After spending over fifteen years focusing on customer experience, I had a profound realisation that I needed to move further up the value chain to the employee's experience. I had found my calling. Having spent the last five years supporting organisations to truly fulfill their duty of care for employees, I am now convinced that it is not possible for any organisation to take good take care of their customers until they first begin to take good care of their people. And, that until leaders begin to take care of themselves, they can't truly take care of others.

Let's take a closer look at the different ways we can think about work.

WORK AS A JOB

We think about our work as a job when we are primarily focused on the perks it provides, such as salary and other benefits. Those who see their work as a job are typically more invested in their lives outside of the office and they see work as the means to do the things they really love.

If we are employed as a casual employee or a shift worker, the value exchange that defines our work is probably something like:

> I give you a fixed amount of time each week to perform the specialised work you tell me to perform and you give me an agreed amount of money for each hour I work. The more time I give you, the more money I get.

If we are salaried employees, perhaps the nature of the value exchange goes something like this:

> I give you my commitment to perform the specialised work you tell me to perform, no matter how many hours it takes me each week and you give me an agreed amount of money each fortnight plus money towards my retirement and perhaps the opportunity to earn a bonus at the end of the year. The harder I work, the more money, status, recognition and sense of worthiness I receive.

WORK AS A CAREER

Those who see their work as a career are not only motivated by the money they earn, they are also driven to seek out opportunities for development and advancement. People who see themselves as having a career often have a long-term aspiration for their working lives and work-related goals. This is a different version of value exchange.

WORK AS A CALLING

Those who experience their work as a calling are most likely to feel a sense of alignment between their chosen area of work and who they are as a person. They have a strong emotional connection to their work and generally experience strong levels of enthusiasm. Although people who see their work as a calling are much more susceptible to experiencing heartbreak as a result of work-related setbacks, research indicates that people who see their work as a calling experience more satisfaction than people who see their work as a job or a career.[5] When my work has felt like a calling, this has certainly been the case for me, no matter what challenges I have faced along the way.

WORK AS A MEANS OF GROWTH

Another way to think about our work is as a vehicle for our growth and self-expression. John Sculley, a former leader at Apple, once said, 'the new corporate contract is that we'll offer you an opportunity to express yourself and grow, if you promise to leash yourself to our dream at least for a while.'[6] Work can be seen as an experience of discovery and personal development – a vehicle for the exploration of how our selves can best serve the organisations we are part of and the world those organisations occupy.

WORK AS SOURCE OF WELLBEING

One of my closest friends, after recovering from a long period of chronic pain, was encouraged by many of the doctors that supported her during her recovery to get back to work. At the time she resisted this advice, but later after returning to work she realised how important working was to her recovery. There is a growing body of evidence that tells us that work can be a source of wellbeing. Positive experiences at work play an important role in our mental health and overall happiness. One of the ways work can directly contribute to our happiness is through the production of the four main 'feel-good' chemicals that boost our mood – dopamine, serotonin, oxytocin and endorphins.

Dopamine is released when we feel we have accomplished something. Serotonin is linked to feeling important or significant in life – work can be a vehicle for feeling that our life really counts, and that we are contributing in meaningful ways to something bigger than ourselves. Oxytocin is released during physical contact with another person. Oxytocin supports us to build trust and foster good relationships. Oxytocin has been found to reduce cardiovascular stress and improve immunity. Experiencing moments of warmth and connection with colleagues and customers through our work can elevate our oxytocin levels. Finally, endorphins help to reduce discomfort in our body. In addition to physical activity, laughter is a great way to release endorphins. By taking a playful approach to our work, we can experience the uplift of endorphins.

Research shows that our work is more likely to be a source of wellbeing when we feel that, through our work, we are helping to make life better for customers, colleagues and other stakeholders.[7]

WORK AS LOVE MADE VISIBLE

The expression 'work is love made visible'[8] was first used by the Lebanese-American poet Khalil Gibran. In 1923 he published his book *The Prophet* which contained a collection of prose poetry fables, including the following words:

> *When you work you fulfill a part of earth's furthest dream, assigned to you when that dream was born. And what is it to work with love? Work is love made visible.*[9]

In my own working life, I aspire to create harmony between all of my big loves – my love for myself, my love for my family and friends and my love for my work.

WORK AS A PATH OF SERVICE

Finally, we can also think about our work as a path of service. We can serve our colleagues, our organisations and the customers and communities they serve. We serve the fragile ecosystems we inhabit to help sustain all forms of life.

I don't subscribe to the view that to serve is to sacrifice. It is my belief that we best serve by bringing forth all that is within us – not by slaughtering even the tiniest part of ourselves. And, that to be of service is our highest calling.

Just think about the possibilities that will emerge as more people begin to think about work as an opportunity to serve – and as a pathway to doing what they love from a place of love. The highest aspiration I hold for my work is to generously serve in order to uplift life.

Our goal is to commit to practices, habits, thoughts and actions that grow our faith in ourselves – our worthy, vulnerable, caring, creative, playful selves.

How work shapes us

When we shape our social institutions
- our schools, our communities and yes, our workplaces -
we also shape human nature.

Barry Schwartz[1]

The environments in which we work shape us. From the first moments of entering the world of work, it began to shape me.

When I joined the most junior ranks of my local bakery Donaldson's Cakes as a 'cake shop girl', I didn't realise I had entered the shallows of the murky waters of organisational dynamics that often encouraged me to hang my values at the door and to follow hard instructions without asking hard questions. A short time after being employed, I was promoted to taking the lead on the prized Sunday shift. It was prized because it was the longest shift of the week and one paid at 1.5 times the normal hourly rate. I worked that shift for years. I started at 5am every Sunday morning. My first task each shift was to move all the cakes that had been baked from the back racks near the ovens out into the shop. Early one Sunday morning, I discovered that a rack of large sweet buns had been nibbled by rats in the wee hours of the morning. Upon reporting this shocking situation to Mrs Donaldson, I was firmly instructed to get a knife, trim away all evidence of rat teeth marks, brush off the poo and stick a half-price sign on each one. Selling those buns to people I knew in my local neighbourhood was a test of my true commitment. I am sad to report that I passed with flying colours. I continued to give my unquestioning, iron-stomached loyalty to Donaldson's Cakes all throughout high school and university. The money I earned paid for my first car, and a countless number of White Sambuca shots at the university bar. I did not leave that job until after I had graduated from university with a Manufacturing Management degree, and landed a full-time job as a production assistant at a lighting company. Rod, the manufacturing manager, explained that he had chosen me for the role, despite the fact I had zero manufacturing industry experience because of the dedication and loyalty I had demonstrated through my long-standing job at Donaldson's Cakes. I learnt that the system rewards those who stay in the muck and deal with the crap. The problem is that staying in the muck can damage us in really serious ways.

As much as we might like to think of ourselves as somehow immune to the environments we expose ourselves to when we are working, the inconvenient truth is that we are not immune. While we have been conditioned to treat ourselves and each other like robots, the reality is that humans are living systems and so are the organisations we work within.

As Deborah Frieze explains in her TEDx Talk 'How I Became a Localist':

> *Somewhere along the way, we got confused about how life works. We convinced ourselves that the world was causal, linear and predictable. And so, we began to treat our bodies, our communities and our ecologies as if they were machines... A machine would never criticise the five-year-plan or lose faith in the boss. Thankfully, that is not how we are – and that's not how life is. Natural systems, living systems are complex, emergent and unpredictable. And every system humans participate in, is a living system.*[2]

In the same way plants needs fertile, nutrient-rich soil in order to sustain growth and health over the long term, humans need this too. Sunflowers have adapted to be heliotropic, orienting themselves throughout the day to soak in maximum sunlight. In the Royal Botanic Gardens in Melbourne, I recently discovered a type of jasmine flowering in the middle of winter, its fragrance delicate yet defiant in the chilly air. In much the same way humans can be strong, adaptive and resilient – but if any element of our environment is toxic, over the long term we cannot prosper. We may try to fool ourselves into believing if we just try hard enough, we can move through our working days with a force field bubble around us repelling any toxins that may be present in our environment. The truth is that we are not superheroes. We are susceptible, vulnerable living creatures that are connected to and influenced by our environments.

A single acorn can grow into a tiny, twisted bonsai or a towering, mighty oak tree. Both organisms share the same DNA and potential. The only difference is that the bonsai's growth has been diminished through root constraint and branch pruning. In the same way, certain roles and environments can stunt our growth if we allow ourselves to have long-term exposure to them. It is important to be aware of the nature of the environments and roles we choose to 'plant' ourselves in, and to exercise discernment around how long we remain 'planted' in any particular spot. Unlike an acorn, we can all exercise some degree of freedom about where we choose to grow. With this awareness and freedom, we can ensure we allow enough room for our roots to spread, our branches to extend and our leaves to unfurl. Then we avoid the pain of realising that we have a become a stunted, twisted bonsai-sized version of ourselves.

I have worked with thousands of good people over the years. Sadly, too many of these good people were living what Henry David Thoreau has described as 'a life of quiet desperation'.[3] On a good day at work we would achieve great work together. However, we would also experience so many moments of feeling mistrusted, diminished, disempowered or underappreciated. On bad days we would feel damaged. We might occasionally feel buoyed through our shared experiences as workplace warriors soldiering on in a marathon version of the Hunger Games – but it was pretty crazy stuff. Looking back with the benefit of hindsight, I wish I had a stronger day-to-day awareness of the elements of my environment that were undermining my innate capacity to thrive.

If there are elements of our work environment that are toxic, planning to make changes (on our terms) would be a wise course of action. We must each find the courage to rescue ourselves from damaging work environments – even if this means radical simplification of our lifestyle. In the meantime, the practice of self-fidelity will support us to work with greater awareness so that we can take steps to minimise our exposure, reduce the rate of absorption and soak in nourishment from other sources.

For those of us who work in an organisation, there are many invisible 'forces' at play that are shaping our experiences at work. Our experience at work, and our mindset, is influenced by the dominant paradigm, organisational culture, our direct manager and other leaders within our organisation. The below diagram shows how the forces at play nest to create the environments we work within.

The forces at play

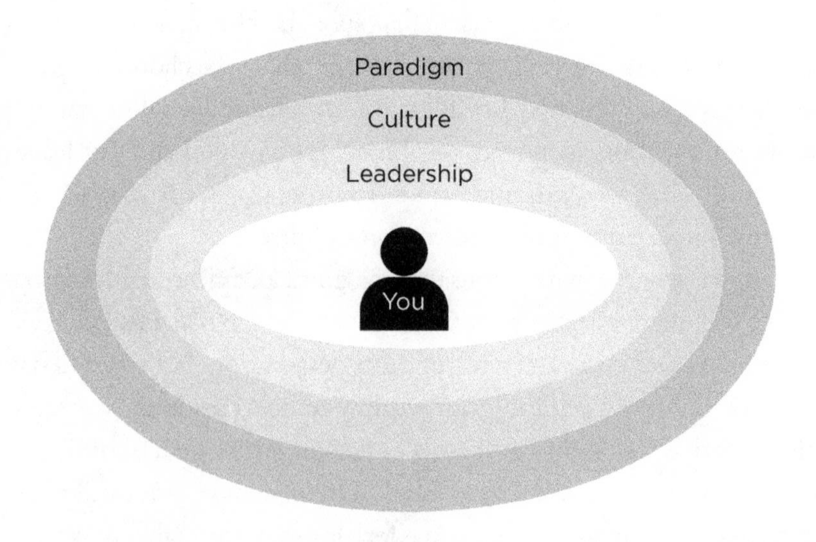

PARADIGM

A paradigm, or 'world view' influences the way we think, talk and behave. All organisations have a dominant paradigm. Of course, organisations also exist within broader economic, social, political and perhaps religious paradigms. We will explore organisation paradigms in greater depth a little later.

CULTURE

Carolyn Taylor describes culture as 'the patterns of behaviour that establish what is required to fit in'.[4] The culture of the organisation we work for is an invisible force that has the potential to both uplift and drag down our vitality and performance. Unfortunately, in many organisations today the culture acts more like a high-pressure system than an updraft.

Culture gives rise to 'behavioural norms'. Norms are the 'rules that prescribe what people should and should not do'.[5] These unwritten 'rules' exist in all organisations – and they are powerful. They can slow down organisational change initiatives, stifle creativity and innovation and wear people out. If they contradict our official organisational values, they can also make us feel like we are slowly going insane and increase risk of burnout. In the book *Walking the Talk*, Carolyn Taylor shares the following observation:

> *I have observed cultures which lift people to operate at the highest level of their intellectual and emotional potential ... I have seen others which turn fairly normal and well-meaning individuals into selfish, political, back-stabbing monsters.*[6]

I have worked at an organisation that espoused a commitment to innovation, but where one of the most powerful unwritten rules was 'it is unacceptable to question or challenge those in power'. Unsurprisingly, this climate was not exactly conducive to innovation – which is exactly what I had been hired to deliver. The stifling nature of the environment meant that I knew I could not stay for long. I did my best to lay some basic foundations, collect some new skills, mature organisational capability and grow my team's resilience – and then I moved onto greener pastures where I could grow, contribute and thrive.

Organisational systems also underpin culture and the associated norms. Throughout *Self-Fidelity* I will also refer to the systems we work within. Within our organisations there are many systems in place to incentivise, manage, measure and control people, resources and processes. Humans are living systems and our organisations are a type of living system. Organisations are also nested within natural ecosystems.

LEADERSHIP

Leadership also plays a significant role in shaping our experiences at work. In particular, the person we report to can have a tremendous influence on our capacity to grow, thrive and experience uplifting work. Our one-up manager has the power to either deflect or amplify the forces at play within the broader organisation. As a rule of thumb, I always do thorough due diligence on who I will be reporting to when considering any new role. Platforms like Glassdoor and LinkedIn are making this easier and easier to do.

There have been times when I have chosen to take a role that was 'too good to refuse' knowing that the person I would be reporting to was unlikely to inspire and uplift me – but I have made that decision eyes-wide-open and with a big toolbox of practices to nourish and support myself during the period I would be reporting to them. In all my leadership roles, I have always made sure I have a clear Personal Sustainability Strategy. This is simply a one-pager that outlines how I will support my vitality and sanity. The more challenging the role and the environment I am working in – the more there is on the page. As a leader, I know that unless I feel uplifted and inspired, I am failing in my duty of care for those I am leading. The same applies for my work as a coach, facilitator and co-creator.

A CLOSER LOOK AT ORGANISATIONAL PARADIGMS

> When people are seen as just like each other and treated as cogs in a machine, it is difficult for them to feel that they are valued contributors and therefore difficult for them to care about work.
>
> Carol Sanford[7]

Organisational paradigms are worthy of further exploration, because they are rarely discussed, yet can have a significant impact on our working lives. The dominant paradigm in any organisation influences the way leaders and employees think, feel and act.

Our current dominant paradigm, the machine paradigm, arose in the eighteenth century during the Industrial Revolution, a time when machines were celebrated and organisations were designed to operate like them. In this paradigm, organisations are seen as value-extraction machines that must be optimised. Humans are seen as interchangeable resources to be re-arranged, leveraged and depleted. The machine paradigm relies on elaborate systems of sticks and carrots to incentivise humans to conform, comply and work towards the primary goal of more and more value extraction at all costs.

This paradigm has resulted in many unfortunate consequences for humans, given we are unique, growing beings and not fixed, interchangeable parts. For many years, humans have crunched and compressed themselves like contortionists to survive the machine paradigm. The reason why so many of us feel uninspired, disengaged, exhausted, undervalued, disconnected, lost and diminished is because this paradigm is fundamentally discordant with our essential nature.

In the book *Why We Work*, Barry Schwartz explains:

> *If we want to help design a human nature that seeks and finds challenge, engagement, meaning and satisfaction from work, we have to start building our way out of the deep hole that almost*

> *three centuries of misconception about human motivation and human nature have put us in, and help foster workplaces in which challenge, engagement, meaning and satisfaction are possible.*[8]

As we begin to see the error of our ways, and the machine paradigm falls away, several new paradigms are emerging – the *behavioural paradigm*, the *human potential paradigm* and the *regenerative paradigm.*

Our exploration of self-fidelity takes place within the context of a transitional period from the machine paradigm to these emerging paradigms. For an emerging paradigm to begin to re-shape the organisations we work within, two forms of development must occur – the development of organisational potential and the development of human potential. The practices of self-fidelity focus on the latter – the development of human potential.

Our practice of self-fidelity will be enhanced by an awareness of the dominant paradigm we have operated in for the last few centuries and the new paradigms that are emerging. These are described in the table below.

Organisational paradigms

Goal	Thinking	Unintended consequences
MACHINE PARADIGM		
To maximise value extraction and to invest energy and resources to receive value in return.	Humans are resources and interchangeable cogs. Self-interest and wealth creation are the primary drivers for expansion, discovery and experimentation.	This paradigm has led to dehumanising workplaces, damaged ecosystems, human suffering and environmental degradation.

Goal	Thinking	Unintended consequences
BEHAVIOURAL PARADIGM		
To shape and control employee behaviour towards 'ideal standards' in order to produce the desired outcomes.	Humans must be incentivised to behave in ideal, desired ways. Ranking and rating is the best way to reward and recognise those who meet the ideal standards.	This paradigm is also destructive to the development of free, independent, thriving human beings. This paradigm also leads to an inward-focused culture that is not conducive to innovation and prone to unhealthy internal rivalry. It also does not solve the problem of environmental degradation.
HUMAN POTENTIAL PARADIGM		
The pursuit of the potential inherent in each human.	Humans are inherently worthy and perform at their best through self-determination and self-expression.	The primary focus on human development and expression has a major blind-spot - the relationships between humans and the larger systems we interact with, specially the natural systems. Environmental degradation continues to be an unintended consequence of this paradigm.

Goal	Thinking	Unintended consequences
REGENERATIVE PARADIGM		
Humans serving as an instrument for the evolution of all beings.	To evolve the capacity and grow the capability of humans we must express our unique essence in a way that contributes in a meaningful way, and serves the development of others.	The false assumption that one is already working regeneratively can prevent people from orienting to this paradigm, resulting in organisations remaining stuck in the old paradigms.

Source: *The Regenerative Business - Redesign Work, Cultivate Human Potential, Achieve Extraordinary Outcomes* by Carol Sanford[9]

THE ROLES WE CAN PLAY IN A PARADIGM SHIFT

Deborah Frieze shares the insight that 'it's not possible to change big systems – we can only abandon them and start over or offer hospice to what's dying.'[10] Deborah's work outlines four key roles we can play during the break-down of a no-longer-good-enough paradigm and the emergence of something new. We don't necessarily have to all be 'early adopters' or originators of new ideas in order to play an important role in the shift that is occurring. However, sitting on the sidelines as a passive observer, a heckler or a helpless victim is neither good for our organisations or for us. Our participation in the shaping of the emerging paradigm does not mean we are anti-capitalism – it means that we understand that true prosperity requires us to work together in new ways that better support all life.

We can all support new paradigms of work to emerge with ease, the machine paradigm to dissolve with dignity, and the shift to unfold with grace.

The four roles required in order for this to happen are:

Trailblazers – pioneering path-finders who are eager to experiment with a healthier and more resilient future.

Hospice Workers – compassionately stay within the collapsing system and guide its people through the transition to the emerging alternatives.

Illuminators – tell the stories of the emerging systems so others can find them and make wiser choices about their future.

Protectors – hold power in the dominant system to create space for innovation and experimentation.

The four roles

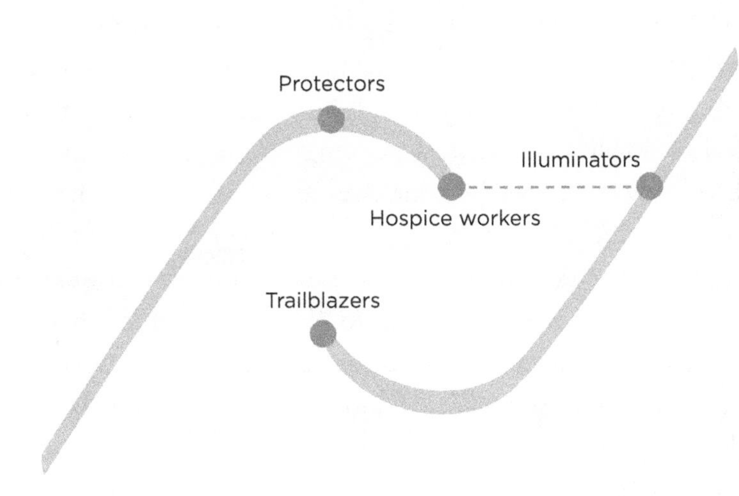

ORIENTING TO THE EMERGING PARADIGM

Our dominant systems of work are inclined towards self-preservation and may attack the virus of innovation. During the time between the collapse of the old and the full emergence of the new we will need to cultivate the capacity to sit in the not-knowing, the confusion and the uncertainty – perhaps for long periods of time. This means that our own mindset and orientation will be essential. Just like the woman I once saw eating M&Ms while walking on a treadmill at the gym, without the right mindset and orientation, it doesn't matter how hard we work or how long we persevere – we will never get where we want to be. Our mindset must be one of openness, sensing, learning, collaboration and discovery. Through this connection, orientation and mindset, we can course-correct when needed and skilfully navigate the hazards we encounter.

To succeed, we must remain connected with our essential nature and oriented towards the emerging paradigms. It is also important to maintain a broad perspective. From this vantage point, we can begin familiarising ourselves with both the fresh qualities of the emerging paradigms and the undertow of the dissolving paradigm.

The paradigm we orient towards will shape the way we receive and perceive information – and as a result it shapes the experiences we have and the possibilities we can imagine. The same experience – for example a one-on-one meeting with our manager – will look and feel completely different, depending on the paradigm through which we view it. In orienting ourselves to a new paradigm, it is vital that we consciously engage new ways of thinking – a new mindset – about familiar tasks and habits. By orienting ourselves towards the new emerging paradigms, we begin to see our work through a radically altered perspective. We can begin to break free of the shackles of redundant, diminishing beliefs. Just one small, careful twist of the kaleidoscope can open us to an entirely different perspective, a new working reality.

The emerging paradigm that best harmonises with the practices of self-fidelity is the regenerative paradigm. This paradigm awakens within us a commitment and a connection to our collective evolution.

Here is how Carol describes the experience of working from the regenerative paradigm:

> *One comes to understand oneself as a living process, embedded and intertwined within all of the other processes that make up a living world. The sense of personal identity drops away, to be*

replaced by a deep and caring resonance with each specific living being one encounters. This resonance creates an unshakeable commitment to enabling all living entities to awaken and express their indwelling potential in service to life's evolution.[11]

As humans we like to cling to the familiar, yet it is not possible for us to live simultaneously in multiple paradigms while maintaining coherence. It is imperative to the practice of self-fidelity that we override our tendency to cling to what is familiar and wake-up to the emerging paradigms so that we can work with skill, awareness and discernment.

OUR EMERGING FUTURE

The ability to shift from reacting against the past to leaning into and 'presencing' an emerging future is probably the single most important leadership capacity today.

Otto Scharmer[12]

The 2020 coronavirus pandemic certainly accelerated the emergence of more humane work practices. During the lockdowns that occurred across the world, even the most controlling members of the old guard of leadership who had staunchly resisted flexible working 'privileges' were finally forced to open their minds to the reality that work is an activity and not a location.

In the book *Cult Status* Tim Duggan describes the emergence of two more powerful forces that are having a big impact on all organisations today:

On one side we have millennials demanding more and on the other we have the same cohort taking control of the vehicles that can give them that. These twin trends of demand and supply are crashing into each other creating circumstances ripe for combustion.[13]

I find it extremely hopeful to think about millennials moving into leadership positions in organisations across the world. Millennials tend to care deeply about the big issues of our times. We have recently seen the resurgence of 'wokeness' among millennials. Wide-awake millennials are demanding that decision-makers in the organisations they work for and purchase from not only care about the big issues of our times but are genuine and active in contributing to a better world.

Self-fidelity is about learning to understand, harness and ride the winds of change – and knowing when and how to find shelter. It is the understanding that clinging to the edge will tear us apart. Venturing beyond the edge of the world of work as we know it can feel scary – or exhilarating – it all depends on how we look at it.

THE DANGERS OF CONFORMING

> We shift ourselves not in sweeping pivots, but in
> movements so tiny that they are hardly perceptible,
> even in our view. Years pass before we finally discover that,
> after handing over our power piece by piece,
> we no longer even look like ourselves.
>
> Alicia Keys[14]

Very early in my leadership career, my 'bible' was the book *Nice Girls Don't Get the Corner Office.*[15] Looking back, I cringe. At the time, I was convinced that the fastest way to get the corner office was to behave and look like a man. Every morning I scraped my hair back into a tight bun. I wore only collared shirts and tailored pants to work. I was quick to dish-out well-meaning, but completely misguided advice to younger female colleagues – suggesting that to be taken seriously they needed to reconsider wearing their hair down or applying lipstick in public and that big dangly earrings were potentially career-limiting. I feel deeply sorry for my former self and for the former female colleagues I may have misled. Not only was my understanding of success completely corrupted by my conditioning (being a man-impersonating-woman sitting in a corner office now feels more like a nightmare than a dream goal), so was my thinking around how to be 'successful'. Today, I understand how uplifting it is to express my zest and playfulness through my wardrobe. I love wearing bright, bold colours with a touch of sparkle. Instead of my wardrobe being part of my armoury, today, my clothes celebrate the truth of who I am.

Given the many invisible forces that influence us at work and in life, it is easy to conform, little by little, only to suddenly realise one day that we no longer remember who we *really* are or what we *really* believe anymore. We conform in ways that are small and subtle, but over time, our choices accumulate.

The world of work can encourage us to squeeze ourselves into small spaces where it thinks we best fit. Over time we can begin to believe we *should* fit, even when deep down, we feel like a chunky square peg being jammed into a small round hole. Conforming happens little by little, driven by our desire to fit in or by internalising other people's incomplete and inaccurate assessment of our potential. We conform when we mould ourselves to the expectations of others or to perceived 'ideals' that we buy into. We conform in an attempt to belong. And as humans we have a fundamental need to belong. At times, of course, we must conform in order to maintain a peaceful and civil society – but so often our choice to conform is one that stifles our potential.

The small spaces we squeeze ourselves into can take many forms. Perhaps we crunch ourselves down to squeeze into the footsteps of our parents. Maybe we override our individual sense of style to comply with the dress code deemed to be 'business appropriate' by the powers-that-be in our organisation. Perhaps we become conditioned to prioritise the list of values espoused by our organisation over our own core values. Perhaps we limit our potential at work to the contents of our two-page job description. Maybe we feel forced to comply with our company's preferred work hours or work

Conforming happens little by little, driven by our desire to fit in or by internalising other people's incomplete and inaccurate assessment of our potential.

location. Perhaps we dare not expand our sphere of influence to a level that exceeds the shadow of our insecure manager. Perhaps the 'us and them' office politics means that we suppress our desire to connect and collaborate with others. Or perhaps we crunch down our yearning to do big, meaningful work in the world to conform with society's expectations for parents to maintain lives that tightly orbit the lives of their children.

For those of us who work for organisations, perhaps it is a drive for simplicity that can lead to the loss of our individuality. In *Nine Lies about Work: A Freethinking Leader's Guide to the Real World,* Marcus Buckingham shares this observation:

> *Large organisations are complex places and a strong and understandable instinct of their leaders is to seek simplicity and order… But the desire for simplicity easily shades into a desire for conformity, and before long this conformity threatens to extinguish individuality. Before we know it, the particular talents and interests of each person are seen as an inconvenience, and the organisation treats people as essentially interchangeable.*[16]

The problem is that our decisions to conform can become our default setting, and therefore go untested and unchecked. This is when suffering can occur and the personal costs mount. Whenever we allow any external constraining factors to suppress the embodiment of our full potential, without challenge, we are doing ourselves (and the world) a great disservice.

Cultivating self-fidelity and self-trust supports us to break free of oppressive and unnecessary conformity. If we have worked as part of a large organisation for some time, it can take time to rebuild self-trust because we have become reliant on being told what is important and often what to do. If we are honest with ourselves, we may actually like being told what to do – because we no longer trust in our own judgement.

Or perhaps we have never had the opportunity to build a foundation of self-trust. We are not alone in this. This can be the natural outcome of conformity-based schooling systems and over-protective parenting. Jen Hatmaker powerfully described her childhood experience that led to the absence of self-trust:

> *I was assured from a young age that I could not trust myself. That something was bad about me. So, it never occurred to me that I could trust anything about myself – my instinct, my own good eyes and ears paying attention to the systems and rhythms that were breaking people's hearts. I couldn't trust my gut. I couldn't trust what felt true.*[17]

CORRUPT SYSTEMS

Our human tendency to try to fit in as a misguided attempt to belong can become particularly dangerous if we find ourselves in the gravitational pull of a corrupt system. A corrupt system is a system that exists to serve only the interest of the powerful few, rather than serving the interests of customers, employees and communities in which they operate. Any system that places the protection of the system and the reputations of those in power over the dignity of the people within the system is a corrupt system. Corrupt systems depend on finding enough people who are willing to conform to this unspoken value exchange – keep quiet and don't question those powers and we will bestow you with status, money and a sense of belonging.

These systems can offer rich rewards to those willing to give unquestioning loyalty to power. These rewards are addictive and over time it is easy to start to attach our sense of self-worth, perhaps even our identity to them. The problem is that power, status and financial gain are not enough to sustain us. It does not matter how rich and powerful we become – we will eventually pay a high price. We will sacrifice our health and happiness, and on our way down, steal health and happiness from those we love the most.

Corrupt systems are really good at pretending to be something they are not – so they have the potential to really mess with our minds. Over my career I have had a close encounter with a corrupt system. Once I was free of the system, I had a new awareness – I came to see the generous salary the organisation had been paying me as a form of hush money. My paid-for silence meant I was complicit in the corruption. It was not until months after I left that I realised that I felt so much lighter. My chiropractor remarked that all the tension in my jaw and shoulders had disappeared.

So, what can we do when we find ourselves in the pull of a system where conformity is corrosive to our health and happiness? Playing the long game is essential. Systems have a powerful capacity for self-preservation – any perceived threats can be abruptly rejected. Before we take any action, big or small, it is important to carefully consider what we have to lose should the system reject us. Timing is everything here. We may already know that the price of remaining in a particular system is too high, but I would warn against taking bold action unless we are confident that we are financially and emotionally strong enough to survive the possibility of being rejected by the system. Make a plan and take the steps required to extract ourselves with dignity – and on our terms.

UNDERSTANDING OUR POWER AND WHAT WE ARE UP AGAINST

As humans we like to think that we have the power to control the world around us. We convince ourselves that, if we are vigilant enough, we can protect ourselves and those we care about from pain and heartbreak – but we can't. The harsh reality is that the only thing we can control is ourselves. When we cling to the belief that we can control other people or the world around us, we waste precious energy. This is energy we could have spent focusing on what we can control – our own thinking, beliefs and actions.

The laws of systems dynamics tell us that in any system the power of any one individual is dwarfed by the strength of the system and the dynamics within that system. And yet, we still each have power – especially when we work together with wide-awake awareness.

The answer is not to blame the system and to give up our power, but rather to skilfully amplify our collective power while maintaining a strong awareness of our thinking and the larger-scale forces at play. Awareness will enable us to move from *reacting* to *responding* to the world around us. Together through communities of practice, we can begin the work of *creating* an entirely new world of work.

The American poet Mary Oliver said that 'the greatest way we give up our power is to believe we don't have any.'[18] I would add that the greatest waste of our power is by not working with wide-awake awareness of what we're up against.

Growing our inner resources

My mission in life is not merely to survive, but to thrive;
and to do so with some passion, some compassion,
some humour, and some style.

Maya Angelou[1]

To navigate the challenges we encounter at work and in life we need *resources.* Resources can be found outside of us and inside of us – in our bodies and minds. To cope with increasing challenges, our resources must also increase.

The practice of self-fidelity focuses primarily on growing the resources inside of us – in our minds. We will call these *inner resources.* We can all grow our inner resources to better cope with the growing challenges we are navigating in our working lives and experience lower stress and less overwhelm.[2]

Challenges and resources

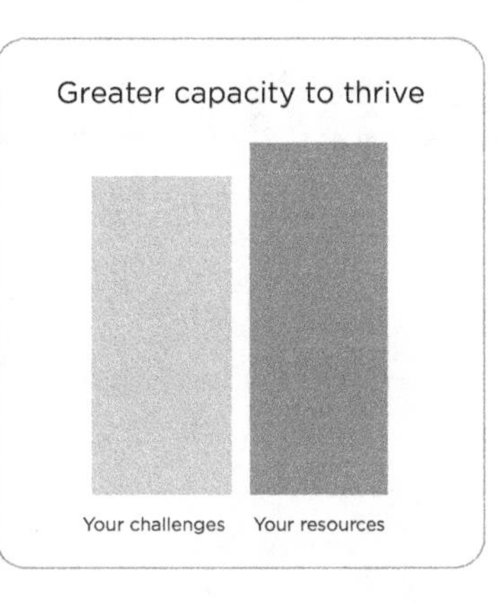

By reconnecting with our essential nature and harnessing the power of our inner natural resources, we can all be the sort of leader that awakens and inspires others.

The core practice of self-fidelity focuses on increasing the inner resources in our minds because we often have more influence in this area. As the resources in our minds grow, they help us build resources in our body as well as external resources.[3]

While we will primarily focus on growing the inner resources in our minds, it's also beneficial to increase the inner resources in our bodies – by improving physical fitness or reducing alcohol consumption, for example. We can also increase our external resources – by nurturing a friendship with a kindred spirit at work, for example.

The five elements of our essential nature we will focus on throughout the book are all inner resources. We will grow: our worthiness, our vulnerability, our caring nature, our creativity and our playfulness. These inner resources will support and stabilise us throughout our working lives. And these natural resources already exist in great abundance inside each of us.

Just like the seeds of a lotus flower, with attention, patience and care the natural resources that dwell inside of us will begin to grow – even if they have been lying dormant and forgotten for long periods of time. (Fun fact: scientists have germinated lotus seeds that were 1200 years old.)

I was fortunate to train in Positive Neuroplasticity with Dr Rick Hanson when he was in Melbourne in 2018. Rick is a man who embodies a strong, warm-hearted blend of wisdom, kindness and generosity. During our training, Rick explained that if our mind is like a sailboat, growing our inner resources is like lengthening and strengthening the keel. Inner resources enable us to live more boldly, trusting we can explore and even enjoy the waves of life, and handle any storms that can come our way. If inner resources are like the keel on a sailboat, these five elements of our essential nature combine to create the 'winged keel's' equivalent of inner resources. (The winged keel increased stability, reduced drag and was a key factor in Australia II's much celebrated 1983 America's Cup victory.)

When we think about the people who have had the greatest impact on the world in their lifetimes, we quickly realise that their source of power and influence comes not only from *what they achieved* but from *who they were.* The source of their power is their capacity to embody an awakened way of being that inspires and awakens the hearts of others – often in the face of tremendous challenges.

By reconnecting with our essential nature and harnessing the power of our inner natural resources, we can all be the sort of leader that awakens and inspires others.

Transforming our mindset

When people learn how to evolve their own thinking – their beliefs, perspectives, aspirations, and thought patterns – they become change catalysts in all parts of their lives and with everyone they touch.

Carol Sanford[1]

Human development can happen in two different directions.[2] The first direction is *horizontal development.* In horizontal development, we add new skills and knowledge within our current view of ourselves and the world around us. Over time, horizontal development enables us to grow and improve. The second direction is *vertical development.* In vertical development, we transform our view of reality so we can see our lives and the world around us through a new lens.

Horizontal development *transfers knowledge,* whereas vertical development *transforms us.* When it comes to uplifting our working life, trying to get there through horizontal development is like buying ourselves bigger and bigger bunches of helium balloons. Taking a vertical development approach would see us climbing aboard a hot air balloon.

Our own mindset determines what we perceive, how we make sense of what we perceive, and therefore how we act and how we experience work. The evolution of our mindset and our thinking is vertical development. At the heart of the regenerative paradigm is an understanding of the new possibilities that would emerge if we were to grow our most powerful human capabilities – and each figure out how the expression of our unique essence might best contribute to the evolution of all life on our planet.

This same evolution in our thinking – from the individual to the collective – infuses the emerging work of Ash Buchanan – the *Benefit Mindset.* This work does not diminish Carol Dweck's work around Growth Mindset,[3] but rather evolves it.

The Benefit Mindset:

> *is concerned with the life-long process of learning how we can be the transformation and realise our unique potential in a way that serves the wellbeing of all.*[4]

At its core, the Benefit Mindset is about shifting our mindsets towards more *caring, inclusive and interdependent* perspectives. It recognises the reality that our personal wellbeing must be considered in a way that is nested within societal and ecological wellbeing – and the wellbeing of future generations. The table opposite provides more information on the Benefit Mindset, which is enormously relevant and helpful in the context of self-fidelity.

As our mindset evolves from a focus on our individual growth to the wellbeing of all present and future beings, we will experience an evolution in how we work together and how we live together.

	Fixed Mindset	Growth Mindset	Benefit Mindset
Engagement	We are resistant to growth and change	We have an open mind, ready to learn	We have an open heart, ready to contribute to the collective
Development	We believe that intelligence and abilities can't be developed	We believe that intelligence and abilities can be developed	We create the conditions for everyone's development
Focus	We focus on maintaining what is familiar	We focus on improving how we do things and what we do	We focus on who we are being and why we do what we do
Relationships	We hold set expectations about our relationships	We practise learning and growing together	We practise flowing together in resonance
Challenges	We avoid challenge, or give up and see failure as proof of our inability	We embrace challenges and persist, seeing failure as an opportunity to learn	We use learning to transform our understanding of ourselves and the world around us
Success of others	We feel threatened by the success of others	We are likely to feel inspired by the success of others	We engage as a partner in everyone's flourishing
Culture	Authority and experts	Growth and learning	Collective transformation and co-evolution

Source: Ash Buchanan[5]

Embracing paradox

Human beings are constantly choosing
too early in the conversation.

David Whyte[1]

Some of the most powerful moments of personal growth I have facilitated and experienced have emerged from the experience of zooming out enough to realise that conflicting parts of ourselves become reconciled through the awareness of a bigger picture. With enough perspective, two parts that appear to be in direct opposition to each other can always become integrated into a bigger whole. Contemplative traditions teach us that awareness to the non-duality of our reality – or the oneness of all things – lies at the heart of true awakening.

While the practice of self-fidelity does not require us to become fully enlightened beings, it does require us to be open to a great many paradoxes. The successful exploration of self-fidelity requires us to embrace the mysterious alchemy that arises from holding the tension of opposing ideas, resisting the urge to succumb to an easier, simpler but less accurate understanding of the true, complex nature of things. We must cultivate the capacity to zoom out enough to engage *and/also* thinking – a richer, far more helpful alternative to *either/or* thinking.

The poem 'Paradox of Noise'[2] by Gunilla Norris invites us to tap into 'a deeper level of being' within ourselves that has the capacity to embrace paradox.

Our minds do not like paradoxes.

We want things to be clear, so we can maintain our illusions of safety.

Certainty breeds tremendous smugness.

We each possess a deeper level of being, however, which loves paradox.[3]

One of the central tensions of self-fidelity is the paradox of our desperate desire to fulfill our own individual wants and needs alongside our deeper desire to contribute in some meaningful way to the common good. With enough perspective we can come to appreciate the bigger picture – that to truly accept and honour ourselves, we are also honouring and accepting others. In creating an accurate and peaceful definition of self-fidelity, it was essential to encompass the idea of bringing about 'the widest possible freedom'[4] for all – not just for ourselves. Self-fidelity is grounded in unwavering faith in our own unique potential and the unique potential of others. True self-fidelity cannot be attained through individualism, isolation or elitism – it is bound up in healthy relatedness to ourselves, others and the world around us. It is not possible to truly honour our own potential, worthiness, uniqueness, goodness and imperfectness, without also honouring these same things in others. In the words of Harriet Lerner, 'only through our connectedness to others can we really know and enhance the self and only through working on the self can we enhance and improve our connectedness with others.'[5]

Another paradox of self-fidelity is its direct association with true belonging. Until we feel we truly belong to ourselves we won't feel like we truly belong in any team or organisation. Many of us experience feelings of disconnection and loneliness. As Brené Brown's research has shown, one of the factors that contribute to this lack of belonging is our tendency to confuse belonging with fitting in.[6] Fitting in is about conforming, contorting and suppressing the truth of who we are in order to earn acceptance from others – it is externally referencing and does not truly serve us. Whereas *true* belonging is internally referencing – it is about believing in and belonging to ourselves so deeply that we cultivate the strength and courage to stand alone if needed.

It is also helpful to work with awareness of the emotional tensions that exist within our wild hearts – the qualities of being both fierce *and* kind, strong *and* soft. Self-fidelity requires us to work with awareness of both our yin and yang qualities within ourselves. Our yin qualities allow us to nurture and comfort ourselves and our yang qualities embolden us to take protective or remedial actions with strength, courage and wisdom. Having an open yet discerning heart means that we work with awareness of the energies that others bring and the effect those energies are having on us, and those around us. Practising discernment means that we take the necessary steps to minimise our exposure to harmful energies and energy vampires.

There is also, of course, a very real tension between our longing to experience freedom and our reliance on existing systems of work to pay our mortgage and put food on the table. Irene Claremont De Castillejo captured the heroic feat of holding these conflicting parts of ourselves together when she said, 'Only a few achieve the colossal task of holding together, without being split asunder, the clarity of their vision alongside an ability to take their place in a materialistic world. They are the modern heroes.'[7] This book aims to inspire and activate many, many more everyday modern heroes.

This is by no means a full catalogue of the paradoxes we will navigate on the exhilarating pilgrimage ahead. We might also be called to navigate the intersection of many more very-real tensions including the paradox that work does not expect enough of us, yet it exhausts us. Then there is the small matter of our sanity depending on the acceptance of a myriad of uniquely human *in*sanities. We might also ponder the tension between simultaneously thriving *and* struggling, of being *and* doing, of optimism *and* realism.

The reality that self-fidelity is by its very nature both challenging and complex does not make it any less worthy of earnest practice. In fact, it makes it even more worthy.

Why self-fidelity matters

Our very human fears and grasping, combined
with our cognitive ability, make us the greatest danger
on earth to ourselves and all other species. Living true to
ourselves becomes, in its fullness, living true to our
collective path of healing and freedom, our shared
yearning for a peaceful, loving world.

Tara Brach[1]

The work of restoring our faith in ourselves and each other is arguably our most important and urgent work – it is also challenging work. The practice requires commitment, courage and patience.

WHY BEING TRUE TO OURSELVES AT WORK REALLY MATTERS

I believe there are a number of reasons why being true to ourselves at work matters an awful lot.

We spend the majority of our waking hours working

Over the course of our lifetime, most of us will spend around 90,000 hours working. The experiences we have while we are working, particularly the extent to which we feel truly seen and feel we belong, have a profound impact on us and the people we care about. In the book *Workings* Studs Turkel shares firsthand accounts of people working in a diverse range of jobs exploring what makes work meaningful. Studs makes the poignant observation, 'In all instances, there is felt more than a slight ache. In all instances there dangles the impertinent question: Ought not there be an increment, earnt though not received, from one's daily work – an acknowledgement of [one's] *being*?'[2]

Many senior leaders are abdicating their responsibility

Unlike the generations of workers before us, we want much more than a steady salary.[3] Contrary to the Silicon Valley inspired stereotype of employees wanting yoga classes, fruit boxes, casual dress policies and ping-pong tables, what we really want is to thrive, to have the opportunity to learn and grow, to work with people who care about us and to do something that matters. We want to be part of organisations that are making a positive difference on the big issues of our time. Sadly, this is not what most people working in organisations experience. There are too many executives today using tokenistic gestures such as fruit boxes and weekly yoga classes to relieve their moral tension. I once spoke to an HR executive I was working with about the opportunity I saw to do much more to address the low levels of employee engagement across the organisation. He replied, quite genuinely perplexed, 'What do you mean we need to do more? We are now offering Pilates *twice* a week!'

The shocking reality is that a mere 15% of the global workforce is engaged at work[4] – 'engaged' meaning highly involved in and enthusiastic about their work and workplace. Only 2 in 10 employees 'strongly agree' that their performance is managed in a way that motivates them to do outstanding work.[5] In 2019 the World Health Organization (WHO) declared burnout an occupational phenomenon and 76% of employees have experienced some level of burnout on the job.[6] As much as I love Pilates and bananas, approving invoices for fitness classes and fruit boxes is a complete abdication of the moral responsibility leaders have to engage in real conversations and real solutions. We cannot afford to wait for the old guard of senior leaders to lift their heads from the feeding trough – we must become the sort of leaders we need and take creative, brave, empowered action to participate in the ushering in of a new work paradigm.

The cost of not changing is huge

The machine paradigm is a significant health risk factor. Many aspects of our current ways of working are making so many of us sick, sad and lonely. As a society we are facing an epidemic of burnout, anxiety, depression and loneliness. Every 40 seconds, someone somewhere takes their own life and it is estimated that every 40 seconds 20 people attempt suicide. The dominant dehumanising work paradigm is built upon harmful and flawed ideals of individualism, competition, conformity, ranking, relentless profit growth and short-termism. In the words of Margaret J Wheatley, 'If we look honestly at our current world, the values of [our] culture become brutally clear – self-interest, greed, power.'[7] The original meaning of the term 'corporation' comes from the Latin root *corpus* – meaning a body. The original intention behind the formation of organisations was to enable a group of people to do something that none of them could achieve alone. The irony is that, for many of us who work in large organisations today, our day-to-day experience is that the organisation diminishes what we can achieve as much as it amplifies it.

We must proactively reduce our risk of economic vulnerability

At a time when job security is rapidly declining across all organisations, we must take proactive steps to increase our likelihood of secure, future income. While I believe that organisations have a duty of care to empower their people with the mindset and skillset to access the broadest possible range of work options in the future, ultimately we need to take personal accountability to access the broadest possible array of future work opportunities. Gone are the days when we can expect to have a job for life. It is predicted that by 2050 even the idea of a 'profession for life' will be obsolete.[8] We must embrace life-long growth and learning.

The people we love the most are suffering

Any hurt, sadness or anger that we experience at work cannot be contained. It bleeds into all facets of our lives. Our hurt ricochets out of our hearts to smite the hearts of those we care about the most. We spend our working hours hiding our hurt, putting on a brave face, chugging down cans of harden-up, grinning and bearing it while we take another one for the team – all the while suppressing the overwhelming urge to hurl our crappy laptop across the office. Then we come home, the dam walls burst and the people we love the most are swept up in the deluge. Alternatively, we find ourselves lost in afternoon fantasies about that first sip of beer or wine – or as one of my coaching client's daughters calls it, 'daddy juice'. We rush home to the warm embrace of our secret liquid love and transform ourselves into zombies, our hearts numb and our minds dulled – the people we love fading into the background. Alternatively, we numb ourselves with life-leeching television, social media or crappy food. Either way, the very people most deserving of the best of us often get left with the dregs.

Activating human potential at work is a win-win-win-win-win-win

Organisations are being buffeted by external crisis, rapidly changing technology and ever-evolving customer and employee expectations. We operate in the context of low levels of trust in institutions compounded by a challenging economic environment and the uncertainty of local and global disruption. Many organisations around the world are struggling. There are many studies that link happier, more engaged, more satisfied employees with improved productivity, profitability, customer loyalty, innovation and growth. A study by the Wharton School of the University of Pennsylvania found a long-term link between job satisfaction and improved shareholder returns.[9] Research shows that when we are working in a way that is aligned with our personal values, we experience a greater sense of wellbeing,

Our workplaces must become the arenas to truly liberate and harness the full goodness and power of our human potential.

lower levels of depression and we tend to be more satisfied with life.[10] Activating our potential at work is good for us, good for our families, good for our organisations, good for the customers, good for key stakeholders and good for the ecosystems all those people inhabit – it's a win-win-win-win-win-win.

Changing how we work together will save us

Just in case those six reasons are not quite compelling enough, there is also the small matter of the fast-approaching global ecological catastrophe. We find ourselves at a key moment in history. For the first time in human history our home planet is teetering on the edge of a catastrophic tipping point. No phase of humanity has ever encountered the scale, severity and urgency of the problems we are facing today. The world's wildlife has halved in less than a generation. Our oceans, rivers and forests are struggling to cope under growing strain. The rate of Antarctic ice mass loss has tripled in the last decade. Unless we experience a radical shift, global warming will soon become irreversible. Most of us are too caught up in the minutia of our daily existence to really think about any of this. We scurry around, tiny busy specks on a melting, flooding blue marble that is hurtling through space. However, we cannot afford to be absent on the matter of halting and repairing the devastating damage we have done to our home planet. Each one of us must find the strength and the courage to lean into the reality – our systems of work and industry are quickly bringing about outcomes that no one individual wants but all individuals will suffer from greatly.

Organisations across the world have a moral and ethical obligation to step up now in this period of transition. In the words of Willis Harman, 'Business has become, in the last half century, the most powerful institution on the planet. The dominant institution in any society needs to take responsibility for the whole.'[11]

In summary, work is our primary vehicle for environmental, economic and social progress. To continue to evolve, we must learn how to work together in ways we have never worked before. Our workplaces must become the arenas to truly liberate and harness the full goodness and power of our human potential. We must fully engage in our most creative, collaborative and courageous work yet. There is enormous upside and enormous urgency. We can't afford to keep tinkering around the edges in ways that are disconnected and ineffective. Now is the time to come together to think and work in entirely new ways. Now is the time to begin the practice of self-fidelity in earnest and usher in a new work paradigm – one that truly uplifts all life. In the words of Jean Houston, 'In this time of whole-system transition we can no longer afford to live as half-light versions of ourselves. The complexity of our time requires a greater and wiser use of our capacities', 'the world can thrive only if we can grow.'[12]

THE TIME TO ACT IS NOW

> If you think adventure is dangerous,
> try routine, it's lethal.
>
> Paulo Coelho[13]

When we step back from the minutia of our busy working lives, we might remember that humans' work endeavours have only existed for a relative nanosecond in the context of our evolutionary past as a human species. It is no exaggeration to say that our Stone Age hunter and gatherer brains are dazed and confused by the complex workplace environments we suddenly find ourselves navigating every day. The workplace environments that feel so familiar to us are only a few centuries old, and the digital elements of work only one generation old.

In the past, there have been valid economic and competitive-market-driven reasons to squash multitudinous humans into small compartments. Before large-scale automation, the best way to maximise output was for humans to behave like robots – completing well-defined, repetitive work following standard protocols. Now that real robots work among us, we really need humans to behave like humans. To do this we must remember all we have forgotten and set free all we have suppressed.

Another unfortunate element of our current working reality is that the survival of our dominant paradigms depends on the perpetuation of the pandemic of low self-worth we are experiencing. In the frank words of Harriet Lerner, 'Capitalism would fall if we liked ourselves the way we are now.'[14]

Conditioned by the systems in which we work to conform and comply, we understandably lose touch with the power of our individualism. Because so many workplaces value and reward narrow single-minded dedication to work, we may find ourselves working crazy hours, sacrificing our personal relationships and interests or doing 'whatever it takes' to get the job done. This oppression may manifest in quiet, unquestioning subservience and over time it may metastasise into more serious forms of dis-ease.

I know how easy it is to become caught up in the pursuit of more and more achievements and the amassing of material and status-based rewards. Looking back on my working life, especially the middle chapter of my corporate career, I can see now that my profile made me the perfect worker bee. I was smart, resilient and hard-working, and I had that 'ideal' combination of being extremely conscientious paired with low self-worth. A pairing that meant I spent years enthusiastically (sometimes feverishly) jumping through all the burning hoops, chasing down those gold stars, all the while believing that amassing my achievements meant I had value in the world. It felt like I was on a roller-coaster that was getting faster and faster. I knew deep down that my way of living and working was not sustainable, but I had no idea how to get off the ride.

There were certainly a few kind souls along the way who tried to help me see that I could make different choices. I once had an insightful coach who challenged me to 'break some rules' in my organisation. At the time, I was so fully indoctrinated and so fearful of authority that this idea felt way too crazy.

I will also never forget the kindness of a colleague, Mark, who pulled me aside one Monday after I proudly announced that I had spent my entire Sunday working. He said, 'Cassie, working on the weekends is like pissing in your wetsuit. It makes you feel all warm and fuzzy, but no one else notices.' I remember thinking that I just needed to work harder at making *sure* people noticed. I had missed the point completely. It took me years to understand what Mark was trying to tell me.

There is a popular saying, 'hurt people hurt people'. I have experienced numerous workplace psychological injuries through the callous actions of downtrodden colleagues and managers. I know I am not alone in these experiences. In the words of Seth Godin, 'Every day I meet people who have so much to give but have been bullied enough or frightened enough to hold it back.'[15] My deepest psychological injuries were inflicted by leaders who were so corrupted by workplace conditioning, so intoxicated by power and a need to control that they had lost touch with their hearts. It is easy to become hardened by long-term exposure to workplaces designed to treat us like robots.

Those of us working for large organisations may feel trapped in a hamster-wheel of being busy and important, spending our days in mind-numbing meetings where key people don't even bother to show up, and most of the people who are there are either half-listening or engaging in self-serving politicking. We spend hours reading and creating emails that hot-potato responsibility between siloed departments to cover butts. We lose entire days creating and tweaking PowerPoint presentations that tell carefully curated half-truths to executives and boards. We expend vast amounts of energy complying with stupid policies or navigating minefields of subtle but potentially career-ending politics of shadowy alliances and self-protectionism. We fire-fight the same fires over and over again because we don't have the time, energy or the permission to address the root cause once and for all. In the tiny fragments of time in between all that, we compulsively check our phones hundreds of times a day.

But perhaps the greatest tragedy of all is that much of the human suffering being experienced every day in so many workplaces across the world is avoidable. It is absolutely possible for us to discover greater freedom and meaning and to work together harmoniously, harnessing the best of our humanity to deliver great outcomes for the customers and communities we serve in a way that supports sustainable performance and prosperity, rather than destroys it.

Many of the 'rules of the game' that we see as fixed and beyond question have only existed for a few decades. For example, the unquestioned notion that the needs of boards and shareholders must always reign supreme has only existed for a relatively short time. The emergence of more and more B-Corps is shining a light on the prosperity that can be created for all stakeholders when we break free from the structures that no longer serve us.

The challenges we are facing are very real. Transforming the way we work and supporting ourselves and each other is of the utmost importance.

From understanding to uplift

Every action you take is like a vote for the type of person you wish to become.

James Clear[1]

Often when it comes to our personal growth, we tell ourselves that we are going to try something new or do something differently – only for life to get in the way of our good intentions. Simply reading this book and writing in our journal will not sustainably uplift our working life – it is only through playful, inspired action that we experience growth and sustainable change. Action converts *in*sights to *out*sights. Through playing with different ways of thinking and being we will sense, learn and discover how best to reconnect with our essential nature, grow our inner resources and nourish our vitality. Only through inspired, playful action can we move from *cognitive understanding* to a lived experience of *feeling uplifted.* This creates an upward spiral of growth.

There are a range of specific practices and tools this book offers to support us to activate this upward spiral. By harnessing the power of these practices and tools and by staying playful we are far more likely to do what we say we are going to do – or promise ourselves we will do.

This means that we will:

- reduce victim thinking and procrastination
- increase self-trust

- improve our sense of personal agency
- become less likely to blame others or the system for our own situation
- understand that learning requires trial and error
- create a sense of progress, and therefore motivation
- experience lasting change.

BURNING QUESTIONS

In his poem 'Sometimes' David Whyte talks about the 'questions that can make or unmake a life … questions that have no right to go away.'[2] David explains that these types of questions open us to:

> *conversations that will happen with or without our conscious participation [that] have something to do with timing: when we might step through the doorway into something bigger, better – both beyond ourselves and yet more of ourselves at the same time.*[3]

When a question of this nature becomes known to us, we simply can't 'unknow' it. I call these burning questions.

Burning questions have the power to:

Burn what no longer serves us
Illuminate new thinking
Ignite new ways of being
Generate energy to rise.

By finding the courage to uncover the most truthful answer to a burning question, we illuminate our next best action to move towards greater presence, acceptance, belonging and freedom. The act of asking ourselves the right burning question at the right time will lead us to insights that may feel both familiar and surprising. This is the goosebump territory we are aiming for when we contemplate the burning questions contained in this book.

The idea of burning what no longer serves us may sound scary and feel disorienting, but it is part of an essential and natural process of regeneration. To create something new for ourselves, we must let go of what no longer serves us. As we release ourselves from ways of thinking and working that are no longer truly serving us, we usher in the possibility of something better – something that feels truer to us.

I still remember the exact moment when my most powerful burning question to date entered my mind in my mid-thirties. I was walking alone along a beach when the question came to me: *Why did I knowingly commit to a relationship with a violent man and why did I stay in the relationship for so long?* If I had never asked this question of myself and found the courage to answer it, I would not be able to do the work I do today. While this question related to my personal life, the answers it uncovered affected every facet of my existence and led me on a journey of self-worth building that continues to this day.

Throughout *Self-Fidelity* we will be invited to ask and begin to find answers to burning questions that have 'no right to go away'. These questions propel us forward. When we muster the courage to answer them truthfully, they burn redundant ways of being and thinking to the ground so that we can create something new and better. We may choose to allow ourselves to uncover answers so powerful that they ignite complete and spontaneous combustion of the old. We may prefer a far more controlled slow burn. Either way we are inspired to take thoughtful action towards building something newer, better and truer.

There will be lots of burning questions for us to ponder. Each one has the same goal – to create within us a desire to take inspired action in a spirit of playful discovery.

The burning questions I offer will guide us to enquire about every single layer of our life. At the core of all these intentions lies the invitation to reflect on one central question: *Who do I choose to be?* The act of discovering an answer to this burning question may feel like our final destination but is actually our starting point.

In the words of Indigenous Ceremonial Leader Arkan Lushwala:

> *Once you know what you can be, you know what you can do. We can't afford to waste time, we have little time. We need to be precise now. When someone sincerely asks me 'what can we do?' my humble answer is 'first, find out what you can be.' Action is extremely necessary at this time. This is not a time just to talk about it. And still this action needs to be born from a place in ourselves that has real talent, real intelligence, real power and real connection.*[4]

Burning questions

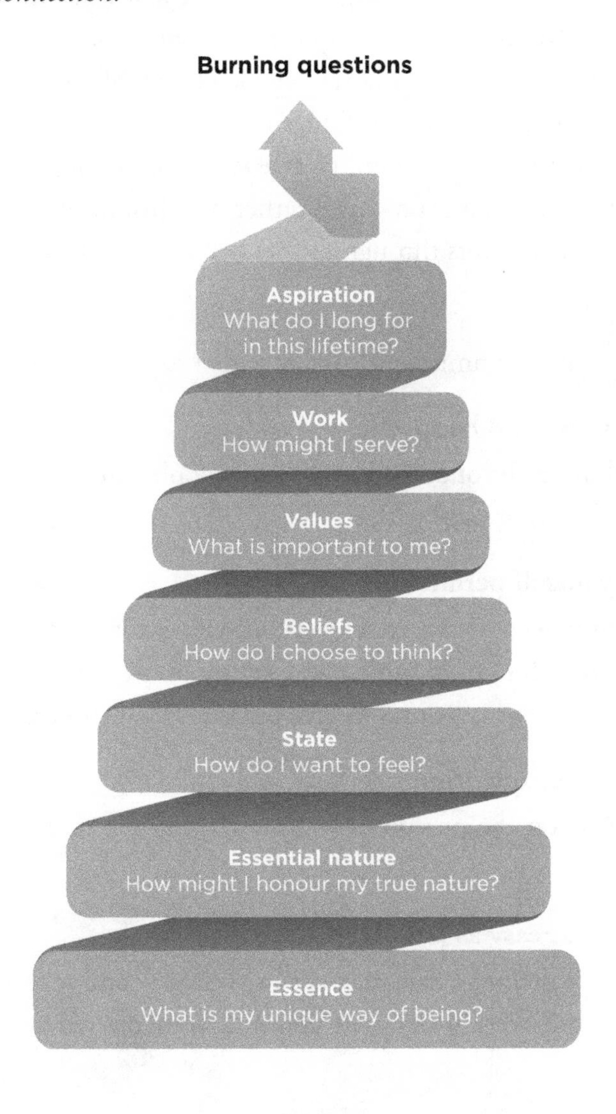

TAKING INSPIRED ACTION

Our truest answers to burning questions emerge and crystalise through taking inspired action. We all experience resistance in moving from thinking to action. Perhaps we have not allowed ourselves to really examine the dangers posed by our current state and therefore deny that change is really necessary. Perhaps we fear losing control in some way. Perhaps we feel that we have too much of an investment in the status-quo. Maybe we feel hopeless about change and overwhelmed by the energy we imagine it will require. Perhaps we tell ourselves that the status-quo is good enough.

We can significantly boost the likelihood of taking inspired action by doing a few simple things to grow our sense of empowerment and personal accountability. It always makes a big difference to write these things down on paper, rather than just think about them. I will provide prompts throughout the book for journalling.

Commit
Make a firm commitment to play with a new behaviour.

Start small and be specific
Get clear on the one small thing you will play around and *when* you will play around with it.

Give yourself permission
Figure out what you need to give yourself permission for in order to honour this commitment and get the most out of the experience. Often it is helpful to give ourselves explicit permission.

Know your intention
Get clear on the outcomes you are hoping for, and why they matter.

Make it as easy as possible
Identify the things that may get in your way and take steps to reduce any friction between you and your desired outcomes,

including distractions. Be intentional about choosing an environment that is conducive to your success.

Tell someone
Share the one small thing you have committed to with another person (a colleague, friend, mentor or coach) and commit to sharing the learnings of your experience with that same person in the not-too-distant future.

UPLIFTING HABITS

> Habits deliver numerous benefits, but the downside is that they can lock us into previous patterns of thinking and acting - even when the world is shifting around us.
>
> James Clear[5]

A habit is a behaviour that has been repeated so many times it has become automatic. Jason Hreha, one of the world's leading applied behavioural scientists, described habits as 'reliable solutions to recurring problems in our environment.'[6]

However, habits that appear to solve a problem in the short term can create negative consequences over the longer term. An unhelpful habit is one where the long-term outcomes are unfavourable. An uplifting habit is one where the long-term outcomes are favourable, even though in the present moment, the habit *may* feel effortful or uncomfortable at first. One reason why it is easy to slide into bad habits is because they feel good in the moment. As James Clear says, 'the cost of your good habits is in the present and the cost of your bad habits is in the future.'[7]

For example, drinking a glass or two of wine each night may seem like a reliable solution to our recurring problem of work-related stress, however over the long term it is more likely to exacerbate our problems rather than offer any real solution. Choosing instead to drink a kombucha with dinner may feel less satisfying in the short-term, but over the long-term it may trigger an upward spiral of positive behaviours that uplift our mood and overall vitality. For example, switching wine for kombucha may support us to be more present with our family in the evenings, sleep better, be more likely to exercise in the mornings and make better food choices throughout the day.

To switch an unhelpful habit with an uplifting one, we must first awaken to the long-term consequences of that habit and, from a place of full presence, make a different choice. Unless we are able to wake up, we are unable to discontinue unhelpful habits and form new, uplifting habits.

Our daily beliefs, mindset, practices, rituals, goals, habits and choices come together to largely determine our long-term outcomes. There are lots of great books that can support us to create new uplifting habits. The focus of *Self-Fidelity* is on powerful practices, beliefs and mindsets and ways of being to complement uplifting habits. Over times, new uplifting practices can become new uplifting daily habits.

James Clear says that 'every action you take is like a vote for the type of person you wish to become'.[8] Our goal is to commit to practices, habits, thoughts and actions that grow our faith in ourselves – our worthy, vulnerable, caring, creative, playful selves.

FOUNDATIONAL PRACTICE: MEDITATION

> Meditation is not about getting rid of all your thoughts; it's learning not to get so lost in them that you forget what your goal is.
>
> Kelly McGonigal[9]

Meditation, simply put, is the deliberate training of attention through direct observation of one's mind. The goal of our meditation practice is not to become a great meditator. Rather, the goal of our meditation practice is to become better at tapping into the feelings of awareness, clarity and freedom that we experience through meditation in the moments that matter in our everyday lives. A regular meditation practice also supports us to more frequently remember that we are not our thoughts.

Meditation also supports us to harmonise our body, mind and breath and supports us to let go of tension in our bodies. A common misconception about meditation is that it is about stopping our thoughts. I have met a lot of people who have tried meditation but have unfortunately decided that it was not for them. Often, they have given up because of a false belief that if they still have thoughts while meditating, they are not doing it properly. This is not the case. The busier our minds, the more essential and helpful our meditation practice becomes.

One thing I know for sure is that without my meditation practice – albeit patchy at times – this book would not have been possibile. For me, meditation is not only a way to clarify my thinking and to allow space for my best ideas to emerge – it is also a practice of remembrance – remembering that the voices in my head are in fact *not* providing reliable instructions on what I should do next.

Like many, I am someone who has been conditioned to measure my self-worth through my achievements. The upside of this is that I am very action-oriented – I am great at getting stuff done. The downside is that I find it hard to rest and experience contentment. When I am able to successfully sit and meditate for 15 or 20 minutes despite the voices in my head telling me that I am too busy to just sit there, almost compelling me to get up and do one of the million things on my never-ending to-do list – it is a small victory. I am far more likely to be victorious if I meditate away from my laptop, kitchen sink and laundry basket. In addition to being a small victory, it is also a small but important reminder that my constant self-generated sense of urgency is an illusion and that I can be with this inner urgency without reacting to it.

My most accessible form of meditation is a moving meditation. I find it soothing to focus on my breath or on the rhythmic movement of my body while running, swimming or doing yoga. Moving quietens my mind. My aspiration, with more practice, is to experience a greater sense of peace in my formal seated meditation practice.

In exploring the topic of meditation, it is helpful to briefly touch on what we know about the human mind. The brain and the mind are two different things. Our brains are physical networks of neurons, synapses and biochemicals. Our minds are the flow of our subjective experiences, such as pain, happiness, anger and love. Science tells us that our mind somehow emerges from our brain, but the reality is that we currently have very little understanding of how.[10] Not only do we have very little understanding of exactly what the human mind is and how it works – we have very little understanding of how our *own* minds work. We will never figure out how our own unique minds work by reading second-hand accounts of others' pilgrimages of self-discovery. The bad news is that we have to do the work. We must undertake our own pilgrimage of discovery into the uncharted and often turbulent weather patterns of our own minds.

The final chapter of the powerful book *21 Lessons for the 21st Century* by Yuval Noah Harari is dedicated to the power of meditation as a vital pathway for all of us to understand the essential work of observing, exploring and understanding our minds. And through this, we learn how to focus our minds. Yuval shares his own experience of coming to the realisation of how little he understood his own mind during his first experience of meditation on a vipassana meditation retreat:

> *The first thing I learnt from observing my breath was that not withstanding all the books I had read and all the classes I had attended at university, I know almost nothing about my mind, and had very little control over it. Despite my best efforts, I couldn't observe the reality of my breath coming in and out of my nostrils for more than ten seconds before the mind wandered away. For years I lived under the impression that I was the master of my life, and the CEO of my own personal brand. But a few hours of meditation were enough to show me that I had*

> *hardly any control of myself. I was not the CEO – I was barely the gatekeeper.*[11]

Meditation teaches us how to change our relationship with our thoughts. If we imagine that our thinking mind is like a waterfall – the constantly flowing thoughts, stories and voices in our heads are the water. At times the waterfall is calm and smooth-flowing, for example, when we experience a state of flow, relax, tune into one of our senses or exercise. Other times, the waterfall becomes a raging torrent, for example, when we experience strong emotions of fear, shame or anger, replay past hurts or catastrophise about imagined future disasters. Through a meditation practice it is possible to build the capacity to notice the state of the flow and, even more importantly, to notice when we are caught up in the swirling deluge of our mind, and develop the ability to step back into the quiet space behind the waterfall. Every time we notice we have been swept away in our thoughts and bring ourselves back to present-moment awareness we are performing the equivalent of one bicep curl for our minds.

By learning how to access this quiet space behind the waterfall, it becomes possible to learn how to observe the thoughts and stories knowing that we are separate from all of them.

The old saying 'come to our senses' provides powerful instructions on how to get out of the whitewash and wake up to our present-moment reality. Many meditation techniques are based on the gentle, vigilant redirection of our attention away from the voices in our heads back to something we can see, touch, hear, feel or taste. Guided meditations often start by prompting us to feel our feet on the floor, the clothes on our skin or the chair supporting us. We might be guided to notice the sounds inside the room and the sounds outside the room. Tuning into one sense at a time – such as what we can see, taste, smell or hear – is a form of meditation.

Becoming familiar with our minds and understanding the simple yet profound truth that we are not our thoughts – and that we can cultivate the capacity to choose our response – is nothing short of life-changing. As we really *get* the fact that we are separate to our thinking minds, our potential becomes limitless. Through regular practice anyone can develop the capacity to more easily remember that they are not their thoughts, but rather they are the awareness of those thoughts.

Meditation helps us to understand what Pema Chodron meant when she said, 'You are the sky. Everything else – it's just the weather.'[12] Experiencing, even for a few fleeting moments, feeling like the sky and not the weather can be transformative. Even though we may continue to get caught up in the weather patterns of our mind, the understanding that at our essence, we are the sky and not the weather is life-changing.

There are a wide range of great meditation apps available. Visit self-fidelity.com to find the ones I use and recommend.

FOUNDATIONAL PRACTICE: SOAKING

By taking just a few extra seconds to stay with a positive experience - even a single breath - you'll help turn a passing mental state into lasting neural structures.

Dr Rick Hanson[13]

One particularly powerful way to creating lasting uplift and grow our inner natural resources is through a practice known as *soaking*. This practice comes from the emerging field of *experience-dependent neuroplasticity* – the study of the ways our experiences change our brains.

Dr Rick Hanson is one of the pioneers in this field. Rick has taught thousands of people around the world how to convert passing positive experiences into lasting changes to their neural networks. By using this simple foundational practice, we can all convert passing positive feelings and emotions into lasting inner resources.

Rick's book *Hardwiring Happiness* provides compelling evidence of the benefits of the practice of 'soaking in the good' to build the inner resources we need to navigate the challenges we are facing.

Here is how Rick describes the essence of his teaching:

> *Your brain has a negativity bias that makes it like Velcro for negative experiences and Teflon for positive ones. This bias evolved to help ancient animals survive, but today it makes us feel needlessly frazzled, worried, irritated, lonely, inadequate, and blue. The good news is that in just a few seconds at a time in the flow of daily life, you can turn your experiences – the pleasure in a cup of coffee, the accomplishment in finishing a tricky email, the warmth from a friend's smile – into lasting inner strengths built into your brain, such as resilience, balance, and positive emotions.*[14]

Rick uses a wonderful analogy of scurvy and vitamin C (stay with me here). Let's say we were suffering from scurvy – that would mean that our body would be in desperate need of vitamin C. If we were given an orange, we would not cut out one small slice and tentatively nibble on it. We would tear off the rind and relish every morsel of that orange and slurp every last drop of its juice.

In this same way, by getting clear on the nature of our dis-ease, we can figure out what we need to heal ourselves – our vitamin C equivalent.

Through this dual awareness of both our dis-ease and its cure, we can intentionally forage for and savour what we most need – with the gusto of a sailor devouring an orange at the end of a long sea voyage, or in the same way a five-year-old would devour a juicy slice of cold watermelon on a hot summer day.

For example, if we feel lonely, we can become more attuned to any small moments of warm-heartedness and caring we experience throughout our day. In these moments, we can use the practice of soaking to amplify and absorb this passing positive emotional state. Perhaps we might notice and soak in a moment of caring connection we experience with a work colleague, a family member or even the barista at our favourite cafe as he carefully pours warm milk into our favourite coffee.

We can use this foundational practice to support us to *Wake up* by soaking in feelings of calm presence. Soaking can also help us *Let be* and feel more worthy, caring, open, playful and creative more often. We can also use it to *Let in* our vitamin C equivalents in the modern workplace, by soaking in feelings such as love, gratitude, appreciation, connection, patience, peacefulness or contentment. These inner resources are especially valuable during times of challenge.

THE PRACTICE OF SOAKING

It only takes a few breaths to soak in positive emotions. I like to use an adaptation of Tara Brach's RAIN technique to soak in positive emotions.[15] RAIN serves as a memorable prompt for a simple four-step soaking process that we can do in under two minutes: **R**ecognise, **A**mplify, **I**nvestigate and **N**ourish.

Recognise – when a positive emotion is present for us, or bring to mind a past experience when a positive emotion was present.

Amplify – and intensify the positive feeling by focusing our attention on it for three to five breaths. In this second step, I like to imagine that my positive feeling is growing from a small spark of light in my heart-space into a powerful radiance that fills my entire body.

Investigate – the feeling for just a few more breaths, see if we can notice something that is unique or fresh about it this time, or a specific reason why this feeling is particularly nourishing for us right now. Consider how it will make a difference for us and the people we care about.

Nourish – ourselves with this positive experience – sense its goodness really soaking into us. In this final step, we might like to imagine that our heart is a sponge absorbing this good feeling and visualise the feeling soaking into us.

My kids love this practice as much as I do. I recently asked my two young sons if they wanted to soak in some goodness while we were walking to school. That particular morning they were both onboard and so we chose to focus on the feeling of love. I helped them to remember a time when they felt really loved, when they were snuggled up in bed listening to stories feeling safe, warm and loved. I helped them to make the feeling really 'juicy' by asking them to recall as many details as they could of that experience of feeling really loved – what could they see, feel, smell and hear? Once their feelings of love were strong, I asked them to imagine that their hearts were made of sponge and the love was their favourite coloured ink. Finally, I asked them to take a few deep belly breaths while they let all that good, juicy love soak into their hearts. My younger son decided that the love he was soaking in was red and sparkly and that he was going to put his heart sponge in a bucket so that none of the juicy red, sparkly love would drip out during the school day ahead.

Play around with the practice of soaking. Try with different visualisations or embodiment techniques to discover what works best. Don't underestimate the healing power of this simple practice. We can all master the practice of converting passing everyday positive experiences into sustained vitality, inner peace, worthiness and resilience.

FOUNDATIONAL PRACTICE: BREATHING

Feelings come and go like clouds in a windy sky.
Conscious breathing is my anchor.

Thich Nhat Hanh[16]

If left alone, breathing is just for our survival. Alternatively, conscious breathing offers a far greater range of functionality and potential benefits. Learning how to override our automatic ways of breathing in moments that matter can support us in our practice of self-fidelity in a range of very powerful ways.

I first began to really understand the power of conscious breathing while training for a marathon in my 20s. Learning to synchronise my breath with my running cadence was a game-changer for increasing my endurance levels, and supported me to complete training runs of up to 30km in the months leading up to the marathon. I also discovered I could harness my breath to let in and let go during the darkest moments of seventeen hours of labour with my first son. Somehow in the fog and panic of pain that threatened to overwhelm me, my mind offered up an image of a red cloud of pain being drawn up and out of my womb with every inhale and then expelled through my nose as dense black smoke with every exhale. This visualisation really supported me through my labour. Years later, in my first triathlon I was overcome with a sudden panic attack while I was far off shore in deep water during the swim leg. I used my breath to regain control of my panicked mind and finish the race. My marathon, birthing and triathlon days are behind me. These days, I also connect with my breath in less dramatic but no less powerful ways through my yoga and chi running practices.

We breathe around 25,000 breaths a day and some days we are not consciously aware of a single one of those breaths. In the book *Breath* James Nestor said, 'There is nothing more essential to our health and wellbeing than breathing: take air in, let it out, repeat 25,000 times a day. Yet, as a species, humans have lost the ability to breathe correctly, with grave consequences.'[17] When our breath is on auto-pilot mode we can sometimes drift into dysfunctional breathing patterns. If we are not mindful of how we are breathing, dysfunctions in our breathing sever our connection with our essential nature, drain our energy and our vitality.

Waking up to our breath, to the present moment and to what our bodies are trying to tell us are important elements of being true to ourselves. Conscious breathing offers a simple, powerful and always-available way to awaken to the moment in front of us and reinhabit our body. Waking up to being in our breathing body and tuning into the sensations of breath moving through our body is a powerful act of listening – to ourselves.

This is how Buddhist monk Bhante Henepola Gunaratana explains why the breath is such a useful tool for supporting awareness:

> *Breathing ... is common to every human being. We all carry it with us wherever we go. It is always there, constantly available, never ceasing from birth till death, and it costs nothing. Breathing is a non-conceptual process, a thing that can be experienced directly without a need for thought. Furthermore, it is a very living process, an aspect of life that is in constant change.*[18]

CONSCIOUS BREATHING PRACTICES

Consciously inhaling and exhaling through our nose, instead of our mouth, offers significant health benefits.[19] As does taking control of the length and depth of our breathing. Slowing and deepening our breath activates our parasympathetic nervous system, calming and relaxing us.[20]

By intentionally balancing the length of the inhale and exhale we can create a state of calm, clear-headed focus.

Navy SEALs are taught to use a technique called box breathing to prepare themselves for high-stakes encounters, ensuring they are in the optimal zone of being relaxed and alert. Box breathing is really straightforward – simply inhale for four seconds, hold for four seconds, exhale for four seconds and hold for four seconds – and repeat for a few minutes, as long as needed to feel relaxed and focused. This is one of many different conscious breathing techniques that we can use any time to access and amplify the natural vitality that is exists inside us.

We can also practise harnessing our breath to create space within us. When we are feeling 'suffocated' or diminished by the circumstances we find ourselves in, we can call on conscious breathing in any moment to experience a sense of greater inner spaciousness. Experiencing inner spaciousness is a vital element of courageous leadership.

In the words of Peter Senge:

> *The leaders' new work is about developing an interior holding space – a space that allows them to navigate in the midst of conflicting information and interests, in the midst of institutional failure and systemic breakdowns, in the midst of confusion that makes people turn to anger, fear, and despair.*[21]

There's a mechanical aspect to the way our breath opens up space inside of us, as well as a mental, emotional and mind-body opening aspect to it. At the physiological level we expand when we inhale, drawing more oxygen and space into our body to expand our heart space and the cells of our bodies. We can also use our breath to expand the space between stimulus and response, thus allowing a new way of thinking and a new way of being to arise. We might also visualise, imagine or feel inhaling breaths pulling fresh space and energy to our head, heart and guts. We can use our inhaling breath to awaken our warm heart, to embolden the courage in our bellies and activate clarity and creativity in the crown of our heads.

We can also use our breath to support us to let be, let go and let in by focusing on:

- the pauses at the top of the inhale and the bottom of the exhale to *let be*
- our exhaling breath to *let go*
- our inhaling breath to *let in.*

Finally, here are some more powerful words from Thich Nhat Hanh that can help to guide us:

Breathing in, I know I am breathing in.
Breathing out, I know I am breathing out.
Breathing in, I notice my in-breath has become deeper.

Breathing out, I notice that my out-breath has become slower...
Breathing in, I calm myself.
Breathing out, I feel at ease.
Breathing in, I smile.
Breathing out, I release.
Breathing in, I dwell in the present moment.
Breathing out, I feel it is a wonderful moment.[22]

There are so many ways to harness the power of our breath. Play around with different conscious breathing techniques to find one that works. More support to practise conscious breathing is available through a wide range of breathing apps and resources available. Visit **self-fidelity.com** to find the tools I use and recommend.

"Come to the edge," he said.
"We're comfortable back here," they said.

"Come to the edge," he said.
"We're too busy," they said.

"Come to the edge," he said.
"It's too high," they said.

"Come to the edge," he said.
"We're afraid," they said.

"Come to the edge," he said.
"We'll fall," they said.

"Come to the edge," he said.
And they did.

And he pushed them.
And they flew.

Christopher Logue[23]

WAKING UP

Awakening creates a bridge to our authenticity.
With that comes a more honest conversation
inside ourselves and with others.

Zainab Salbi[1]

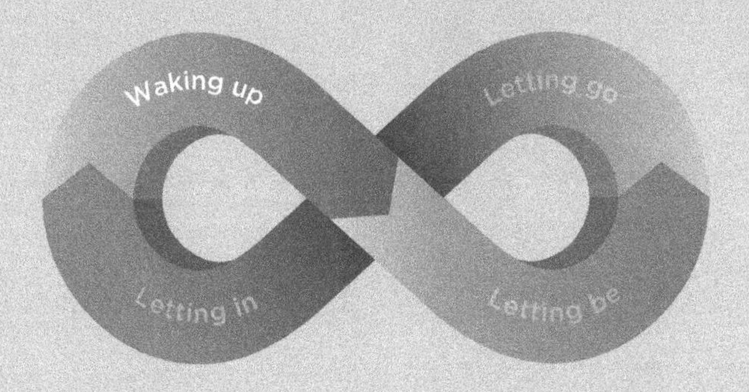

Being present

How we pay attention to the present moment
largely determines the character of our experience
and, therefore, the quality of our lives.

Sam Harris[1]

During the first coronavirus lockdown in Melbourne in early 2020, I was out running one morning. Masks were not yet mandated. I was being careful to abide by physical distancing protocols. The weather was beautiful and I was feeling great. At a certain moment, I approached the back of a woman who was walking on the same side of the path ahead of me. I was about three metres behind her and just about to veer to my right to give her a wide berth when she stopped dead in her tracks, and spun around to face me with an angry look on her face. She yelled, 'Stay away from me! I have a lung condition!' I was taken aback. As I ran away from her my mood had shifted dramatically. I found myself shaking my head and angrily muttering under my breath, 'Get yourself a f-ing mask love and lose the f-ing anger.' Fortunately, I was not lost in my judgement and anger for long. After a few tense minutes, I was able to 'wake-up' to notice the hypocrisy in judging her anger when the same emotion was present in me. I realised that we had both perceived each other as a threat and reminded myself that we were all doing the best we could in extremely difficult circumstances. That morning it became clear to me that the lurking fear of that highly contagious and invisible threat was having a bigger impact on me than I had realised.

Being triggered that morning was out of my control – but what was in my control was the capacity to 'wake up' from my anger rather than spend the rest of the day brooding and suffering.

THE STATE OF TRANCE

Many of us spend most of our working days in a trance-like state. We are in a trance when we mistakenly identify ourselves as the voices in our heads and become lost in all-consuming feelings such as anger, sadness, fear, resentment, powerlessness and frustration. When we are in this trance-like state we are not present in the moment we are experiencing – instead we are mentally time-travelling into an imagined future or into the past. We are going through the motions on auto-pilot.

Being in a trance is not necessarily always bad – we rely on habitual thinking and auto-pilot mode to do familiar tasks efficiently and easily. The problem is that a state of trance can pull us way out of alignment with our integrity, take us off course and block us from accessing our goodness and full potential in moments that matter. It is true that habitual auto-pilot behaviours can certainly uplift us – the danger is that habits can also drag us down. Unless we know how to break free of our trance, we are unable to break the pattern of bad habits and embed good habits instead that uplift us and keep us on track for the long-term outcomes we hope for. Awareness, or waking up, is the gateway to any behaviour change. As Carl Jung said, 'Until you make the subconscious conscious, it will direct your life and you will call it fate.'[2]

In *Radical Compassion* Tara Brach explains that when we are in a state of trance 'our minds are narrow, fixated, and usually immersed in thoughts and our hearts are often defended, anxious or numb.'[3] In a trance, we believe that our thoughts are true and we are disconnected from the reality of our actual moment-to-moment experiences. This really is a trance of separation because when we are in this state of mind we are separated from our reality and from those who are close to us. We are also separated from our own bodies and from our deeper wisdom and potential.

Worrying is a particularly common type of thinking pattern in a trance that drains our energy by pulling us away from the present moment and into an imaginary (often catastrophic) future. Worrying has been likened to praying for what you don't want to happen – but yet we still allow ourselves to burn lots of time and energy doing it. Of course, it would not be helpful or realistic to suggest we try to stop worrying – this would be an impossible expectation and would probably result in us worrying about our inability to stop worrying. Worrying is an important coping strategy. The problem is we are worrying compulsively and incessantly and without awareness.

Pema Chodron said, 'It isn't what happens to us that causes us to suffer; it's what we say to ourselves about what happens.'[4] When we are in a trance, we can't see that most of the time, we are basically all right – it is the stories in our heads that are convincing us otherwise. When we are in a trance we can become convinced that we are a helpless victim, obsess about how to 'fix' other people, catastrophise about imagined worst-case-scenarios or re-live past hurts. The depths of our potential are completely out of our reach, we lose sight of our aspirations and self-care is completely off our radar. We feel like victims – but it is an inside job. Being in a trance can be exhausting. Feeling like a powerless victim, withdrawing, numbing, incessant worrying and self-protection all consume vast amounts of energy and drain hope, resilience and optimism.

I came to really understand that my stress and suffering was an 'inside job' after a particularly nasty experience of workplace bullying that involved being the victim of a premeditated personal attack orchestrated by two senior female colleagues. The actions of these women inflicted a great deal of emotional and psychological pain, however the sad reality was I was the primary perpetuator of the bullying. How did I bully myself? I replayed the experience over and over in my head. I tortured myself about the injustice of it all. About what I could have done differently in the weeks before the incident,

Learning how to wake up and break free from a state of trance is the threshold to a working life well lived.

the steps I could have taken to be more vigilant, to better protect myself. I obsessed about the early warning signs I could have been better attuned to. I mentally role-played the alternative ways I could have handled myself during the experience, crafting and honing the assertive, clear-thinking and calm words I could have spoken during the ordeal – words that, in reality, were way out of my reach in those terrifying moments. In the days following the incident, I dragged innocent bystanders down into my pit of self-righteous anger and pain. Every moment I spent tormenting myself with these harmful thoughts and stories, I continued to see myself as another workplace victim. I was perpetuating and amplifying my own pain. Finally, with the help of a coach, I was able to break the spell of the hurtful story I was telling myself over and over again. From there, I could re-orient myself to all the actions that were within my control to bring about a different, safer working reality for myself. I was also able to see the many ways the experience helped to crystalise and reinforce the work I wanted to do in the world.

When we are stuck in a trance, we are far more likely to settle for good enough rather than engaging in the work of imagining and bringing about our best possible lives. A good-enough life is rarely a life well lived. As Glennon Doyle puts it:

> *Good enough is what makes people drink too much and snark too much and become bitter and sick and live in quiet desperation until they lie on their deathbed and wonder: What might I have created if I had been braver?*[5]

When we are in a trance, we are puppets dancing to the voices in our heads – a limited and predictable soundtrack that keeps us stuck and playing small. Over time, the cumulative effects of replaying old stories can begin to corrode our wellbeing and our sense of agency. We may also become more and more reluctant to challenge and rewrite the stories that perpetuate our suffering.

In the words of Johann Hari:

> *Once you settle into a story about your pain, you are extremely reluctant to challenge it. It was like a leash I had put on my distress to keep it under control. I feared that if I messed with the story I had lived with for so long, the pain would be like an unchained animal, and it would savage me.*[6]

Learning how to wake up from a trance is the threshold to self-fidelity.

WAKING UP: CROSSING THE THRESHOLD

Learning how to wake up and break free from a state of trance is the threshold to a working life well lived. When we break the spell of a trance we move from a *reactive* state into a *responsive* state. We are able to reconnect with our essential nature and respond to the world around us from a place of presence.

Dr Rick Hanson describes awakening as remembering to step back and observe the workings of our minds with 'peaceful detachment':

> *Know your experience without identifying with it. ... Watch the movie without jumping into the screen. We all repeatedly get sucked into our experience and lose the peaceful detachment of observing it. Don't worry, don't scold yourself, just return to an awareness of whatever's arising.*[7]

Play around with this idea of stepping back out of the movie in our mind and into a seat in the movie theatre. Once we experience even a fleeting moment of peaceful detachment watching the movie of our mind instead of being the lead actor, we can't un-experience it.

One of my favourite meditations is Ram Dass's mindfulness meditation. This is the guidance Ram Dass offers for taking the same seat of awareness:

> *Just sit with what is. Neither pushing nor pulling. Just being. Relax. Find within yourself that vast spacious awareness. It is like the sky. Sounds, sensations, feelings, thoughts, they are not disturbances, they're all just part of the natural phenomenon that*

> *are crossing the sky. Keep going back into that part of awareness that is just the sky, resting in spacious awareness … Resting in your natural essence.*[8]

Even though we all continue to get caught up in the weather patterns of our mind, understanding and remembering that, at our essence, we are the sky and not the weather is nothing short of life-changing.

The concept of cognitive fusion and its opposite – cognitive defusion – are helpful in understanding the difference between a state of trance and a fully awakened state. Cognitive fusion is a term that is used in Acceptance and Commitment Therapy (ACT), an evidence-based approach to supporting people to increase psychological flexibility in order to live a full and meaningful life. Cognitive fusion is another way to describe a trance – allowing ourselves to become completely entangled with our thoughts. In a state of cognitive fusion our attention and focus is on our inner dialogue – on the stories in our heads. When we are in a state of cognitive fusion, our actions and decisions are being driven by this internal dialogue instead of being driven by our direct sensory experience of what is *really* going on around us. As Russ Harris explains in his book about ACT, *The Happiness Trap*, 'In a state of fusion a thought can seem like the absolute truth – a command you have to obey or a rule you have to follow.'[9] On the other hand, in a state of cognitive defusion we are in the state of open awareness – we have both awareness and control and are able to observe our thoughts, while also knowing that they are not always instructions on how to behave. In a state of cognitive defusion it becomes possible to respond, rather than blindly react. In the words of Russ, 'in a state of defusion, you recognise that a thought: may or may not be true, is not a command you have to obey, is not a threat to you, is not something happening in the physical world – it's merely words or pictures inside your head and can be allowed to come and go of its own accord.'[10]

RECLAIMING WHAT WE ONCE HAD

We might also like to think about the awakening of the parts of us that we mistakenly left behind in the transition from childhood into adulthood. Many indigenous cultures use rites of passage to teach their young adults that everything they need for their journey through life is already inside them. Unfortunately, growing up, many of us were not given this very important piece of wisdom. Instead, we were conditioned to wrongly believe that adults were always superior and to be child-like in any way was to be naïve and inferior. I like to think that we are living, breathing babushka dolls. Nestled inside me at age 45 lives my six-, seven- and eight-year-old selves. Much of the practice of self-fidelity is about reconnecting the part of ourselves that we unquestionably embodied as children. Those parts of us are pure and very wise.

My two young sons are, without doubt, my greatest teachers. One day I was having a little cry after this book was rejected by a publisher. My five-year-old son asked me why I was so sad. When I explained that my book had been rejected, he said without a moment of hesitation, 'But Mum, it doesn't matter how they feel about your book, all that matters is how you feel about it.' Pure gold.

We can think about awakening as the process of reconnecting with the wisdom of our own inner child. I love the way Dr Shefali Tsabary explains that to awaken is to reclaim that which we once were:

> *We awaken when we become who we truly are. But here is grand irony. The great paradox of life. What you are here to reclaim, you had it once. You had it as that child who knew its might. Who had wonder, grace, presence, beauty, worth, significance. That child who could look at its reflection in the mirror and only see beauty, power and perfection. That child to whom it never once occurred that they were lesser than. That you had to become something to be happy. That you had to do something to prove your worthiness. You were that child who was complete, whole, significant, purposeful, connected, present. You were that child.*[11]

BREAKING THE SPELL: BEING PRESENT

Austrian neurologist and psychologist Victor Frankl survived the brutalities of Auschwitz against all odds. Victor famously said, 'Between stimulus and response there is a space. In that space is our power to choose our response. In our response lies our growth and our freedom.'[12] If breaking free of a trance is the threshold to self-fidelity, then expanding these spaces between *what* happens to us and *our response* to what happens to us is what activates it. Victor discovered that accessing the space between stimulus and response was so powerful it offered a sense of freedom inside a Nazi concentration camp. As Victor explained, 'Everything can be taken from a man but one thing: the last of human freedoms – to choose one's attitude in any given set of circumstances, to choose one's own way.'[13]

Otto Scharmer's Theory U teaches that our capacity to awaken, or pay attention is directly proportional to our capacity to co-shape our world.[14] Otto's work is based around a central insight: the thing that prevents us from navigating our lives more effectively is that we aren't fully aware of that interior condition from which our attention and actions originate. Theory U seeks to awaken people to their capacity to shift their inner awareness to co-shape organisations and institutions around the world.

Breaking free from a trance can be described in many different ways in addition to cognitive defusion including being mindful, returning to loving presence, or waking up. Whatever we call it, breaking the spell of a trance returns us to our present-moment reality. Rather than thinking about learning how to let go of a trance, it is more helpful to think about learning how to break the spell of a trance – allowing the state of trance to let go of us. When we break the spell, we return back home to ourselves and back home to our true nature. Throughout *Self-Fidelity* I will describe the non-trance state we are learning to experience as being awakened or present.

Breaking free from a state of trance to become present is not an inherently difficult act. The difficult part is remembering that we can do it. The more we practise, the less time we spend in a trance-like state before we realise that we have, once again, been swept away. It is only through a regular practice we can learn about the trickeries of our own minds and improving our capacity to notice when we are in a trance and remember that we can in any moment lift out of our funk in to a far more resourceful state. We can practise through meditation, conscious breathing, conscious movement (such as yoga, running or swimming) or by spending time in nature really tuned into our senses. There is a range of free meditations specifically designed for awakening at self-fidelity.com.

By learning how to break the spell of trance, we can orient ourselves to the emerging future and respond to the moment we find ourselves in with discernment, precision and wisdom. When we are present, we reconnect in our true nature to each other and to our vast potential.

LIVING LIFE AS IF IT REALLY MATTERS

> Jon: What we are really trying to do is
> live our life as if it really matters.
> Oprah: Because it does matter.
> Jon: It does.
>
> Jon Kabat-Zinn and Oprah Winfrey[15]

The oft-cited most common regret people have in their final days is not having had the courage to live a life that was true to themselves. In his book *The Five Invitations*, Frank Ostaseski, a Buddhist end-of-life carer, shares Sean's story. Sean entered Frank's hospice in the final stages of his battle with disease. He was cranky, irritated and demanding. Frank shared that over his final weeks, in the kind and accepting environment of the hospice, Sean:

...was able to discover and reveal more of himself – parts of his identity that had long been hidden away for safekeeping. As Sean set down his defences and allowed his heart to open, his innate compassion, love and tenderness came forward. With love, Sean finally was able to let go of his fiercely constructed, self-protective, yet ultimately self-limiting identity.[16]

Sadly, Sean only experienced the embodiment of his true nature for just a few, short days before he died.

Upon seeing Earth from space for the first time, many astronauts report an instant and profound shift in perspective. They suddenly experience a deep awareness of a simple truth that we all know, but so often forget – that in the context of an infinite galaxy our busy, important working lives are really not all that important – or long. Neil Armstrong famously said, 'I put up my thumb and shut one eye, my thumb blotted out planet Earth. I didn't feel like a giant. I felt very, very small.'[17]

In contemplating our overall insignificance in the grand scheme of life, we cannot avoid the truth of our own mortality. We so often lament that 'life is short'. Matthew Michalewicz actually does the math on exactly how short our lives are, in the context of the time-span of human evolution. His book title *Life in Half a Second* is the answer.

Everyone knows that life is short – it is. But how short is it, exactly? Planet Earth is four-and-a-half billion years old. The species you and I belong to, Homo sapiens, did not emerge until some 200,000 years ago. The oldest known fossils of modern humans are only 160,000 years old, discovered in Herto, Ethiopia. So out of the four-and-a-half billion years that this planet has been floating through the nothingness of space, we've been around some .0044% of that time. Put another way, if our planet was exactly one year old, then modern humans would have only been around for the last 23 minutes. Measured on

> *the same scale, if our planet was a year old, then your entire life would amount to half a second.*[18]

Steve Jobs had a daily ritual to remind himself of his own mortality as a way to remember what was important to him:

> *For the past 33 years, I have looked in the mirror every morning and asked myself: 'If today were the last day of my life, would I want to do what I am about to do today?' And whenever the answer has been 'No' for too many days in a row, I know I need to change something. Remembering that I'll be dead soon is the most important tool I've ever encountered to help me make the big choices in life. Because almost everything – all external expectations, all pride, all fear of embarrassment or failure – these things just fall away in the face of death, leaving only what is truly important. Remembering that you are going to die is the best way I know to avoid the trap of thinking you have something to lose. You are already naked. There is no reason not to follow your heart.*[19]

Living with the awareness that our lives are short is a good way to avoid joining the ranks of the many people who die with the regret of not having lived a life that was true to themselves. Whenever I find myself struggling to make a difficult course-correction decision to remain true to myself, I remind myself of the alternative – my working life coming to an end and realising that I hadn't ever truly lived it on my terms. That I had drifted through my life afraid, small and half-awake waiting for a sense of enough-ness that never arrived. Let's make our half a second really count.

LIVING A LIFE WE FEEL PROUD OF

In the book *Die Empty – Unleash Your Best Work Every Day*, Todd Henry suggests that the question we often hear – 'what would you do if today was your last day on earth?' does not often lead us to an illuminating insight.[20] This is because most people imagine that they would choose to spend their last day on earth enjoying themselves as much as possible with their loved ones without any concern for long-term consequences. My answer to this question, for example, would most certainly include my family, a beautiful beach and a large esky packed with a bottle of very expensive champagne, copious amounts of soft cheese and every single flavour of Ben & Jerry's ice-cream – and that is just for starters.

Todd suggests that it would be more useful to imagine that tomorrow, we will have an 'observer' accompany us through our entire day. This observer will follow us from the moment we wake up to the moment we go to sleep, creating a detailed log describing every single thing we do. This log would capture every detail of how we behaved in the morning with our loved ones, how we spend our work day, how we were in the evenings and our mindset and attitude throughout it all. After the log was complete, this observer would then analyse all the data that they had collected from this one representative day and use it to compile a book that will stand as the definitive record of our work and our life. Todd invites us to consider two key questions:

> How would you act differently tomorrow if you knew that your actions and attitude on that *one day* were going to be a permanent testament to your life?
>
> How does your *imagined behaviour* compare with how you are living your life today?[21]

I would add two more questions:

> What would you need to change in order to experience a way of working and living that you felt proud of?
>
> What might be possible if, starting today, you began living a life you felt more proud of?

The sooner we begin to play with new ways of thinking, being, working and living, the sooner we begin to create a working life that uplifts us and the people we care about most. We don't have to wait for tragedy or crisis to make changes. We don't have to stare death in the face. We don't have to wait until we are more experienced, more accomplished, more senior, more wealthy, more educated – or more *anything*. Making the changes necessary to living a working life that is true is of the highest urgency and importance, so let's start right now.

Steven Pressfield said, 'Most of us have two lives. The life we live and the unlived life within us. Between the two stands resistance.'[22] The practice of self-fidelity dissolves this resistance and supports the discovery of an exhilarating answer to Mary Oliver's exhilarating question, 'Tell me, what is it you plan to do with your one wild and precious life?'[23]

Waking up: **Being present**

Understanding to uplift

INSIGHTS

When we are in a trance, we are not fully aware
of our present-moment inner or outer reality.

We can learn to break the spell of a trance to become present.

When we are present, we can reconnect to our true nature.

When we reconnect to our true nature,
life is vivid and we can access our vast potential.

PLAY

Which of the waking up practices resonate the most for you?

How will you practise experiencing presence?

Is there something you need to give yourself
permission to feel or experience?

How will you support yourself to honour your
commitment to practice?

OUTSIGHTS

What does it feel like to be present?

What do you now know in a deeper way?

GETTING TO THE HEART OF THE MATTER

What new possibilities might emerge
if you were to experience presence more often?

How might being present more often uplift your working life?

How might being present more often uplift others in your life?

**In moments of true presence,
what is your experience of who you *really* are?**

Attachments

I bring an undefended heart to our meeting place.
I have no cherished outcomes,
I will not negotiate by withholding,
I am not subject to disappointment.

A native prayer of approach[1]

Building on our understanding of what it means to become present, we can now explore the concept of attachments – or more specifically, unhelpful attachments. Attachments create expectations. And in a world that is tumultuous, unpredictable and out of our control, expectations can cause suffering. As Anne Lamott wisely said, 'expectations are resentments waiting to happen.'[2]

In the context of self-fidelity, we have an unhelpful attachment when we cling to a thought, belief, story, outcome, plan or relationship that no longer serves us.

UNDERSTANDING ATTACHMENT

When we are in a state of trance, we feel separated from the world around us and disconnected from others. One of the coping strategies our brains employ in reaction to these feelings is clinging and attachment. This reaction served as an important survival instinct for our ancestors, given exclusion meant death. However, in the modern world, reactive clinging and attaching is usually unnecessary and often unhelpful. Today, we are constantly triggered by things that are not life-threatening. Something as innocuous as our boss not smiling at us one morning, our idea being dismissed in a team meeting or office politics derailing our project can trigger an unhelpful reaction of clinging to the story in our head or to what we think *should be.* By clinging to what we think *should be,* we resist *what is* – causing suffering and stress. This form of clinging prevents us from accepting and navigating the reality of our situation *as it is.* Of course, in the same way that a state of trance is not always bad, attachments are not always bad for us. Our wellbeing depends on healthy attachments to others. Healthy striving towards an outcome is fuelled by a desire for personal growth. The problem is that humans have a tendency to cling to things that no longer serve us.

Many years ago, I participated in a workshop run by psychologist Dr Carrie Hayward. During the workshop Carrie physically demonstrated a tug-of-war, straining and pulling an imaginary rope. She explained that the tug-of-war represented the way we struggle with and against our reality. She explained how it is so easy to get single-mindedly caught up in our desire to win the battle. We pull harder and harder believing that through enough resistance and brute force we can bring about the outcomes that we desperately want in our lives. Carrie really threw her whole body into the demonstration, crouching, grunting and straining. It was exhausting just watching her. Suddenly, she stopped and said, 'by learning to be aware when we are caught up in a tug-of-war with reality… we remember that we can simply drop the rope.' As she said 'drop the rope' and unclenched her fists, the room fell completely silent. She had also dropped a truth bomb and we all felt it. Practising non-attachment is about remembering that we can simply let go of the rope. Dropping the rope is about accepting and allowing *what is* instead of wishing it were different.

Contemplative traditions teach us that the root of all human suffering is unhealthy attachment. Letting go of how things *should* be and awakening to the true nature of our reality is an ongoing practice. There are entire books dedicated to the practices of awakening to attachment. The most important and the first step towards awakening to unhealthy attachments is becoming aware of them.

We experience moments of micro-awakening whenever we wake up to the reality that an attachment is no longer serving us. Through awareness, we can begin to become aware of alternative, more liberating perspectives that are available to us in any moment. If we patiently string together small moments of awakening, like a beautiful strand of pearls, we slowly build confidence in our capacity to liberate our hearts and our minds.

PRACTISING LOVING DETACHMENT

A practice that can support letting go of attachments is the practice of *loving detachment*. I learnt this practice at the Al-Anon meetings that were my lifeline during the period I was untangling myself from an abusive relationship. It is no exaggeration to say it was a life-changing revelation to learn that it was possible for me to choose to emotionally detach myself from my unhealthy, alcohol-fuelled merry-go-round relationship without being cruel or callous. I realised that I could honour myself and my right to live without fear, and that this honouring need not be cruel and cold, but instead rooted in loving respect for one another's struggles and individuality.

As we awaken to our unhealthy attachments, we can begin to meet our current reality and wisely navigate our way forward to discover something new – something truer and better. Whether we are awakening to an unhealthy relationship, a constraining belief, a limiting identity or a cherished outcome, practising both compassion and self-compassion is vital. We can choose to be thoughtful about what is said and what remains unsaid. We can embody discreet, calm silence instead of cold, distant resentment. We can choose to speak to ourselves and others with patience, kindness, love and respect. We can gently break free and return ourselves to a centred place of wisdom and strength.

Waking up: **Attachments**

Understanding to uplift

INSIGHTS

Attachments become unhelpful when they no longer serve us.

We can let go of beliefs, stories or relationships
that no longer serve us.

It is possible to detach in a way that is loving.

Awareness is the first step in letting go.

Every small moment of awakening
builds confidence and clarity.

PLAY

How might you become more aware of your attachments
and whether they serve you?

Is there something you need to give yourself
permission to feel or experience?

OUTSIGHTS

How do you know when an attachment is not good for you?

What else do you now know in a deeper way?

GETTING TO THE HEART OF THE MATTER

What are your heaviest attachments?

How might letting them go uplift your working life?

How might it uplift others in your life?

**What might be possible
if you were no longer constrained?**

Beliefs

Human beings have a great capacity for sticking to false beliefs with great passion and tenacity.

Bruce H. Lipton[1]

A belief is simply a repeated thought. Our human tendency to attach to our beliefs is worthy of closer examination and the importance of our beliefs cannot be overstated.

Our beliefs are invisible forces that operate often below our levels of conscious awareness. Our beliefs drive our behaviour. Limiting beliefs can act like invisible heavy sandbags that are working against our desire and natural capacity to rise. Often, we cannot see that we are being held back and held down by these beliefs. This is because our patterns of thinking become so ingrained in us, that over time we become blind to the reality that there are alternative ways to think. By becoming conscious of our thinking, it is possible to create new beliefs and let go of beliefs that no longer serve us.

The poet Rumi said, 'Why do you stay in prison when the door is wide open?'[2] The bars of our personal prisons are our own limiting beliefs. We can spend years believing these bars are real, and then suddenly awaken one day to the reality that they are merely a reflection of our thinking.

Our beliefs want to be proven right. They determine what we notice in the world around us and they drive our behaviour – they become a self-fulfilling prophecy. How do our beliefs determine what we notice in the world around us? One way is through the part of our brain called the Reticular Activating System (or RAS). The RAS is a small bundle of neurons at the top of our spinal column. One of the things our RAS does is act as a filter of the vast amounts of sensory information we are receiving in any moment. The RAS makes sure our brain doesn't get bombarded with more information than it can handle. It decides which bits of incoming information to let into our brains. One of the ways it does this is by determining which elements of the incoming information are most important for us to pay attention to – based on the beliefs we hold. So, for example, if I have a belief that I am not intelligent, the RAS will very efficiently filter out the incoming data that may suggest otherwise – over time reinforcing this belief. This reinforcing loop that strengthens our beliefs is also referred to as confirmation bias. This is how Professor Ellen Langer of Harvard University describes how our beliefs continue to prove themselves true:

> *You have a belief, and then you seek out a confirmation for it. My belief is that our beliefs are not inconsequential. It's not that they matter a little, they're almost the only thing that does matter.*[3]

Ellen's decades of work involve some truly extraordinary experiments that demonstrate the power of our beliefs. In her well-known chambermaid experiment, Ellen divided a group of women who worked in hotels cleaning and servicing rooms into two sub-groups. She educated one of the sub-groups about how their work met the Surgeon General's definition of exercise, embedding a new belief that by doing their jobs they were in fact exercising. There were no changes made to their activity level or the work they were doing – the *only* thing that changed was their belief about the work they were doing. The results were astounding. At the end of the experiment the sub-group who perceived themselves to be getting regular exercise at work showed a significant decrease in weight, blood pressure, body fat, waist-to-hip ratio and body mass index compared with the control group.

A belief is simply a repeated thought.

Johann Hari's work provides another perspective that illuminates the tremendous power of beliefs.[4] In his book *The Lost Connections*, Johann explores the healing power of the placebo effect (which is essentially a belief that you are getting help, usually in the form of a drug which is not actually a drug but a harmless, inactive substance.) After examining the clinical trial data for the drugs most often prescribed for managing depression, Johann discovered that the belief that a placebo drug was a form of help accounted for the vast majority of cases of reduced symptoms of depression. He discovered that the data suggested the drugs themselves were having 'no meaningful effect at all'.[5] Johann also shares the story of Henry Beecher, an American anaesthetist, who ran out of morphine on the frontline in World War II. Henry was worried he would 'kill soldiers by inducing heart failure if he tried to operate on them without anything to numb them',[6] so he decided to use a saltwater drip and tell the soldiers he was giving them morphine. It worked. The patients who believed they were being administered morphine during their operations 'reacted just as if they had been given morphine. They didn't scream, or howl and they didn't go into full-blown shock.'[7]

We are still in the process of really understanding the complex networks of connection processes that happen within our bodies to activate familiar patterns of thinking. Repeated patterns of thinking create well-worn neural pathways. From a neuroscience perspective, the neural connections associated with beliefs have 'fired and wired together' many times. Over time, these default ways of thinking about ourselves and the world around us combine to create our paradigms. Generally speaking, creating and embedding a new way of thinking – and new beliefs and paradigms – takes perseverance. Although with enough emotion, new ways of thinking can become embedded very quickly.

I once planted the seeds for a new belief – that I could run a full marathon – in a split second. This was the second after my ex-partner told me I was most definitely not capable of running a marathon (based on the logic that he had not been able to finish one). Six months later, with many hours of training under my belt, the strength of that belief was still so strong, it triumphed over extreme physical pain and two completely cramped quadriceps to propel my body in a forward direction (albeit slowly) for four and half hours and 42.2 kilometres. In retrospect, perhaps there was a smidge of unhealthy proving in the mix there also.

The process of letting go of our limiting beliefs and choosing instead to orient towards uplifting thinking and beliefs begins with awareness. Once we surface the limiting beliefs that are lurking, below the level of conscious awareness, we can consciously choose alternative ways of thinking – and over time create more uplifting beliefs. To do this requires a combination of awareness and full presence. At the heart of an uplifting belief system is the core belief in our own worthiness. In the words of Oprah Winfrey,

> *The first question to ask yourself is, What do I believe? Do you believe that you are worthy of happiness, success, abundance, fulfillment, peace, joy and love? What I know for sure is you become what you believe.*[8]

When a new way of thinking worms its way through the tofu in our heads to forge new neural connections, we must strengthen these new connections through repeated, intentional effort. Over time, the new patterns of thinking and the associated belief can become our default way of thinking. The process of shedding a limiting belief starts with the emergence of new awareness. While we often talk about having light bulb moments, in my experience awareness feels more like, as Malcolm Gladwell describes it, the flame of 'a flickering candle that can easily be snuffed out.'[9]

Later, in *Letting go* we will illuminate and begin to release the limiting beliefs so many of us carry.

Waking up: **Beliefs**

Understanding to uplift

INSIGHTS

Beliefs are just thoughts we keep on thinking.

Our beliefs prove themselves right.

Beliefs can weigh us down or lift us up.

Humans have a strong tendency to cling to our beliefs.

We can choose different thoughts and form new beliefs.

Choosing different thinking begins with awareness.

PLAY

How might you become more aware of your beliefs?

How might you choose different ways to think,
as a result of this awareness?

Is there something you need to give yourself
permission to feel or experience?

OUTSIGHTS

How do you know when a certain way of thinking
is weighing you down?

What else do you now know in a deeper way?

GETTING TO THE HEART OF THE MATTER

What are the heaviest beliefs you carry?

How might letting them go uplift your working life?

How might letting them go uplift others in your life?

**What might be possible
if you refused to weigh yourself down?**

The voices in our heads

...it was in this moment, lying in bed late at night, that I first realized that the voice in my head - the running commentary that had dominated my field of consciousness since I could remember - was kind of an asshole.

Dan Harris[1]

As we become more familiar with the experience of wide-awake awareness, we also become more familiar with our inner worlds – especially the voices in our heads – and the ways these voices can keep us stuck, small and over time, make us sick. Stress is not something that physically exists in the world – there are only stressful thoughts and stories peddled by the voices in our heads.

When we were children, we were so much more confident in ourselves. We believed that we could sing, dance and paint. And so we did all these things and much, much more. As we get older, this confidence fades. Why? It's not because we grow out of our innate creativity and playfulness. It's because the voices in our head take residence and get louder – and we believe what they tell us. Too many fabulous people are held back by the voices in their heads. For many of us, the shocking reality is that if a family member spoke to us in the way the voices in our heads speak to us, they would be charged with emotional abuse.

During the 2020 coronavirus pandemic, like a lot of people, I watched many webinars. One webinar in particular rocked me to the core – but not for the reasons you might expect. It was a TED-talk style webinar and I had paid to watch a talk about how the pandemic was impacting job security in female-dominated sectors. The presenter was incredible. She was smart. She was strong. She was articulate, savvy, well-researched and passionate. I was mesmerised for the full twenty minutes she spoke. Then something extraordinary happened. The moment she finished her talk (not realising she was still broadcasting) she immediately gave a huge sigh. She blurted out to the host, 'Oh my gosh! Was that okay? That whole time I was talking I just kept thinking to myself, "you are talking such total crap!"' I sat there dumbstruck for quite a long time – I think I may have even said aloud – W T F.

Now we are in pretty deep water when we start to contemplate the voices in our heads – who are they and why do they exist? When we figure out that we are, in fact, not the voices in our heads and we are not even our thoughts – then we hit the big kahuna of questions. If I am not my thoughts and I am not the voices in my head… then who the hell am I?

Because this central question 'who am I?' blows our tiny minds, we can very easily put this entire line of self-enquiry right at the bottom of the too-hard basket and leave it there under our dusty collection of orphaned socks forevermore. What a waste of a life this would be. As Michael A Singer says, 'There is nothing more important to true growth than realizing that you are not the voice of the mind – you are the one who hears it.'[2]

As overwhelming and confusing as the question of 'who am I?' is, we can still start to engage with it. We start by simply getting just a little bit familiar with the 'I' that sits behind and in between the stories and voices in our heads. We can grow our *awareness of* those voices, stories and thoughts, understanding that voices, tracks, stories and thoughts in our heads are the weather – and we are the sky. To start with, we can focus on becoming more and more familiar with the answers to the following two foundational questions.

- What are the most common weather patterns in my inner world?
- How might I notice fleeting experiences of being the clear blue sky that sits behind and between these weather patterns?

Our essential nature transcends all the voices in our heads. It is the vast, sky-like presence that these voices so often cloud.

BECOMING FAMILIAR WITH THE VOICES IN OUR HEADS

A great way to begin to uncover the answers to these questions is by observing the voices in our heads and starting to become really familiar with the limited tracks they tend to play and the lies they tell us. Occasionally the voices in my head interrupt my precious evening family time at home with this breaking fake-news bulletin:

> Be alert and alarmed! No one in your family has asked you how your day was! This is absolute proof that not one of them *really* loves you or cares about you. This confirms your deepest suspicion that you are, in fact, unworthy of love. It would probably be best if you found a small, affordable apartment nearby and moved out.

If I allow myself to get sucked-in by the growing vortex of BS forming in my head, I can quite easily become fully engulfed in a protracted trance of unworthiness. In this trance, I can spend the entire dinner engulfed by feelings of shame, sadness, self-righteousness, resentment and loneliness – all while the people who love me the most in the world are telling me about their day and asking me to pass the salt. I may be physically sitting at the same table as my loved ones, but my heart is closed and I am in another realm – shadow-boxing in my own virtual crappy-apartment-imagining reality.

We are all susceptible to being spirited away from our present-moment reality by the pesky voices in our heads. If we allow ourselves to remain away for too long – it can have serious consequences.

OUR INNER DJ CREW

I think of the voices in my head like a panel of washed-up DJs who run a 24/7 radio station that provides the background soundtrack of my life. If this inner radio station had a catch-phrase it would be: *Easy listening, hard living.* I am becoming more and more familiar with the DJs who live in my head and their small, stale repertoire, which includes catchy little numbers like:

- Everything is urgent.
- I can't cope with this.

The voices in our heads have honed their repertoire over time. They have cleverly learnt and adapted the strategies employed by our parents, relatives, teachers, coaches, siblings, peers or bosses to try to make us conform and keep us safe. Here are some of the most common members of our inner DJ crew and the tracks they just love to play:

DJ Pleaser: always put the needs of others first

DJ Pusher: work harder, faster and better

DJ Blamer: it's all your fault that things have gone wrong

DJ Comparer: it's already been done, so don't even bother

DJ Impossible-standards-setter: it's not perfect – work harder

DJ Fixed mindset: you'll never learn

DJ Comfort zone: don't even try – you can't handle it

DJ Just lucky: you just got lucky this one time

DJ Imposter: you are a fraud – just wait until they find out

DJ Should-er: you really should…

DJ If only: if only you had done (or not done) …

DJ Shame-er: you'll never be good enough

DJ Insulter: you're stupid/weak/naïve/selfish/ugly/fat

DJ Fear: you will just fail, make a fool of yourself or get hurt

By awakening to the voices in our heads we can begin to get familiar with their limited playlist. We can't turn them off but, with practice, we can learn how to change the channel for a little while or turn down the volume when we are doing something important – or just need a cuddle.

It can be helpful to give your inner DJ crew a name that works for you. Perhaps you might think of them as 'The-know-it-alls' or 'The inner critics'. The simple act of naming and addressing the voices in our heads when we notice their presence separates us from them and gives you some power back. 'Ah, hello crew, welcome back! You guys are right on time. Now quiet down, please. I am in the middle of something important right now.'

While I know for sure that the tunes my inner DJs spin and the fake news they broadcast are not instructions on how to behave – I still find myself often forgetting. One of the little hacks I like to play with is imagining these inner fake news flash updates to uplifting music. 'I can't cope with this' quickly loses its power when I imagine these same words to the tune of MC Hammer's 'You can't touch this'[3] (doo na na na, you can't cope with this, doo na na na …). The inner newsflash of 'Everything is urgent!' feels far less heavy when I imagine it to the tune of the Lego movie theme song 'Everything is awesome'. Play around with different ways of relating to the voices in your heads to see how you can dial-down their power.

A PRACTICE OF SELF-ENQUIRY: IS IT TRUE?

> Byron Katie's Work is a great blessing for our planet.
> It acts like a razor-sharp sword that cuts through illusion
> and enables you to know for yourself the
> timeless essence of your being.
>
> Eckhard Tolle[4]

The work of Byron Katie provides a wonderful method of enquiry that we can use to dial-down the power held by the voices in our heads and their 24/7 fake-news-feed. Katie invites us to isolate one particular thought to enquire about, asking four simple but powerful questions. This process of enquiry is a form of guided meditation practice. The four questions are:

Is it true?

Can you absolutely know that it's true?

How do you react, what happens, when you believe that thought?

Who would you be without that thought?

If you keep a dedicated journal to capture and reflect on the answers that emerge when you ask yourself these four questions, predictable patterns and themes will quickly emerge.

MAKING FRIENDS WITH THE VOICES IN OUR HEADS

This work is not about rejecting or suppressing these parts of ourselves. At its core, this work is about embracing the sometimes opposing parts of ourselves. It's about making friends with the residents in our heads. It's important that we don't see our inner residents as enemies that must be conquered but rather as potential allies on our pilgrimage of discovery.

As we unveil the voices in our heads, we come to better understand their motivations and the consequences of allowing them to get behind the helm. Empowered with this understanding and awareness, we can get on with our most important work of practising how to be true to ourselves.

Sometimes we need help to familiarise ourselves with the voices in our head and safely engage in dialogue with them. Also, if you experience an inner voice that is more extreme, pervasive or nasty than what I have described in this chapter, please seek professional help.

HOW WAKING UP LEADS TO DIFFERENT OUTCOMES

When we are awake to the voices in our heads, we are no longer stuck in a state of trance, wrongly believing that the voices in our heads are our instructions on what we should do next. This awareness – in very practical terms – leads us to make different choices and experience different outcomes.

Here is an example of how the dominoes can fall quickly – from thought to outcomes – when we are unable to break free from the spell of a trance.

While this example may be a little extreme, it certainly illustrates the point.

Experience
Our boss dismisses a suggestion that we make in a team meeting.

↓

Thought
What an asshole, I really think I need to start looking for another job.

↓

Choice
That's it. I am just going to keep my mouth shut. Why should I bother wasting my breath with this guy. This whole team meeting is a joke.

↓

Action
We lean back from the table, cross our arms over our chest. We only give one-word answers for the rest of the meeting.

↓

Outcome
Our boss spends the afternoon avoiding us. That evening, over dinner, we drink two large glasses of wine while venting to our partner about what an asshole our boss is. Our partner goes to bed early and we stay up late eating chocolate and watching Netflix.

This is how waking up and becoming *present* builds in a circuit-breaker. By simply becoming aware of the voices in our head, we can potentially experience very different outcomes.

Experience

Our boss dismisses a suggestion that we make in a team meeting.

↓

Thought

What an asshole, I really think I need to start looking for another job.

↓

!! AWARENESS !!

Oh gosh, I just had the thought that my boss is an asshole. That seems a little harsh. He loved the suggestion I made in our last team meeting. Perhaps he knows something I don't know. Actually, he looks a little tired.

↓

Choice

I am not going to let what just happened ruin the rest of my day or damage my work relationships.

↓

Action

We maintain our composure and participate in the rest of the meeting.

↓

Outcome

Walking out of the office at the end of the day, we have an informal chat with our boss and he shares that his eldest son is really struggling at school and that he has lost a lot of sleep over it. That evening we think about how we might be able to step up at work for the rest of the week, given what he is experiencing.

Waking up: **The voices in our heads**

Understanding to uplift

INSIGHTS

The voices in our heads can keep us
stuck, small and over time, make us sick.

None of the voices in your head are the 'real you'.

We can get to know the voices in our heads.

Identifying predictable stories and songs is the first step.

With awareness, presence and practice
the voices in our head lose their power.

PLAY

How might you become more aware of the thoughts,
voices and stories in your head?

How will you practise observing them?

How will you support yourself to honour this commitment?

Is there something you need to give yourself
permission to feel or experience?

OUTSIGHTS

How do you know when the voices in your heads
are influencing you?

What else do you now know in a deeper way?

GETTING TO THE HEART OF THE MATTER

What are the most limiting inner stories and songs in your head?

How might observing your inner dialogue
(rather than seeing it as instructions on how to behave)
uplift your working life?

How might observing your inner dialogue uplift others in your life?

What might be possible
if you stopped believing the voices in your head?

Connecting to our essential nature: a deeper understanding

You live like this, sheltered, in a delicate world,
and you believe you are living.
Then you read a book... or you take a trip...
and you discover that you are not living,
that you are hibernating.

Anaïs Nin[1]

Through an understanding of what it means to wake up we can deepen our understanding of what it means to be true to ourselves, building on what we covered in the *Foundations* section. Once again, do not be concerned if all of this does not make complete sense just yet, it will all become clearer as we work through the remaining core practices of *Letting be*, *Letting go* and *Letting in.*

When we are connected to our essential nature

We are present.

We have the capacity to respond to the world around us, rather than react to it.

Our thinking is spacious, clear and inspired.

Our self-worth is not in question.

Our hearts are open yet discerning.

We can inhabit our vulnerability.

We can work in ways that are creative and playful.

We are open to alternative perspectives.

Life is vivid.

Our potential is vast.

AND

We can observe our thoughts.

We know that our thoughts are not always the truth.

We can investigate our thoughts and beliefs.

We can let go of unhelpful attachments and beliefs.

We remember that we are not any of the voices in our heads.

We can notice uncomfortable feelings without being entangled in them.

We are open to the voices of others, but with discernment.

Dear you,

You who always have
so many things to do
so many places to be
your mind spinning like
fan blades at high speed
each moment always a blur
because you're never still.

I know you're tired.
I also know it's not your fault.
The constant brain-buzz is like
a swarm of bees threatening
to sting if you close your eyes.
You've forgotten something again.
You need to prepare for that or else.
You should have done that differently.

What if you closed your eyes?
Would the world fall
apart without you?

Or would your mind
become the open sky
flock of thoughts
flying across the sunrise
as you just watched and smiled.

Kaveri Patel[2]

LETTING BE

To be yourself in a world that is constantly trying to make you something else is the greatest accomplishment.

Ralph Waldo Emerson[1]

Being worthy

Self-worth comes from one thing –
thinking you are worthy.

Dr Wayne Dyer[1]

Several years ago, I experienced my first professional photo shoot with the fabulous Melbourne-based photographer Fi Mims. Leading up to the shoot I noticed a slight feeling of nervousness. The big day arrived, and we started the process with getting my hair and makeup professionally done. As I sat in the makeup chair looking at myself in the mirror, the voices in my head began getting louder and louder. I became more and more convinced that I was not worthy of all the fuss and attention. My mind raced into the future to manufacture even more anxiety by imagining meeting new people and seeing the looks of surprise on their faces upon realising that the in-real-life version of me was significantly less polished and glamorous than the version of me in the images we were about to create. I put on a brave face and soldiered on. As we started the shoot, I began to calm down a bit. Fi's warmth and humour helped me to remember my playfulness, and the voices in my head began to fade. That was until the moment when Fi wheeled in her wind machine. Within a split second of seeing the machine and then realising what it was, a loud voice inside my head boomed, 'who the *hell* do you think you are, love?' I lost it. Luckily Fi had seen it all before. She was patient and kind and she told me about the many times she has seen the same reaction from her other clients. We managed to get through the shoot and the images we created that day hold a very special meaning for me. This experience taught me that we are all 'wind-machine-worthy'. It also brought into sharp focus the truth of Marianne Williamson's words:

> *It is our light not our darkness that most frightens us. We ask ourselves, who am I to be brilliant, talented and fabulous? Actually, who are you not to be? Playing small does not serve the world ... We are all meant to shine, as children do.*[2]

Many of us are blind to the truth of who we are because we have mistakenly come to believe that we are not enough or that we are in some way unworthy. We may be hurting, we may be afraid, we may be exhausted, we may have made terrible mistakes, we are imperfect. But we are all enough and we are all worthy. And true belonging only comes to those who learn how to honour their enough-ness.

We can all experience feelings of unworthiness. For some of us, these feelings surface occasionally, for others they are a constant companion. When we are in the trance of unworthiness we are out of touch with reality and we lose the capacity to accurately discern strengths, limitations, opportunities and threats. Whether we feel trapped in the land of low self-worth or are just an occasional visitor, every moment we spend there causes us to miss opportunities and suffer.

Self-worth is not something we achieve – there is no finish-line we can cross, arms in the air declaring, 'Finally, I will forever feel worthy!' The cultivation of self-worth is a commitment to the ongoing practice of reminding ourselves over and over again of our worthiness – and choosing to believe it every time.

Over time, we can learn to source a sense of enough-ness from within us, rather than continuing in vain to fill the void in our hearts by collecting gold stars or striving to prove ourselves by climbing the corporate ladder, earning big bonuses, having well-behaved kids, the perfect marriage or attracting a certain number of followers or likes on social media.

At its core, accepting our own intrinsic worthiness is about learning that we can't *do* our way to *being* someone. Instead, we must *do* from a place of knowing that we already *are* someone. That we have *always been* someone. We truly let be when we embody the knowing that we are all born worthy. In the words of Mark Dooley, 'contrary to popular thinking, worthiness is not something you earn, it's something you recognise.'[3]

I have suffered greatly from a deep belief that my achievements were the only measure of my worth in the world. I spent the first decade of my career being propelled forward by an urge to prove my worth through my achievements. Always striving, never really feeling content with just being. Always doing. I felt like I was being propelled by a hidden force that was beyond my control. It was not until my mid-30s that I began to make progress with the support of a psychologist. Looking back at my working life over that period, I now believe that the string of painful workplace experiences was the 'unseen order of things' asking me, 'Are you ready to back yourself yet, Cassie? Are you going to find the courage to honour your worthiness? Not yet? Okay – let's turn up the heat a little!'

THE SHADOW-SIDE OF HIGH PERFORMANCE

Low self-worth can be the shadow-side of high performance. In fact, for many people feelings of low self-worth are the primary fuel that drives our performance. While this type of fuel can be powerful, it is also heavily polluting. Over time, it can be toxic to our wellbeing, relationships and long-term performance. This became clear to me during a women's leadership retreat I participated in many years ago. It was a pivotal experience for me, but not for the reasons I expected. During the retreat I had the privilege of spending several days with a group of highly accomplished senior female leaders. The cohort consisted of incredible women doing difficult and important work across a broad spectrum of industries and government departments. As trust grew, many of the participants began sharing that they

Embracing our own worthiness and the worthiness of others is a vital element of being true to ourselves and living into our ethical potential as humans.

secretly wrestled with omnipresent feelings of low self-worth. Their inability to make sense of these feelings alongside their drive to keep performing in their senior, high-profile positions further amplified their secret suffering. It deeply saddened me that many of the wonderful women at the retreat felt like something was wrong with them and they were suppressing their feelings or beating themselves up about them. The teary confessions of one of the women – Debra – whose job put her in charge of an emergency department at a large hospital will always stay with me. Debra was quite *literally* saving lives every single day, yet she revealed that she felt like she had absolutely no value in the world.

Carl Jung coined the term 'shadow', using it to refer to the parts of our personality that we have rejected or put walls around – describing the shadow as 'the person you would rather not be'.[4] He, and many others after him, believe that the process of integrating our shadow has a profound impact on us. This process is really a process of forgiveness – forgiving ourselves for our imperfection, for our cracks. As Debbie Ford said:

> *Our shadows exist to teach us, to guide us ... They are resources for us to expose and explore. The feelings we have suppressed are desperate to be integrated into ourselves. They are only harmful when they are repressed: then they can pop up at the least opportune times. Their sneak attacks will handicap you in the areas of your life that mean the most. Your life will be transformed when you make peace with your shadow.*[5]

It may sound counter-intuitive, but the integration of our darkest shadows activates our brightest light. Our greatest flaws are often a corrupt or extreme version of our greatest strengths. When we suppress or disown the 'bad' part of ourselves, we also suppress their opposite. Accepting our wholeness means that we understand, for example, by denying our fear we diminish our courage, or by denying our naïvety we diminish our openness.

'What you resist persists' is a common mantra popular in addiction support groups. Making peace with our fullness doesn't mean that we condone actions that hurt others. Instead we understand where they come from and have the courage to recognise the same tendencies within ourselves. From this place of compassionate awareness, we discover ways to heal and do better together. The alternative of mounting the high-horse of self-righteous judgement is corrosive to our wellbeing, wholeness and connections.

Honouring our wholeness and our shadows does not mean that we walk past unethical or cruel behaviour – in ourselves and others. Rather, it is about working with these behaviours from a place of compassion and understanding. Sometimes when we react with harsh condemnation, judgement and criticism towards the behaviours of others, it is because these behaviours mirror the part of ourselves we have disowned.

Embracing our shadows is essential if we are to make peace with the best of human nature and the worst of human nature and become truly faithful to our own imperfect fullness and the imperfect fullness of others. The acceptance of our wholeness, our shadows, our past mistakes, our struggles and our sharp edges, means that shame cannot thrive. Accepting our wholeness can dissolve a great deal of resistance and salvage a tremendous amount of energy.

As we are beginning to see, the work of cultivating self-fidelity is as much about unlearning as it is learning. The key is to take some small action to soften and activate these parts of ourselves. When we stop suppressing and denying the parts of ourselves that we have come to believe are not-good-enough, we begin to take positive actions to return ourselves to wholeness. I love how Lisa Messenger speaks about her journey back to wholeness and how it has allowed her to redirect her energy to making a positive impact on the world:

> *In the past, at times, I may have [been a] different Lisa, depending on the situation. Today, I'm all the same – the over-sharer at the dinner table and from the stage, the visionary around the office*

and when planning holidays, the caring friend who also cares about my staff. I know who I am and I don't have to keep shifting my energy to suit a new environment. Instead, I can focus all my energy on engaging with the world and making a positive impact on it.[6]

ACCEPTING OUR IMPERFECTIONS

Wabi sabi is the Japanese philosophy of accepting our imperfections to make the most of life. It celebrates the way things are – rather than how we think they should be. As Richard Powell explains in *Wabi Sabi Simple*, wabi sabi is 'a way of life that appreciates and accepts complexity while at the same time values simplicity'.[7] This honours three simple realities – 'Nothing lasts, nothing is finished, and nothing is perfect.' A beautiful example of wabi sabi is the Japanese art of *kinsukuroi* or 'golden repair'. This artform involves repairing broken pottery by mending the areas of breakage with lacquer mixed with powdered gold, silver or platinum. It integrates the cracks as part of the history and beauty of an object, rather than something to disguise.

Wabi sabi reminds me of the words of Leonard Cohen:

Ring the bells that still can ring
Forget your perfect offering
There is a crack, a crack in everything
That's how the light gets in.[8]

People pay attention to what we do, not what we say. Wholehearted leaders engage with the world from a place of worthiness and this is obvious to everyone who comes into contact with them. When we have done the work that enables us to lead from a place of unwavering faith in our own worthiness and the worthiness of others – it changes everything.

Terry Real describes self-esteem as 'our ability to see ourselves as a flawed individual and still hold ourselves in high regard'.[9] When we work with awareness, self-compassion and patience to own our story and still believe in our worthiness – new realms of possibilities open up to us. Embracing our own worthiness and the worthiness of others is a vital element of being true to ourselves and living up to our ethical potential as humans. It grants both us and others permission to show up and be seen, just as we are – with our cracks, our battle scars, our rich tapestry of stories, stuff-ups and shadows.

Letting be: **Being worthy**

Understanding to uplift

INSIGHTS

Remembering our worthiness is an ongoing practice.

Learning to accept all of ourselves supports us
to *think* we are worthy, and to *feel* worthy.

We feel worthy when we remember our enough-ness.

PLAY

In what situations at work might you benefit from feeling worthy?

How might you remember your enough-ness in these situations?

What will you play around with to help you remember?
When will you do this?

How will you support yourself to honour this commitment?

Is there something you need to give yourself permission for?

OUTSIGHTS

How do you know when you are in touch with
your inherent worthiness?

What else do you now know in a deeper way?

GETTING TO THE HEART OF THE MATTER

What new possibilities might emerge
if you felt worthy more often?

How might being connected with your worthiness
uplift your working life?

How might being connected with your worthiness
uplift others in your life?

When you remember your worthiness,
what other elements of your essential nature emerge?

**If, in your own mind, your worthiness was irrefutable,
what would this mean?**

Being vulnerable

It is a great paradox that when we let ourselves be undefended we find our true strength.

Toko-pa Turner[1]

There has been much discussion of late on the topic of vulnerability in the workplace. Often, I feel that these conversations are missing an important nuance. It is not about learning how to *be more vulnerable* at work. It's about learning to *be with* our inherent vulnerability in all facets of our lives – including while we are working. Being vulnerable is not about acquiring a new skill. Being vulnerable is about coming to terms with the truth of our human-ness. It's about acceptance. It's also about being brave enough to remain open and undefended. It's about finding the courage not to close our hearts in a working world that has the potential to be heartbreaking.

As David Whtye so powerfully expresses in his essay on vulnerability, it's about choosing how to inhabit our vulnerability.

> *Vulnerability is not a weakness, a passing indisposition, or something we can arrange to do without, vulnerability is not a choice, vulnerability is the underlying, ever present and abiding undercurrent of our natural state. To run from vulnerability is to run from the essence of our nature... The only choice we have as we mature is how we inhabit our vulnerability.*[2]

A good working definition of vulnerability is: Uncertainty, risk and emotional exposure.[3] Inhabiting our vulnerability requires us to learn how to be with all three of these things. Navigating uncertainty feels disorientating and scary. Playing with new ways of being feels risky, uncomfortable, and at times downright terrifying. The same goes for opening our hearts to care, to connect and to love. Speaking our truth requires us to inhabit our vulnerability – especially when we are speaking our truth to good friends, family members and people who hold greater positional power.

Importantly, when we are inhabiting our vulnerability it *feels* scary and risky – but in the eyes and hearts of others it *looks* like courage and *feels* like inspiration.

DISCOMFORT-TOLERANCE

As much as we might prefer to avoid the uncomfortable feelings that accompany the inhabitation of our vulnerability, navigating uncertainty, risk and emotional exposure are essential elements of our self-fidelity practice. A desire to avoid discomfort while practising self-fidelity is as nonsensical as a desire to avoid the wind while flying a kite.

When we resist uncomfortable feelings, we resist doing anything that we don't know for sure we can do well. And this is incredibly limiting, given we all have the opportunity to try so many new things. Taking gentle steps to increase our discomfort-tolerance is essential. As we increase our levels of discomfort-tolerance, we free ourselves from the stifling no-growth confines of our comfort zone. We will talk about the common belief 'I can't handle this' later in *Letting go.*

We grow our capacity to inhabit our vulnerability by growing our self-awareness and over time, increasing our discomfort-tolerance. By normalising discomfort, we lay the bedrock of our courage and creativity. We also reduce the risk that we will lash out and hurt others when we are experiencing or trying to avoid discomfort.

VULNERABILITY AND COURAGE

Courage lies at the heart of our capacity to embrace our vulnerability. Courage is being brave despite our fear and vulnerability. Our courage is fuelled by our faith in our worthiness. Courage makes it possible to show up, to speak our truth and to be seen. It takes courage to inhabit our vulnerability and through this courage we build trust and connection with ourselves and others.

Courage is about learning how to be with discomfort so that we can take inspired action despite it. Courage is essential to the practice of self-fidelity because it makes it possible to play with new ways of being, to speak our truth and to be truly seen. In the words of Maya Angelou, 'Courage is the most important of all the virtues because without courage, you can't practise any other virtue consistently.'[4]

Courage requires us to journey through the heartland of vulnerability. Our success will hinge on our capacity to be with our fears and to embody a spirit of adventure and discovery. We are going to feel the discomfort of vulnerability often. But the more we practise small acts of courage despite feeling exposed, the better we get at it.

One of my most treasured memories of my children's development milestones was accompanying my older son on his first roller-coaster ride when he was six. While we were lining up, I gently encouraged him to keep moving forwards, step by step despite the churning tension inside him – the tension between his desire to be brave and the near-overwhelming fear of the unknown. After his first ride, the fear of the unknown was transformed into the anticipation of exhilaration. We went on the roller-coaster ride another four times. I did not hesitate

in buying the expensive photo on offer at the theme park exit gates that day. Looking at this photo floods me with pride and joy.

VULNERABILITY AND SHAME

The root meaning of the word 'shame' is 'to cover'. Shame can cause us to cover the things that make us who we are based on a belief that something is fundamentally wrong with us – and that this flaw makes us unworthy of love. Shame is often described as the 'master emotion'. If left undetected, shame can sabotage our efforts to be true to ourselves. Carl Jung describes shame as 'a soul-eating emotion'.[5] Whereas guilt – the belief that we have *made* a mistake – inspires us to become better. Shame can lead to depression, anxiety, numbing and bullying.[6] Shame is excruciating and (somewhat ironically) isolating. The antidote to shame lies in skilfully illuminating and revealing the truth of who we are.

The discomfort we may experience when the parts of ourselves and our stories that we perceive as shameful are exposed is particularly painful. Shame thrives on remaining undetected – on silence and secrecy. Shame cannot survive where there is empathy. When we find the courage to share our experiences of shame with people we trust not to judge us, and we allow ourselves to experience their empathy, our shame cannot survive. By sharing our truth, we transform our secrets into struggles – and struggles we can work with. In the book *Freedom is an Inside Job*, Zainab Salbi said:

> *If we all speak our truth, no matter how heavy or how trivial our stories seem, then together we can light the way toward a new future and a new story, one that is no longer based on silence and shame.*[7]

It took me many years to understand what shame felt like. For me, the most helpful pointer is that shame is not mild discomfort – it is excruciating. When I was living with domestic violence, whenever I was in the company of friends and my partner's behaviour became even

When we are inhabiting our vulnerability it feels scary and risky – but in the eyes and hearts of others it looks like courage and feels like inspiration.

slightly erratic, I was flooded with terror that the secret of his violent behaviour would become public knowledge – and along with it, the reality of how worthless and unlovable I was would also be exposed. Even the thought of the *impending* shame was utterly excruciating.

For many years shaming was a standard element of our parenting toolkit. In the past, shame has been used as a tool of social control to shun certain people who were perceived to be a threat to the safety of the community. Despite the ongoing prevalence of shaming language in political arenas, using shame as a weapon against each other is neither necessary nor ethical today.

In addition to being unethical, shame is also not an effective way to influence our own behaviour or the behaviour of others. To paraphrase Brené Brown, we may be conditioned to use shame as a weapon when we feel dehumanised, but at the end of our rampage, the world is just more dehumanised.[8]

Shame does not work in our homes and it does not work in our workplaces. Many of us have experienced the pain of being shamed at work. A CEO earning many million dollars a year once shamed me in front of the entire extended leadership team of the organisation I worked for because I dared to ask him a tough question about our strategy. A particularly lonely and bitter female manager once shamed me in a Monday morning team meeting after I shared the news of my engagement. 'God, you are just so bloody predictable, Cassie! And that diamond ring is a complete waste of money – now you won't be able to afford a home deposit!' Both these experiences had a significant impact on my levels of motivation and work and resulted in erosion of the respect I felt for these highly paid leaders through their abdication of their duty of care.

SHAME AND SECRETS

It is also relevant here to talk more about secrets. Secrets weigh us down and create feelings of shame and reinforce a false belief that there is something wrong with us – and that we are not worthy. As the AA slogan says, 'we are only as sick as our secrets.' One of the big upsides of increasing our discomfort tolerance is the opportunity to transform our secrets into struggles – by sharing them with people we trust.

Our secrets may relate to past traumas, how we speak to ourselves, how we numb ourselves with over-working, food, shopping, alcohol or other drugs. Our secret may relate to an addiction. Perhaps our secret is the real behind-closed-doors dynamic of our family relationships. Whatever our secrets, they make us sick. By sharing a secret with someone we trust deeply in a way that feels safe for us – we transform that secret into a struggle – and struggles we can work though. We know that shame cannot survive empathy.

Sharing a shameful secret (in an appropriate way) and experiencing another human's empathy and compassion can be transformative. I have learnt this from experience and research confirms that I am not alone.

Michael Slepian, a psychologist and associate professor at Columbia Business School has spent a decade studying the psychology of secrets. He wanted to better understand why we refer to a secret as a burden. His research revealed that for those of us preoccupied with a secret, the experience of feeling burdened is very real. His research has found that people who are preoccupied with an important secret estimate that a hill is steeper and a target further away.[9] Our secrets weigh us down. The research of Michael and his colleagues has also confirmed that secrets can hurt our health, relationships and sense of wellbeing and lead to depression and anxiety. He also discovered that 97% of us have at least one big secret at any time and the average person has 13 secrets.[10] Secrets are like black pearls lodged in our hearts, coated by feelings of shame, they grow larger slowly but surely, layer upon layer.

In her book *Freedom is an Inside Job*, Zainab Salbi vividly describes her experience of sharing her secrets in her first book:

> *I had locked my past into my heart for so many years that it had turned into a black stone, weighing heavily in the centre of*

my chest. It suffocated me and sapped me of energy. But when I unlocked my secrets, that dark stone turned into a crystal: clear, transparent and beautiful. In my utter vulnerability lay my protection and my power. No secrets, no hiding, no shame.[11]

Living with domestic violence was, for many years, my big dirty secret. I hid this secret from the world for a long time. When I finally packed a tiny overnight bag and fled to the safety of a nearby hotel, my decision to leave home was not driven by seeing a L'Oréal commercial and suddenly realising that 'because I was worth it' I deserved better. My actions were driven by a fear of my secret being revealed to my colleagues, family and friends through physical injuries I could no longer hide. My decision to flee was driven by a fear that my carefully crafted image of a confident, high-achieving professional would be shattered. My decision to leave that night was driven by the fear of the impending shame of people knowing the truth of how little I valued myself. The sad truth is that I had actually intended to go back home once my partner had sobered up and calmed down and I had figured out some new negotiation tactics to keep the situation on the down-low.

I am so very grateful that I had the sense to call the Employee Assistance Hotline my workplace provided for 'a little bit of relationship advice'. I made an appointment with a psychologist and in that first session I shared my secret. With good support, I embarked on the long road of disentanglement and self-worth building. I believe that I shared the truth of my situation in that first meeting with a psychologist because I had already shared my secret with one trusted work friend about six months prior to things coming to a head. I did not realise it at the time, but Andrea's kindness and empathy had begun to work like magic on dissolving the shame I felt. I will never forget the day I shared the truth of what I was experiencing with Andrea. She did not judge. She did not admonish me. She simply said, 'Cassie, you are a sparkling diamond'. Over a decade later, I am incredibly grateful for this life experience. I am grateful for the hard questions it forced me to ask and answer. And I am incredibly grateful for the path of growth and personal development it has led me down.

It is really hard to prosper at work or in life when we are carrying the burden of a big secret. The idea of sharing our story, our struggles or our secrets with a trusted friend, coach or therapist may sound terrifying. However, in my experience, the upside is tremendous. There is something so transformative about sharing the truth of our situation (in a safe and appropriate way) and experiencing the wonder of feeling no judgement, releasing the hurt and shame and allowing help and compassion to flood in.

Secrets and shame undermine our inspiration and our wellbeing. Keeping big secrets sucks enormous amounts of energy, stifles our growth and contributes to feelings of low self-worth, isolation, depression, being unloved, unlovable and inadequate. Shame thrives on secret-keeping.

THE VOICES OF FEAR

Becoming familiar with the way our fear communicates with us is an important aspect of growing courage. The DJ fear may play tracks like 'you are not good enough' or 'you will fail and make a fool of yourself or get hurt'. The soundtrack of our fear might become particularly loud and disturbing when we are about to cross a significant threshold in our growth journey or when we are attempting something for the first time. Given the practice of self-fidelity will often take us beyond our comfort zones, normalising and finding ways to work with the inner soundtrack of fear is essential.

DJ fear is commonly referred to as our 'inner critic'. In their book *Embracing Your Inner Critic*, Hal Stone and Sidra Stone compare the inner critic to a renegade CIA agent, explaining:

> *It developed to protect your vulnerability by helping you to adapt to the world around you and to meet its requirements, whatever*

they might be. It makes you acceptable to others by criticizing and correcting your behavior before other people could criticize or reject you. In this way, it reasoned, it could earn love and protection for you as well as save you much shame and hurt. [However] like a renegade CIA agent, the Critic oversteps its bounds, takes matters into its own hands and begins to operate on its own agenda. The information (your weaknesses and imperfections), which was originally supposed to be for your overall defense and to promote your general well-being, is now being used against you, the very person it was meant to protect.[12]

Scilla Elworthy, author of *Pioneering the Possible* and Nobel Peace Prize nominee, has developed a powerful practice of sitting in dialogue with her inner critic while visualising it as a huge, fire-breathing dragon with a large diamond under its claw. The diamond represents an important insight she needs to understand that is eluding her. During her dialogue, she asks direct questions to the dragon such as 'Please tell me what it is that you know that I need to know' and 'What is this *really* about?' At times, she may speak sternly to the dragon saying, 'that is not really helpful'. She asks a series of questions while holding the firm intention of coaxing the jewel – the key insight she needs to understand – from beneath its sharp claws. In a 2020 interview Scilla said, 'I have learnt some of the most important things in my whole life from that fire-breathing dragon'.[13]

Elizabeth Gilbert has been very open about her struggles with the voice of fear, particularly when it comes to taking on creative projects. Her 'Open letter to fear' in *Big Magic* is a great example of an empowering way to relate to fear – respectfully acknowledging its presence but never allowing it to take control of the wheel.

Dearest Fear:

Creativity and I are about to go on a road trip together. I understand you'll be joining us, because you always do. I acknowledge that you believe you have an important job to do in my life, and

> *that you take your job seriously. Apparently, your job is to induce complete panic whenever I'm about to do anything interesting – and, may I say, you are superb at your job. So by all means, keep doing your job, if you feel you must. But I will also be doing my job on this road trip, which is to work hard and stay focused. And Creativity will be doing its job, which is to remain stimulating and inspiring. There's plenty of room in this vehicle for all of us, so make yourself at home, but understand this: Creativity and I are the only ones who will be making any decisions along the way. I recognize and respect that you are part of this family, and so I will never exclude you from our activities, but still – your suggestions will never be followed. You're allowed to have a seat, and you're allowed to have a voice, but you are not allowed to have a vote. You're not allowed to touch the road maps; you're not allowed to suggest detours; you're not allowed to fiddle with the temperature. Dude, you're not even allowed to touch the radio. But above all else, my dear old familiar friend, you are absolutely forbidden to drive.*[14]

We can all grow our capacity to be with fear while remaining connected to a sense of 'all-right-ness' and 'enough-ness'. We can become better at recognising and acknowledging the presence of fear in our bodies perhaps through sensations of tightening or contracting. When we are tuned into our bodies and we notice the tell-tale signs of fear we can remember to say to ourselves, 'Ah, fear is here. Welcome – you are right on time.' From this place of awareness, we can allow the fear to be there, by simply asking ourselves, 'Can I just be with this fear right now? Can I make space inside me for it – just for a few breaths?' Once we have created some inner wiggle-room there is space to become curious about the story that has triggered the fear – is it a familiar one? Can we be absolutely sure it is true? Finally we can nurture ourselves, perhaps by turning our awareness to sensing that we are basically alright in the moment and taking a few deep breaths while kindly reassuring ourselves that we are, in fact, basically alright, despite the presence of fear. From this place of calm, we can discern our next best step.

Be on the lookout for opportunities to practise small, everyday acts of courage. We can practise courage by reaching out to connect with someone who is suffering. We might not know what to say, we might be terrified of making things worse or feeling inadequate, but we can rise above these fears by simply letting them know we are there for them. One of the earliest meanings of courage was 'to speak one's mind by telling all one's heart.'[15] So calmly speaking our truth with warmth and respect is another way to practise courage. Coco Chanel said, 'The most courageous act is still to think for yourself. Aloud.'[16] We can practise courage by thinking for ourselves and putting our ideas out into the world despite knowing that not everyone will agree with them. Finally, another great way to practise courage is by keeping our hearts open when it would be easier to give up on someone.

Letting be: **Being vulnerable**

Understanding to uplift

INSIGHTS

Inhabiting our vulnerability is an ongoing practice.

Connecting to a sense of all-right-ness can help us to handle discomfort, risk and uncertainty.

We can all increase our discomfort-tolerance.

Our discomfort and inner voices of fear are loudest when we are crossing important thresholds.

We can also ask ourselves: can I be with this discomfort?

PLAY

What do you believe to be true about vulnerability at work?

Are there situations at work where inhabiting your vulnerability may be of benefit?

What will you play with in order to inhabit your vulnerability?

How will you support yourself to honour this commitment?

Is there something you need to give yourself permission for?

OUTSIGHTS

How do you know when you are inhabiting vulnerability?

What else do you now know in a deeper way?

GETTING TO THE HEART OF THE MATTER

What new possibilities might emerge if you were to inhabit your vulnerability more often?

How might inhabiting your vulnerability uplift your working life?

How might inhabiting your vulnerability uplift others in your life?

When you inhabit your vulnerability, what other elements of your essential nature emerge?

If, in your own mind, your vulnerability was an unquestioned source of strength, what would this mean?

Being caring

The antidote to exhaustion is not necessarily rest.
The antidote to exhaustion is wholeheartedness.

Brother David Steindl-Rast[1]

Many years ago, I had a manager who gave me the following feedback during my annual performance review: 'The problem with you, Cassie, is that you care too much. If you want to progress to an executive position, you really have to learn to care less.' He did not deliver this feedback in a patronising or mean way. He genuinely felt he was sharing his secret to success with me. Fortunately, I was clear in my core values – zest, honesty and kindness. And I know that for me, trying to care less about the work I do and the people I do it with is about as realistic as trying not to feel hungry at lunchtime. Thanks to this self-awareness, I was able to respectfully deflect this well-meaning but ill-informed advice. As my manager was imparting these words of wisdom, I actually felt really sorry for him. By all the traditional measures he was extremely successful – he was highly paid, was holding a top-rung position in the organisational hierarchy and he held a great deal of positional power. However, according to more sane measures of success he was not doing so well. Those of us who worked closely with him knew him well enough to know that the things he cared most about were his own status, reputation and promotion prospects and that he had a tendency to be openly cruel towards those he perceived as a threat. He was not someone others trusted. The people who reported to him never *really* brought their full potential to work. Last I checked, he was still ascending up the corporate ladder, flying closer and closer to the sun.

INSPIRING HEARTCOUNT

One of the great tragedies of the modern workplace is that, over time the hearts of so many leaders become closed and hardened. To be courageous is to lead with heart. The resurrection of courageous leadership is vital to the work of being true to ourselves at work. Great leadership is about finding the courage to care.

For so many years, the term leadership was synonymous with power and control and workforce optimisation. Today, the best leaders have no desire to optimise headcount – their aspiration is to inspire *heart*count.

Leadership exists in the eye of the beholders – it is the people we lead and inspire who judge the quality of our leadership. Research has identified that truly inspirational leaders share four unexpected qualities[2] – all of which sit right at the heart of self-fidelity. Inspiring leaders:

- understand and leverage their uniqueness
- care intensely about their work
- don't hide areas of vulnerability, instead reveal their humanity
- rely on their intuition to gauge the best course of action.

Inspiring leaders lead with awakened hearts to awaken the hearts of others. Our current climate demands that we work from a state of presence in the moments that matter. When we are operating on cruise-control, we are not connected with our essential nature and our hearts are off-line. McKinsey & Co captured this powerfully when they published the article 'Leading with inner agility' which said:

> *The very nature of disruption means that even the best, most prescient leaders will be steering their company into, and through, a*

> *fog of uncertainty. You aren't alone if you feel threatened by this – everyone does, whether consciously or subconsciously... You can't steer your company through constant change if you are relying on the safety of your own cruise control.*[3]

There are countless ways to describe inspiring, courageous leadership. For me, the people who I find most inspiring are people who:

Believe in themselves – I find it deeply inspiring when I see people embody 100% conviction in what they stand for. For me, Malala Yousafzai epitomises strength in one's own beliefs. I had full-body goosebumps for most of her talk when I saw her in Melbourne. When she said, 'if you want others to believe in you, *you* must believe in *you*,' her words struck right at the core of my being.

Have the courage to speak their truth – I also am deeply inspired by people who have the courage to speak their truth, even when they risk ridicule or being shunned by people who think differently. For me, the late Dr Wayne Dyer epitomised a person who embodied true courage and conviction in this way.

Have allowed themselves the space to think deeply – those who manage to rise above the busyness of our modern existence to invest the time in contemplation and the discovery of inner wisdom are also very inspiring. For me, David Whyte is a person who epitomises the embodied wisdom that comes from commitment to ongoing deep contemplation of life.

Here are some of the ways others have described inspiring leadership.

> *Your first and foremost job as a leader is to take charge of your own energy and then help to orchestrate the energy of those around you.* Peter Drucker[4]

> *Leadership is about making others feel better as a result of your presence and making sure that impact lasts in your absence.* Sheryl Sandberg[5]

> *A leader is someone who takes responsibility for finding the potential in people and processes, and who has the courage to develop that potential.* Brené Brown[6]

The reality in many organisations is that the old guard of leadership still holds much of the power. We can't change the rigid, narrow views of the 'more experienced'. Trying to change their minds is both futile and exhausting. Instead, we must channel our energy into becoming the sort of leaders we yearn to work for and with. Only through out-shining and out-living the old guard will we be successful. We must be the change we want to see in the world. Nobel Peace Laureate Wangari Maathai said, 'I was doing the right thing. But they didn't want me to do it because it was inconveniencing them, and I knew that.'[7] The work of self-fidelity will often be an inconvenience to the old guard. This is not a valid reason to stop trying to transform the ways we work – with respect but without apology.

Acts of self-fidelity are essentially acts of courageous leadership because they inspire others to also be true to themselves. When we give ourselves permission to figure out how to be truer, better versions of ourselves at work, we grant others permission to do the same. When we choose self-betrayal over self-fidelity, we steal permission from other people to begin their own unique journeys towards a fuller embodiment of the truth of who they are at work. If you are reading this, then you are a pioneering leader. So, whenever I use the word 'leader' in the book, know that I am talking about you.

CREATING ISLANDS OF SANITY

For me, the work of Margaret Wheatley is a clarion call for courageous leadership. Margaret describes our call to courage as 'bravely standing in contrast to the current practices and dynamics of this age'.[8] She calls forth leaders to create 'islands of sanity'[9] and 'to use their power and influence, their insight and compassion, to lead people back to an understanding of who we are as human beings, to create the conditions for our basic human qualities of generosity, contribution, community and love to be evoked no matter what.'[10]

When we care, are courageous and work with open hearts – it is also important to practise discernment and work with an awareness of the forces at play that can mess with our minds. Many of us encounter situations that can potentially cause us to lose trust in the soundness of our own judgement and sanity. To support ourselves, I love the idea of intentionally creating 'islands of sanity' – places of refuge in the midst of the madness.

I once facilitated a wellbeing workshop for a professional services organisation. By the mid-morning-mark I was feeling quietly confident that we were making good progress. We had covered all the latest insights from the science of wellbeing. It seemed that no one in the room was disputing the growing body of evidence linking wellbeing with sustained performance. Just before the morning-tea break, I asked if there were any final questions. Thankfully, one very brave (and very weary) account manager decided it was time to speak his truth. Raising his hand, he said, 'This is all really interesting, but not really that helpful, because the reality is that our clients treat us like their bitches.' It was the comment that finally revealed the *real* conversation that needed to emerge. It was the Eureka moment. The moment when the 1000kg invisible sacred cow that had been stomping around in people's heads was finally out in the open. Thanks to his courage, our conversation shifted from the transfer of knowledge into the realm of transformation. Fortunately, the CEO was in the room. Even more fortunately, he was also courageous enough to place down his own armour and have the conversation his team desperately wanted to have. It was a vital, highly vulnerable conversation about the sort of organisation they wanted to be. About how the CEO wanted his precious, smart and hard-working people to be treated. About how they defined success as an organisation. About whether their stated organisational values were *really* real, or whether they were really just corporate-speak BS. It was a conversation that

Until we learn to take care of ourselves, our capacity to take care of others will continue to be limited.

compelled the CEO to make some brave and important decisions that clearly demonstrated what he stood for as their leader.

I have personally experienced many workplace situations that have led me to doubt my own judgement. There have been times when I have sat in leadership meetings and thought to myself, 'Are we filming a sit-com right now or trying to run an organisation?' I once worked in a particularly dysfunctional organisation and after confiding to a trusted peer, Sally, that I felt I was losing touch with my own judgement, Sally shared a simple practice that she had been using to remain sane. Sally explained that she always brought a small snack-size bag of popcorn to our leadership meetings and when things got really crazy (as they often did), she would quietly open the bag, start eating the popcorn, telling herself to relax and enjoy the show. This was an enormously helpful tip. I started bringing a small bag of popcorn to all our leadership meetings and it worked like a charm. This small creative act created a secret island of sanity for both of us.

It is so essential that we have trusted work friends with whom we can have honest conversations and seek refuge on small 'islands of sanity'. Sometimes we really need to hear someone else say the words, 'Wow – this is really screwed up.' From time to time, we all need reassurance that we are not going crazy – that it's the system that is so often bonkers.

CARING FOR OURSELVES

In order to take care of others, we must first learn to take care of ourselves. In today's busy world it is really easy to lose touch with ourselves. As Arianna Huffington says, 'Being connected in a shallow way to the entire world can prevent us from being connected to those closest to us – including ourselves.'[11] To have any hope of remaining connected with ourselves, it is vital to develop a clear understanding of who we are. Paradoxically, we strengthen our connections with others by strengthening our connection with ourselves. Dr Vivek Murthy reminds us:

> *Reflection and self-awareness play such an important role in preparing us for relationships with others. As we become attuned to our own inner signals and frequencies, we naturally gain an empathic (and largely unconscious) ability to recognise and relate to those signals in others.*[12]

Until we learn to take care of ourselves, our capacity to take care of others will continue to be limited. One very powerful way we can do this is by using the practice of soaking to nourish ourselves. Soaking can support us to absorb the feeling of gratitude and connection we experience in moments of being cared for or cared about.

We will talk more about the many other ways we can care for ourselves in *Letting in.*

CARING FOR OTHERS

Activating our capacity to care is also about understanding that we are one small part of a complex dynamic work system or organisation. A deep belief in our interconnectedness is the foundation for human flourishing and growth. In the words of Harriet Lerner, 'only through our connectedness to others can we really know and enhance the self and only through working on the self can we begin to enhance our connectedness to others.'[13] Knowing that we are not alone supports us to be both caring and courageous.

Harriet Lerner described the goal of healthy, sustainable functioning in an interconnected world as being to 'have relationships that do not occur at the expense of the "self" and to have a "self" that does not operate at the expense of the others.'[14] For this to occur, we must have a strong platform of self-worth to stand on. The challenge of defining our self is in many ways not straightforward. Because we have all been exposed to much conditioning from our schools, our families, our religions, social groups and workplaces to mould ourselves to standards and ideals that have not been defined by us, it can be difficult to begin to form an understanding of who we are and what we stand for. Given this reality, how do we go about gaining an understanding of a clear and authentic self? The act of slowly forming a view of our sense of self allows us to respond to external challenges, rather than react, because we are more anchored by self-awareness and self-acceptance.

The work of Harriet Lerner serves as a reliable guide when it comes to the work of defining a sense of self. Harriet explains that a healthy understanding of self is built upon the awareness of and the ability to *calmly and assertively communicate* in five key areas:

- the things that are important to us
- where we stand on important issues
- the limits of what is acceptable and tolerable to us
- our strengths and achievements
- our vulnerability and struggles.[15]

CARE AND COMPASSION

Research has shown that when we feel compassion our heart-rate slows down, we produce the bonding hormone oxytocin and the part of our brains linked to empathy, caregiving and feelings of pleasure is activated. Compassion makes us want to connect and care for other people.[16] The work of Dr Kristin Neff teaches us that self-compassion allows us to 'give ourselves the same kindness and care we'd give to a good friend'.[17] Self-compassion plays an essential role in self-care, boundary setting and our commitment to ongoing growth.

We honour our caring nature when we honour our need for wholehearted connections – our need to belong and to feel seen. We can all work in a way that honours our vital, invisible bonds to each other and the web of life we occupy.

It does not matter so much *what* you care about – just care deeply about some element of your work that is bigger than yourself. It is not my place (or anyone else's) to convince you what to care about – that is for you to decide. Just care. And care deeply. Convincing yourself that it is better not to care about some element of your work is a type of modern-day self-inflicted flagellation. To spend the majority of your waking hours every day working in a way that is devoid of care, in order to protect your heart is arguably the most damaging thing you can do to your heart, your body and your soul. Convincing yourself that it would be safer not to care about the work you do, the greater outcomes it contributes to, the people you do it with and the implications that work has for all life – is one of the most dangerous things a human can do.

The working world desperately needs more people who are able and willing to take off the masks, shed the armour, and dig deep to find within themselves the courage to care. When we really connect with others, when there is vulnerability, trust and care – we unlock our collective potential and extraordinary outcomes become possible.

Letting be: **Being caring**

Understanding to uplift

INSIGHTS

Remembering our caring, warm-hearted nature
is an ongoing practice.

Great leadership is about finding the courage to care
and inspiring *heart*count.

To thrive we need three types of relationships - with a close
confidant, good friends and a like-minded community.

PLAY

What do you believe to be true about being caring at work?

In what situations at work might being more caring be beneficial?

How might you connect with your warm-heartedness
in these situations?

What specifically will you play around with first?
When will you do this?

How will you support yourself to honour this commitment?

Is there something you need to give yourself permission for?

OUTSIGHTS

How do you know when you are in touch with your caring nature?

What else do you now know in a deeper way?

GETTING TO THE HEART OF THE MATTER

What new possibilities might emerge if you felt free to care?

How might being caring uplift your working life?

How might being caring uplift others in your life?

When you're being caring, what other elements
of your essential nature emerge?

**If, in your own mind, your caring nature was undeniable,
what would this mean?**

Being creative

Creativity isn't the ability to draw or compose or sculpt,
but a way of understanding the world.

David Kelley[1]

We are all innately creative beings. As we grow up, sadly many of us lose touch with our creativity. As a result, our true creative potential remains unexplored. There is no word for 'creativity' in the Tibetan language – the closest translation is 'natural'.[2] By reconnecting with our inherent creative nature, we reconnect in our play nature and rediscover the joy in our work. Creativity, courage and playfulness work in the same way our muscles do – we strengthen these parts of ourselves by using them. As they grow, these strengths support us to experience greater joy and abundance – and rediscover the thrill of working and living.

Psychologist Robert Sternberg has been studying creativity for over thirty years. All the creative people he has studied have one thing in common – at a certain moment, they *decided* to be creative.[3] IDEO founder David Kelley believes that in order to reclaim our creativity and overcome the fears that get in the way we can develop our creative confidence. David explains that 'creative confidence is the belief that everyone is creative.'[4] In the book *Creative Confidence* he explains that 'at its core, creative confidence is about believing in your ability to create change in the world around you [and] the conviction that you can achieve what you set out to do.'[5] I have been fortunate to complete the d.school program *From play to innovation* – a partnership between Stanford University and IDEO. It was an incredible learning experience – every moment of that experience was infused with a basic premise: everyone in this room is a highly creative being and so, we are going to play with different ways to apply that creativity and work together to create extraordinary outcomes.

Science also considers creativity to be a standard functionality of a human brain. It is the functionality that makes new connections between existing knowledge. The different cognitive processes that have been linked to creativity appear to share one feature – they enable us to venture into uncharted waters. There are no guarantees when we are being creative. Seth Godin summarised creativity as 'this might not work.'[6]

Given creativity is a standard design feature of our brains, why are so many people convinced they are not creative? There are a few main reasons:

- the world makes us doubt ourselves
- we are far too distracted
- we're just too bloody exhausted to be creative
- we are conditioned to see failure as something bad, instead of an inherent part of creativity and learning.

In 1992 NASA was searching for a way to measure the creative potential of their rocket scientists and engineers. To help, Dr. George Land and Dr. Beth Jarman developed a test designed to identify the capacity for divergent thinking and creativity. They used this test to assess the creative ability of a sample of 1600 people that comprised of four different age groups.[7] Their findings were startling. The test results showed that 98% of four to five-year-olds were creative geniuses. By the age of ten this number had dropped to 30%. By the age of fifteen it was only 12%. When they conducted the same test on a group of adults they discovered that less than 2% of the adults tested were creative geniuses. Dr Land noted this study proved that we are born as highly creative beings but that 'non-creative behaviour is learned'.

Adobe Systems study of around five thousand people found that while 70 percent of people believed being creative makes us better workers, only 31 percent felt that they were living up to their creative potential.[8] There are vast amounts of creative potential lying dormant in almost every organisation on this planet.

Many of us may have hidden our greatest gifts away for safekeeping when we were children. At a certain moment in primary school, my tender, budding sense of creativity and wonder was trampled during a particular incident at school. Like many childhood traumas the incident was relatively small. It involved being publicly humiliated by a teacher after writing a poem I felt particularly proud of. The poem was about the miracle of an egg transforming into a chick. I don't remember very many details of the incident – but I remember feeling my face burn red-hot with shame as my teacher read my poem, shook her head and loudly exclaimed in a condescending tone, 'Cassie – it is just an egg!' This small but deeply scarring incident resulted in me abandoning my creativity and sense of wonder for many years, wrongly confusing it with childish naïvety.

Over time, we internalise hurtful comments made by others. As adults the voices in our heads effectively play the same role – trampling our creative confidence. Vincent Van Gogh said, 'If you hear a voice within you that says, "You cannot paint," then by all means paint, and that voice will be silenced.'[9] The secret is to start small. If the voice in our head tells us that we are not good at writing, for example, don't attempt to write a fiction novel – start with a blog post.

Not only does the system tend to beat our creativity out of us – it can do the same to our natural and inherent sense of wonder and playfulness. As we get older, many of us develop an unfortunate tendency to avoid doing anything that we have not done before.

And doing only what we have done before is pretty much the definition of anti-creativity.

Another major problem is that we allow ourselves to be constantly distracted, and creativity takes focus and flow. We also have very little tolerance for discomfort – and that includes the discomfort of not knowing if our idea or thing is decent or not – not knowing whether we will valiantly triumph or fail miserably or land somewhere in between.

I know that my natural creativity flows when I focus on what is important for an extended period of time, usually around 50 minutes. I call these 'focus sessions'.

Taking control of our environment to minimise distractions is essential to our capacity to focus and be engaged in meaningful, creative and uplifting work. During my focus sessions I limit all distractions – turning off all notifications on my laptop and ideally putting my phone in another room. When I am working on a significant creative project, I string together a series of focus sessions to dedicate half or full days to focus on one very important thing. There is simply no way this book could have emerged without me doing that. I could have dedicated a million thirty-minute splinters of time to writing a book, but there is no possible way *Self-Fidelity* would have come together in any sort of cohesive form using that method.

BRINGING OUR SOULS TO WORK

A conversation about creativity would not be complete without a conversation about our souls. The idea of putting our heart and soul into our work is a fairly familiar one. We understand that the idea of putting our hearts into our work is about working with courage, passion and compassion – but what exactly does it mean to put our soul into our work? I believe that the activation of our souls at work is key to the activation of our creativity.

The human soul has been described in many different ways – the truth of who we are, our only true source of wealth, the beautiful thing inside of us, the being under the doing. In the lyrics of *Zion Train* Bob Marley warns us, 'Don't gain the world and lose your soul; wisdom is better than silver and gold.'[10] The final lines of William Ernest Henley's well-known poem *Invictus* declare, 'I am the master of my fate: I am the captain of my soul.'[11] Oscar Wilde said, 'In your soul are infinitely precious things that cannot be taken from you.'[12]

Human creativity depends greatly on maintaining a strong connection with our souls, which can prove difficult in the workplace. In *The Heart Aroused*, David Whyte explains:

> *The soul's needs in the workplace have long been ignored, partly because the path the soul takes to fulfill its destiny seems troublesomely unique to each person and refuses to be quantified in a way that satisfies the need to plan everything in advance ... A soulful approach to work is probably the only way an individual can respond creatively to the high-temperature stress of modern work life without burning to a crisp in the heat.*[13]

There is no easy answer to how best to work and live in a way that honours and feeds our soul. However, holding an awareness of our soul's very existence at work is a wonderful place to begin. There have been many moments at work that have fed my soul. I have also experienced many moments at work that have quite literally felt like a cheese grater on my soul. As my career progressed, selling rat-nibbled sweet buns to my neighbours started to feel like a walk in the park.

Preservation of the human spirit and our own souls at work depends on our individual sense of awareness and connectedness to a deeper, unquantifiable, enduring part of ourselves – however we describe and define it. It depends on the preservation of our humanity, calling on the best of our human nature knowing we are all part of something bigger – even when we have to do things that are incredibly hard. It depends on leaders cultivating the courage and wisdom to open the office window to the strong, fresh breeze of human longings, being prepared to deal with aspects of our humanity that are inconveniently lofty, sacred and fragile.

A PROCESS OF UNLEARNING

To activate our innate creativity, we have far more to unlearn than learn. The core of our practice of honouring our creativity is unlearning. We must shed our conditioned patterns of soul-less busyness, and our zero-tolerance for vulnerability or failure.

A good way to start is by committing to small acts of creativity that come with relatively low levels of fear and risk. Perhaps we might like to block out two technology-free hours in a new space to work through a tough problem with paper and pen. Maybe we might try to write a short article and publish it on LinkedIn. The key to success is to set aside some time to focus and really give our chosen creative challenge our full, uninterrupted focus. It is easy to give up and confirm the fake news in our head that we are just not the creative type when in fact the problem is that we have not given ourselves the gift of focus time. The process of creating this book – which was the most challenging creative endeavour of my life to date – taught me about the importance of giving my brain long stretches of uninterrupted time. I loved spending a quiet few hours writing in the wee hours of the morning before the kids woke up, but it quickly became apparent to me that my book would never come together without protecting much longer blocks of focus time. When we work in a busy job this can be hard. If we really want to lash the full power of our creativity we will need to block and vigilantly protect long periods of uninterrupted focus time.

Reconnecting with our innate creativity, sense of play and sense of wonder is a vital element of our self-fidelity practice. Only through our creativity can we activate the best of human ingenuity and passion to solve the problems we face.

Despite the many ways our creativity may have been dismissed and diminished (by others and by the voices in our heads) – it is still inside us. We each have a responsibility to begin to excavate and apply our creativity – because it is needed in our organisations and in the world.

Letting be: **Being creative**

Understanding to uplift

INSIGHTS

Creativity is a standard function of the human brain.

To solve the complex challenges we face,
it is essential we harness our creativity.

Remembering and reconnecting to our inherent creativity
is an ongoing practice.

PLAY

What do you believe to be true about being creative at work?

In what situations at work might you benefit from being creative?

How might you connect with your creativity in these situations?

What specifically will you play around with first?
When will you do this?

How will you support yourself to honour this commitment?

Is there something you need to give yourself permission for?

OUTSIGHTS

How do you know when you are in touch with your creativity?

What else do you now know in a deeper way?

GETTING TO THE HEART OF THE MATTER

What new possibilities might emerge
if you were to harness your creativity more often?

How might being creative uplift your working life?

How might being creative uplift others in your life?

When you are being creative,
what other elements of your essential nature emerge?

**If, in your own mind, your creativity was irrefutable,
what would this mean?**

Being playful

When we play, we are engaged in
the purest expression of our humanity,
the truest expression of our individuality.

Dr Stuart Brown[1]

While we may be conditioned to believe that work is the opposite of play – this is a lie. In the words of Brian Sutton-Smith, 'The opposite of play is not work – the opposite of play is depression.'[2]

I hold an intention to experience my work as a form of productive play. Bringing lightness and play to my work does not mean that I did not take my work seriously. It meant that I understood I am at my best when I am connected with my essential, playful nature. Being playful is essential to creating work that is taken seriously, because without play, I am only skimming the surface of my creative potential.

I will never forget kicking off my heels and dancing like a barefoot crazy lady at 5:30am one morning in the boardroom of my corporate office to the song 'Happy' by Pharrell Williams in order to get myself in the right zone to nail a high-stakes 6am job interview with a panel of London-based executives to get a big promotion. I nailed the interview. I have another very fond memory of a very tense conversation at another place of employment about the implementation of agile ways of working. Extraordinarily, the entire organisation-wide deployment of agile ways of working was being held up by a decision by a powerful individual in the facilities department that we could no longer put post-it notes on walls. I was able to break the tension and ultimately find a solution by playfully suggesting that we could put the post-it notes on the ceiling and have lie-downs instead of stand-ups.

It was not until I had the opportunity of learning from Dr Stuart Brown in 2018 that I fully understood the science behind my innate desire to experience my work as a form of productive play. One of my most treasured life experiences is the time I have spent with Stuart, a man who has dedicated his life to understanding the vitally important role of play in animals and humans. Stuart has studied the play histories of thousands of people from all walks of life, from serial murderers to Nobel Prize winners. He has also established the National Institute for Play in California. This is how Stuart described why play is an essential element of work:

> *Work and play are inseparable, and play is one of our most basic human needs – as vital to our wellbeing as sleep and nutritious food. Play allows us to express our joy and connect with the best in ourselves, and in others. Respecting our biological need for play can transform work. In the long run, work does not work without play.*[3]

In his wonderful book *Play: How it Shapes the Brain, Opens the Imagination and Invigorates the Soul* Stuart shares the indisputable evidence that play is a fundamental human biological drive. Play is just as essential to our ability to thrive as sleep or nutrition. As humans we are designed to flourish through play. Play is essential to our social skills, adaptability, intelligence, creativity and ability to problem-solve. In tough times, we need to play more than ever because, as Stuart explains, 'it's the very means by which we prepare for the unexpected, search out new solutions, and remain optimistic'.[4]

Play is an essential and powerful catalyst for our growth. Unlearning the dangerous, widely held beliefs that confuse playfulness with childishness or folly is an essential step in our journey towards activating our true potential and experiencing joy and fulfillment through our work.

For many adults, the biggest barrier to reconnecting with our essential play nature is fear. Perhaps it is fear of looking silly, fear of being seen as crazy or childish or fear of being judged. The science tells us that if we can understand and reduce the sources of this fear and introduce just small amounts of play back into our lives, we can experience significant benefits.

SECRET SPACES

Elizabeth Goodenough, a professor and expert in play and an advisor to the National Institute for Play, is an advocate for the idea of 'secret spaces' – places and spaces where we feel safe to play.[5]

The practice of creating our own secret space involves both reflection and experimentation. Once we have more awareness (or even a hunch) about the barriers to play that exist for us and what a more play-conducive place would look like, it's time to experiment!

Play around with different spaces and places where we feel safe to play. Perhaps we want to try running along the beach or in a local park. Riding a bike in nature can be a great way to play. Painting, learning a new sport or a musical instrument might also be good options. Perhaps we feel safe to play when it is just us and the kids alone, dancing to the latest silly pop song. The key is to keep testing and learning until we find a space or place we can regularly access for the purposes of unbridled play.

Reconnecting with our playful nature has the potential to activate tremendous healing in workplaces around the world. It's the long-forgotten remedy we all benefit from remembering. As Gabrielle Roth said:

> *In many shamanic societies, if you came to a medicine person complaining of being disheartened, dispirited, or depressed, they would ask one of four questions: "When did you stop dancing? When did you stop singing? When did you stop being enchanted by stories? When did you stop being comforted by the sweet territory of silence?" … Each of us has the power and responsibility to heal ourselves, to be our own medicine man or woman.*[6]

Letting be: **Being playful**

Understanding to uplift

INSIGHTS

Work does not work without play.

The opposite of play is not work – it's depression.

Reconnect with your playful nature by taking small steps and finding a safe place to play.

PLAY

In what situations at work might you benefit from being playful?

How might you connect with your playfulness in these situations?

What specifically will you play around with first? When will you do this?

How will you support yourself to honour this commitment?

Is there something you need to give yourself permission for?

OUTSIGHTS

How do you know when you are in touch with your playfulness?

What else do you now know in a deeper way?

GETTING TO THE HEART OF THE MATTER

What new possibilities might emerge if you were to be playful often?

How might being playful uplift your working life?

How might being playful uplift others in your life?

When you are being playful, what other elements of your essential nature emerge?

If, in your own mind, your playfulness was irrefutable, what would this mean?

And the day came
when the risk to remain tight in a bud
was more painful than the risk it took to blossom.

Anaïs Nin[7]

LETTING GO

If you begin to be what you are,
you will realise everything,
but to begin to be what you are,
you must come out of what you are not.

Swami Shantanand Saraswati[1]

I am not enough

You alone are enough, you have nothing
to prove to anybody.

Maya Angelou[1]

One of the beliefs that can weigh us down is the belief 'I am not enough'.

We are conditioned to attach our self-worth to things outside of ourselves based on the conditioned belief that these things hold the key to our enough-ness, worthiness and happiness. The belief that we are not enough and are somehow unworthy can be buried so deeply we don't realise that it is there. But if it is there, it has the power to influence every action we take or fail to take. We may come to believe that our salary, job title, corner office or annual performance rating is a reflection of our worthiness and a measure of our value in the world. Believing these external things hold the keys to our worthiness creates tremendous suffering. It's like hitching our hearts to a roller-coaster ride because these things are ever-changing, out of our control, unpredictable and often volatile.

There are lots of factors that contribute to the mass forgetting of our enough-ness. Society conditions us to fix our weaknesses and eradicate any areas of so-called imperfection – and when this is not possible, be masterful at hiding them. School and work condition us to conform, comply, compete, prove ourselves and above all – to fit in. We conform with the mainstream pursuits of enough-ness through the accumulation of status, material wealth and achievements, only to discover they are hollow substitutes for true meaning, worthiness and belonging – and lead to stress, anxiety, depression and burnout.

Another trap of believing that we are not enough is the trap of waiting and deferring. This happens when we convince ourselves that we don't have permission to activate our potential until we are more experienced or more educated. The immense challenges we are facing in the world today will not be solved through more qualifications or through more experience. They will be solved by passionate, creative, collaborative and courageous pioneers harnessing and combining the fullness of their potential.

UNHEALTHY STRIVING AND PROVING

When we don't believe in our own enough-ness we are often weighed down by two additional, insidious limiting beliefs. They often come as a pair and together they further corrode our sense of worthiness and sabotage our efforts for self-care. The first is the belief that our value is measured by what we *do*. The second is the belief that our value is measured by what we *have*. These beliefs result in the exhausting and relentless pursuit of doing and having, and make us blind to seeing that who we *are*, and who we are *being and becoming* are our true sources of value in the world.

As young children we are rewarded when we do well at school and sport. Growing up as a straight-A student, my achievements became the primary currency of my value in the world. My hunger to achieve served me well, up until a certain point. It was not until I was in my 30s that I realised that attaching all my worth to my external achievements meant that life was a rocky experience of highs and lows. When things were going well and my achievements were recognised, I was on top of the world, but when things were not going well my mood and mindset plummeted. Another side effect of attaching my self-worth to my doing was that my way of being in the world was one of striving and proving myself. Needless to say, proving and striving as a way of being is not sustainable, fairly unattractive, the epitome of anti-leadership and certainly not playful.

Leaders who narrowly focus on doing can make people feel like human robots. I had a manager whose sense of enough-ness was so strongly tethered to delivery that she was unwilling (or unable) to have the types of conversations that build connections with peers or direct reports. And of course, when leaders are unable to build connections, people are compliant, but they are most certainly not inspired. Compliant people may deliver what is necessary to tick the box, but they are unlikely to harness their full potential to go above and beyond.

Just as we can come to believe that we can prove our enough-ness by *doing*, we might also come to believe we can prove our enough-ness by *having*. The modern world bombards us with many messages that reinforce the belief that who we *are* equates somehow to what we *have*. As kids, in addition to wanting to prove ourselves through good grades and sports trophies, we were also conditioned to yearn for all the stuff we saw on TV commercials. We came to believe that our Kmart branded bike meant that we were in some way lesser than our friend who had the BMX from the bike shop. (A small point of clarification here – back when I was growing up, Kmart was not considered cool.) In the world of business we see leaders overly focused on *having* when people squabble over the perceived seniority of job titles, when we invest an inordinate amount of leadership time debating and explaining the intricacies of bonus structures and payments or when senior leaders act like spoilt toddlers, stubbornly refusing to let go of the status symbol of their office when their organisation transitions to activity-based working.

Decoupling our understanding of our own worthiness from what we do and what we have, and instead learning how to anchor our worthiness in who we are, is transformative. The belief that I could achieve my way to enough-ness was a shadow that followed me for the first decade of my career. It was an exhausting burden to carry, however for many years I was oblivious to the cost of maintaining

Great leadership is about finding the courage to care.

this belief. I remember a courageous older colleague named Geoff pulling me aside into a small meeting room one afternoon when I was in my early 30s. He closed the door gently behind him, looked me in the eye and said kindly, 'Cassie, stop trying to prove yourself.' I remember thinking, 'What are you talking about? Of *course*, I have to prove myself – and by the way, I am just getting started!' It took many more years of personal development work for me to understand what Geoff was trying to tell me that afternoon. It also slowly dawned on me that by trying to prove myself I was not exactly being the best version of myself. I had inadvertently become someone who was pushy, aggressive, impatient. I was not a team player nor a leader (the very things I was so hungry and impatient to become). Thanks, Geoff.

One of my coaching clients who struggled with a constant drive to prove herself was able to identify a recurring story. By becoming more aware of her belief that she needed to prove herself, she was able to identify a familiar story she was telling herself – that she was 'the little kid at the big kids' table'. Getting hooked by this story was a trigger for behaviours she knew were getting in the way of being the sort of leader she wanted to be.

The process of letting go of unhealthy patterns of striving and proving starts by beginning to notice when we are thinking about our work as a means to prove something, prove ourselves, get somewhere else, or get something out of someone else in order to get somewhere or prove something. What are the tell-tale signs for us? Are there certain sensations we feel in our body? Is there a familiar story, emotion or thought pattern that is activated in our mind?

My late grandmother Jean Warne worked at the local council in Condobolin. I have the clipping from the local newspaper article that announced her 'retirement' in 1938. She was getting married to my grandfather at age 22. The article said:

> *Many tributes were paid to Miss Warne when occasion was taken to officially farewell her prior to her retirement in preparation for*

her forthcoming wedding. She had been a great girl for the council. She was described as having proved her worth. Miss Warne in responding spoke very nicely saying "all the nice remarks of me make it even harder to leave."

I am very grateful to my grandma. Not just for all she sacrificed to have my mum and aunty but also for showing me that I do not aspire to being referred to as 'a great girl who has proved my worth'. I want to know that my worth is immeasurable and that I don't have anything to prove to anyone.

Learning how to trust in our own enough-ness and worthiness can transform our lives, and the lives of others. It supports us to assertively claim what we need to thrive, and we avoid wasting our precious energy wearing masks and hiding the truth of who we really are.

Releasing ourselves from the burden of the belief that we are not enough means we don't have to wait until we have eliminated our sharp edges or amassed more experience in order to create a working life that contributes in meaningful ways.

Letting go: **I am not enough**

Understanding to uplift

Does the belief 'I am not enough' influence your choices and actions?

BURNING QUESTIONS

How might letting go of this belief uplift your working life?

How might letting go uplift others in your life?

Is there something you need to give yourself permission for, in order to let it go?

What might shift in your working life if you were to *respond* from worthiness, instead of *reacting* from not-enough-ness?

What new possibilities might emerge if you no longer believed the thought 'I am not enough'?

What might you choose to *think* and *believe* instead?

I can't handle this

Everything you've ever wanted
is sitting on the other side of fear.

George Addair[1]

The work of activating our potential involves, at times, significant amounts of discomfort. Our growth does not happen in our comfort zone. We *become* from struggle, discomfort and pain. Learning how to be with our own discomfort is a key element of self-fidelity because being true to ourselves at work is often uncomfortable at first. This means that letting go of the belief 'I can't handle this' is essential.

The longest period of sustained discomfort I have experienced in my career to date was the three years I spent working in Europe while I was working for General Electric. GE was an organisation who really walked the talk of their motto 'grow yourself to grow others and grow the business'. I fell in love with GE's approach to continuous improvement. It blended the things that I was deeply passionate about – customer-led innovation, challenging the status-quo and working collaboratively. I spent four years mastering and applying GE's continuous improvement toolkit. I attained Black Belt and then Master Black Belt accreditation in Lean, Six Sigma and Change Management methodologies. From there, I set my sights on becoming a Quality Leader. It was the Quality Leader roles that encompassed responsibility not just for training, coaching and execution but also for setting the business strategy for how to apply continuous improvement methodologies to maximise value generation. I quickly discovered that the limited number of Quality Leader roles available in Australia were taken by people with no plans of moving on.

One afternoon I did another search for Quality Leader roles in GE's global internal job vacancy system, this time leaving the country field blank. I will never forget the wonderful surprise I felt the moment when I saw the long list of search results fill the screen. There were dozens of open Quality Leader roles available across the globe. One in particular jumped out – Quality Leader for the GE Security Business. The role was based in Brussels, Belgium and encompassed responsibility for the continuous improvement function across their entire region – Europe, Middle East and Africa. Before I knew it, I was on a plane to Brussels for an interview. And after a gruelling two-day interview process that involved being screened by every single member of the executive team, to my surprise and delight, I was offered the job.

I lived in Brussels for three years. Over that period I struggled in so many ways. The first day, I struggled with how to buy milk. The first week I struggled to drive on the other side of the car on the other side of the road in snow in my first-ever company car. Later I struggled to understand the culture and how an innocent invitation to a weekend BBQ at my house could result in several people complaining to the CEO. I constantly struggled with the language and the way the CEO and CFO often switched to a side conversation in Flemish in the middle of an executive meeting. One day I got a call from the CEO of the Australian GE business I had left three years prior. He was calling to let me know that a Quality Leader role had become available in my hometown of Sydney. I moved back to Australia and spent another wonderful few years at GE working in that role. The last five years of my GE career were the most expansive, most scary, most thrilling and most enriching years of my career

The journey of discovering what we are truly capable of is life's greatest adventure and our greatest gift to the world.

to date. And none of it would have been possible had I stayed in my comfort zone.

THE COSTS OF COMFORT

We are conditioned to see discomfort as something to avoid, and thanks to the wonders of modern life, it has never been easier for humans to avoid discomfort. Every time I visit the US, I find myself captivated by the commercials for drugs on TV. The ads usually start with footage of someone joyfully living their best life, having found the miracle drug that has finally set them free from their debilitating ailment (which strangely, often seems to be restless leg syndrome). The commercials always end with a rapid-fire voice that says something along the lines of: 'May cause diarrhoea, nausea, dizziness, insomnia and death.'

We often choose to ignore any potential side effects of our artificial, always-on comfort. Day after day we choose from a vast menu of remedies to mask any discomfort we may be experiencing day-to-day. We drink, sugar-fix, scroll, pop pills, binge and shop to stay feeling good. While in the short-term these things may seem to keep us safe and in our comfort bubble, long-term they can lead us into a world of pain.

The journey of discovering what we are truly capable of is life's greatest adventure and our greatest gift to the world. But like all great adventures, there is a level of risk involved and there will be inevitable struggles, stumbles and setbacks along the way. At times it may feel more like destruction than growth. On occasions we may get our butts well and truly kicked. The idea of getting comfortable with being uncomfortable is not a new one. Perhaps we have heard this phrase so many times in the context of our volatile, uncertain, complex and ambiguous world that it sounds like a cliche.

Just because this idea might seem cliched or common sense, it does not mean it is common practice. We still cling to comfort and for many of us, our discomfort tolerance is very low.

'BECOMING' PAIN VS 'BETRAYAL' PAIN

It can be tremendously helpful to learn how to discern between different types of pain. More specifically, to learn how to discern between 'becoming pain' and 'self-betrayal pain'. Self-betrayal pain is the pain we experience when, little by little, we allow ourselves to drift away from our core values and aspirations. If unrecognised, this type of pain can hum in the background for long periods of time. It might show up as a low-level reverberation of feeling empty, unfulfilled, lost or off track. Perhaps the pain of self-betrayal manifests as feelings of homesickness, being trapped, sleepwalking or somehow alienated from our own life.

Alternatively, the discomfort of becoming feels scary yet exhilarating. The pain of personal growth is a signal that we are *doing it.* We are in the arena, playing around the fringes of our comfort zone, expanding into all that we are. Contrary to popular belief, thriving and struggling are not two ends of a one-dimensional spectrum. We can thrive through change and struggle. The work of being true to ourselves is no walk in the park, but it sure beats the alternative – a life of quiet desperation, unfulfilled dreams and deep regret.

We can all notice when the belief 'I can't handle this' has been activated in our thinking and instead choose to think something more empowering and uplifting. For example, by being aware that we are having the thought 'I can't handle this', we can remind ourselves that while we don't like discomfort, we understand that avoiding it means we will never understand our full potential. We can remember the huge cost that accompanies living our lives in our comfort zone – and come back to the reality that while we may prefer to remain comfortable, we can most certainly handle discomfort.

The first step to releasing the burden of the belief that we can't handle discomfort is to be aware of its existence. From this place of awareness, we can begin to imagine the possibilities of letting it go.

Letting go: **I can't handle this**

Understanding to uplift

Does the belief 'I can't handle this' influence your choices and actions?

BURNING QUESTIONS

How might letting go of this belief uplift your working life?

How might letting go uplift others in your life?

Is there something you need to give yourself permission for, in order to let it go?

What might shift in your working life if you were to *respond* from self-trust, instead of *reacting* from fear?

What new possibilities might emerge if you no longer believed the thought 'I can't handle this'?

What might you choose to *think* and *believe* instead?

I need to shield my heart

When we protect ourselves so we won't feel pain, that protection becomes armor, like armor that imprisons the softness of the heart.

Pema Chödrön[1]

The working world can condition us to think that we need to shield our hearts – over time this way of thinking forms a belief. We believe that we must shield our hearts to protect ourselves from the slings and arrows of the world. As we all know, these slings and arrows can be particularly prevalent and cutting in our workplaces. However, by shielding our hearts we cut ourselves off from the care and connection we long for.

I will never forget one blood-chilling moment when I was presenting the dismal insights from our latest employee engagement survey to my CEO. During our conversation he latched onto one particular anonymous employee comment in my report that spoke pointedly about his incapacity to sort out the obvious dysfunction, empire-building and in-fighting that was rampant across his executive team. He looked at me, eyes bulging with rage and said, 'If I ever find out who wrote this, they will never work for this organisation again.' I did my best to professionally but quickly wrap things up and scurried out of his office. The comment was mine.

There have been moments in my career when I felt I had to choose between putting my heart into lockdown and transforming myself into a litigation-mitigating droid. In one organisation, the decision was made that we needed to make every role in my team redundant and build an entirely different team with a different set of capabilities. I had the gut-wrenching task one afternoon of delivering the news droid-style to six people, one after the other. HR had instructed me to ask each person to leave the building immediately after the meeting, so the remaining team members would not be alerted about what was happening. The sixth member of my team walked into the meeting room looking bewildered and nervously joked, 'Everyone who has come down here has disappeared – where are you hiding the bodies?' Pushing down my instinct to break from the script in that moment and to show some compassion, I quietly asked him to sit down and transformed myself one last time. I remember drinking quite a lot of red wine that night.

The first step to releasing the burden of the belief that we must shield our hearts is to be aware of its existence. From this place of awareness, we can begin to imagine the possibilities that might emerge if we were to find the courage to lay down our heavy armour and to think differently about our capacity to keep our hearts open, despite the risk of heartbreak.

Letting go: I need to shield my heart

Understanding to uplift

Does the belief 'I need to shield my heart' influence your choices and actions?

BURNING QUESTIONS

How might letting go of this belief uplift your working life?

How might letting go uplift others in your life?

Is there something you need to give yourself permission for, in order to let it go?

What might shift in your working life if you were to *respond* from courageous open-heartedness, instead of *reacting* from self-protection?

What new possibilities might emerge if you no longer believed the thought 'I need to shield my heart'?

What might you choose to *think* and *believe* instead?

Work is the opposite of play

You're going to live once, so you might as well have a full life and try things and make mistakes but try to enjoy what you've learnt. And enjoy work, because work is everything. For me, work is play.

Diane Keaton[1]

The old proverb 'all work and no play makes Jack a dull boy' has got a lot to answer for. It feels like this insidious string of ten little words has wormed its way to the depths of our collective consciousness and given rise to the false belief that work is somehow divorced from play, or perhaps even the opposite of play. Not only is it incredibly misleading to think about work as separate from play, it is also incredibly dangerous.

As we learned in *Letting be*, by suppressing our play nature we suppress our creativity and our joy, and restrict our capacity for connection. Over time, we make ourselves sick.

As our careers progress, we mistakenly believe that we must be serious all the time to be good leaders. We forget that truly inspiring leaders know how to embody a sense of lightness and play, understanding that both are essential to success and vitality.

Over my career I have encountered many leaders who had lost touch with their playfulness and had an unfortunate tendency to beat any glimmer of playfulness out of their colleagues – often by using shame. I remember one powerful executive at an organisation I worked for shaming those of us who were eagerly embracing agile ways of working. He declared that using post-it notes in the office was childish and that 'real leaders' would never degrade themselves to such infantile folly. I could not help but wonder about the trauma he might be still carrying to work every day from his childhood. Shockingly, one powerful individual with a powerful limiting belief about post-it notes was enough to squash the adoption of an incredibly valuable innovation methodology.

Rekindling our innate playfulness can greatly enrich our working lives. The first step to releasing the burden of the belief that work is the opposite of play is to be aware of its existence. From this place of awareness, we can begin to let it go.

Letting go: **Work is the opposite of play**

Understanding to uplift

Does the belief 'work is the opposite of play' influence your choices and actions?

BURNING QUESTIONS

How might letting go of this belief uplift your working life?

How might letting go uplift others in your life?

Is there something you need to give yourself permission for, in order to let it go?

What might shift in your working life if you were to *respond* from your natural playfulness, instead of *reacting* from your conditioned conformity?

What new possibilities might emerge if you no longer believed the thought 'work is the opposite of play'?

What might you choose to *think* and *believe* instead?

Self-care is selfish

If your compassion does not include yourself,
it is incomplete.

Jack Kornfield[1]

So many of us are taught that we should always put others first. For many people in my generation, this way of thinking was modelled by our parents and our grandparents who sacrificed so much for us. If we grew up with a parent who believed and modelled the belief that we must always put others first, and that to take care of oneself is a form of selfishness – then it would be difficult to get through childhood without limiting beliefs around self-care becoming deeply embedded.

Headwinds to self-care are further exacerbated by the reality that we live in a world that tends to tear down tall poppies. As children we learnt not to get too big for our britches. We learnt to fear the most cutting of all criticisms – to be labelled as someone who 'loves themselves'. Tough workplace warriors soldier on day in and day out, proudly declaring that lunch is for wimps and that they will sleep when they are dead. Arianna Huffington said, 'We take better care of our smartphone than ourselves. We know when the battery is depleted and recharge it.'[2]

The truth is that the only person who can really take care of us – is us. As they tell us on planes just before take-off – we must secure our own oxygen mask first. Thinking that self-care is selfish creates enormous amounts of suffering – for us and ultimately for the people we care about the most. Until we let go of the beliefs that get in the way of us putting our oxygen masks on first, we will continue to abuse and neglect our bodies and diminish our vitality and our potential.

As the School Of Life points out in *The Sorrows of Work*, self-care can be especially hard when we are experiencing challenges at work: 'To counterbalance what has happened at work, we may instinctively gravitate towards what is excessively sweet, salty, distracting, [and] easy'.[3] The times when our work (and life) challenges are the most difficult are the very times when we most need to double-down on taking good care of ourselves. Barak Obama managed to run every day during his presidency, so the excuse that we have too much to do really doesn't cut it. We will take a closer look at what we can let in to nourish our vitality later in the book.

Throughout my leadership career, I have held a firm commitment to taking care of myself so that I can take care of others. Even during the busiest period of my corporate career, my morning exercise routine was sacrosanct. My enduring commitment to self-care has meant that I never experienced burnout. Yes, I have navigated through health setbacks. Yes, I have sustained psychological injuries and at times heartbreak. However, because of the strength of my beliefs around the importance of self-care, during times of challenge, I have been able to heal and replenish myself, dust myself off and get my butt back into that arena.

The first step to releasing the burden of the belief that self-care is selfish is to become aware of its existence. From this place of awareness, we can begin to embrace the possibilities that come with letting it go.

Letting go: **Self-care is selfish**

Understanding to uplift

Does the belief 'self-care is selfish' influence your choices and actions?

BURNING QUESTIONS

How might letting go of this belief uplift your working life?

How might letting go uplift others in your life?

Is there something you need to give yourself permission for, in order to let it go?

What might shift in your working life if you were to *respond* from a state of vitality and wellbeing, instead of *reacting* from a state of resentful depletion?

What new possibilities might emerge if you no longer believed the thought 'self-care is selfish'?

What might you choose to *think* and *believe* instead?

I don't have enough time

Lack of time is lack of priorities.

Tim Ferriss[1]

I once facilitated a workshop at an elite top-tier investment firm that had a reputation for their high-performance, dog-eat-dog culture. All the participants wore expensive suits and had very firm handshakes. They all looked bulletproof – but the anonymous pre-workshop survey results painted a very different picture. They were experiencing high levels of work-related stress. Most of them were surviving on a mere five hours' sleep most days. They were jacked-up, high-functioning zombies in a marathon-version of *The Hunger Games.* During our session on sleep, I shared the extensive body of research that shows the significant performance and health risks associated with insufficient sleep. Having established a very compelling case for prioritising sleep, I shared the evidence-based strategies for getting enough sleep. I still recall the look of terror in their eyes as I shared the important recommendation to keep devices out of their bedrooms. Given this was almost inconceivable for everyone in the room, we explored the feasibility of at least turning their devices off 30 minutes before bedtime. I will never forget the moment when one of the participants put up his hand and asked, with genuine bewilderment, 'But… what am I supposed to *do* for those 30 minutes?'

The belief that we don't have enough time is one that pervades our modern-day existence. So many of us feel that we always have so much to do and so little time. When we ask someone how they are doing – more often than not, the answer is 'busy!' Some days we feel we can't even afford the three minutes of steeping time for our mid-morning cup of tea. Our constant thoughts around time scarcity creates powerful limiting beliefs about time – or the lack thereof.

The truth is however, that our true wealth can't even be represented in the currency of time. Our true wealth lies in what we do with our attention. In the end, the quality of our lives will be determined by what we give our attention to – one breath at a time.

HOW MUCH ATTENTION DO WE HAVE TO GIVE?

In Boulder, Colorado there is a monument known as the Salt Monument. The monument was created by Margot Weiss. The monument is a huge glass cube that contains around 7 billion grains of salt. Each unique grain of salt represents a single unique human life on the planet. Every day Margot conducts an elaborate ceremony. She adds one grain of salt for every human born that day – adding about 300,000 grains of salt each day. And, she removes a grain of salt from the bottom of the monument to honour every person who has died that day – around 170,000 grains are removed each day.[2] Once a year, all the grains of salt that been taken out of the cube that year are transformed into a unique salt sculpture. Over our lifetimes, while our unique grain of salt passes through the Salt Monument, we will give around 670 million breaths of attention.

There is a simple three-step calculation you can do to get a reality check on exactly how much attention you have left to give. First, minus your age from 100. Next, multiply the answer by 365. Finally, multiply that number by 14,400.

So, being 45 years old, these are my three calculations:

100 – 45 = 55
55 × 365 = 20,075
20,075 × 14,400 = 290 million.

The resulting answer – in my case, 290 million – is the number of remaining breaths of attention I have left to give in this lifetime. This calculation assumes I will keep nourishing my body enough for it to last a full century. The daily breath count of 14,400 is calculated using the midpoint of the average resting respiratory rate of an adult (15 breaths a minute) and assumes 8 hours of sleep each night. So, 16 waking hours × 60 minutes × 15 breaths per minute = 14,400 breaths of attention each day.

In the words of Stephen Covey, 'Most of us spend too much time on what is urgent and not enough time on what is important.'[3] To experience a working life that leaves us feeling – in our final breaths – that we have lived a life that was true to ourselves, we must choose to give our breaths of attention to what is *truly important* to us – not to what is merely urgent or attention-grabbing.

We might like to think about our attention as a spotlight – no matter how great our work demands, we can always retain control of this spotlight and where we choose to place our attention in each breath. Many of us may hand over control of the spotlight to the myriad of erratic external forces that are constantly competing for our attention. Or perhaps our attention has been conditioned to more closely resemble a mirror ball – splintering our precious attention into hundreds of spinning fragments breath to breath. No wonder so many of us feel frazzled and depleted at the end of each working day.

AVOIDING OVERWHELM

As a coach, the excuse of not having enough time is one that often comes up for my clients. But of course, this is not the real reason why we resist trying something new or doing something different. Often, the *real* reason is that we feel overwhelmed and exhausted. Sometimes we can feel we don't have enough energy to take on one more thing. There have been times in my career when the voices in my head have loudly warned me, 'Be careful! If another single person needs you to do one more tiny thing for them, this whole house of cards is going to come crashing down!' If we hear this sort of story in our head, it is a good sign that we have an opportunity to take back control of the spotlight of our attention.

I have found that thinking about my working day as a stream of sand grains slipping through an hourglass is a helpful perspective. Each grain of sand in the hourglass represents a single breath. At the start of an eight-hour working day, my hourglass begins with around 7000 grains of sand at the top. I can choose what I am going to do with each grain, with each breath. I know that to stay connected with my essential nature I must choose wisely. I must invest some of my daily breaths in moving and nourishing my mind and body. I also know that it would not be wise to try to scatter sequential grains across multiple areas of focus.

FOCUS AND STRESS

Most of us now understand that multi-tasking is a myth, that our brains can actually only perform one task at a time and that the illusion of multi-tasking is really just our brains toggling between multiple things and doing a very average job of them.

Gloria Mark (University of California) has conducted extensive research into stress, productivity and distractions. Her research found that every time we allow ourselves to be interrupted it takes around 25 minutes for our brains to return to the same level of focus we had prior to the interruption. This means that if I were to interrupt working on my book to spend five minutes checking LinkedIn, I have not robbed myself of five minutes of focus time, but a full 30 minutes of focused attention. That's 450 breaths I will never get back. Mark wrote in *The New York Times*, 'Our research has shown that attention distraction can lead to higher stress, a bad mood and lower productivity.'[4]

Not only are interruptions and devices stopping us from doing good, creative work, they are also corroding our relationships at work and at home. In the words of Simon Sinek, 'When we break eye contact to check our phones we degrade trust.' In her column *Life Matters* Jo Stanley shared her views on her husband's smart watch:

> *I hate it because it contributes to the cult of busy, busy, busy. I hate it because it supports the false belief that we can – and should – multi-task, a habit research tells us makes us unproductive, and experience tells us makes us bad company. Mostly, I hate it because human connection should not be taken for granted.*[5]

FOCUSING ON WHAT IS IMPORTANT

Here are some questions we can ask ourselves throughout the day to become more aware of how we are spending our time and check that our choices align with our highest aspirations.

- When I feel my time has been well spent, what have I been doing?
- What are the activities that I am spending time on that drain me? How does this feeling influence other aspects of my life?
- What can I do 'more of' and 'less of' to feel more uplifted today?
- What small first steps can I commit to taking to build momentum and a sense of progress on the things that are most important to me?
- What steps can I take to minimise interruptions during focus time?

Letting go: I don't have enough time

Understanding to uplift

Does the belief 'I don't have enough time' influence your choices and actions?

BURNING QUESTIONS

How might letting go of this belief uplift your working life?

How might letting go uplift others in your life?

Is there something you need to give yourself permission for, in order to let it go?

What might shift in your working life if you were to *respond* from careful, considered prioritisation, instead of *reacting* from constant busyness?

What new possibilities might emerge if you no longer believed the thought 'I don't have enough time?'

What might you choose to *think* and *believe* instead?

I have to go it alone

The time of the lone wolf is over.

The elders of the Hopi Nation[1]

I once had a manager who had a strong tendency to be narrowly focused on tasks, delivery and the protection of her reputation as someone who made things happen. She did not place much value on 'the people stuff' and had a reputation for being cold and aloof. Our one-on-ones often got cancelled and when she did meet with me, she seemed cold, impatient and distracted. These experiences were subtly dehumanising for me. Over time, I observed that staying fit was really important to her. So, I suggested we combine our one-on-one meetings with a brisk walk around a nearby park. Her keenness to exercise meant that she became far less likely to bump my one-on-one meeting. I made certain that these walking catch-up experiences were doubly value-adding for her by being sure to spend the first 20 minutes of the walk telling her about all the work I had recently completed and all the ways I was going to make her look like a rock star. On the days when her thirst for looking good was sufficiently satiated by my update (and the brisk exercise) and she relaxed a little, we sometimes managed to spend the last part of our walking meetings connecting human to human, heart to heart. By patiently connecting with what my boss had been conditioned to care about I was able to occasionally connect with her deeper, more essential nature. However, it really should not take that much effort to feel connected with our colleagues.

THE TIME OF THE LONE WOLF IS OVER

This prophecy offered by the Hopi elders, considered the earth protectors, in the year 2000 warns 'the time of the lone wolf is over'.[2] Their prophecy ends with the line 'we are the ones we have been waiting for.'[3] For me, the key word here is 'we'.

It seems that so many of us, at some point in our lives, have made a solemn post-heartbreak pact with ourselves to lock our hearts away for safekeeping and to forevermore go it alone. The belief that we operate best as lone wolves is further reinforced by the individualist 'every man for himself' undercurrent that flows beneath the surface of many organisational cultures. The under-handed politics and powerful shadowy alliances that operate in the upper echelons I have been privy to in my senior leadership career at times made it seem foolish to trust anyone but myself.

It was not until many years into my leadership career that I realised that my success as a leader was completely dependent on my capacity to form trusted, mutually respectful partnerships with others. I came to realise that the quality, honesty and strengths of the relationships I nurtured with people right across the organisations made the difference between being able to powerfully and easily activate cross-functional change and feeling like I was constantly swimming against a strong tide. I have worked with intellectually brilliant individuals who were so self-righteous and rigid in their views they were virtually impossible to work with. It perplexes me why highly paid, highly credentialled individuals who are terrible collaborators continue to get put on pedestals in organisations. We could hire the best data scientist in the world, but it counts for nothing if they see themselves as superior to everyone else in the organisation.

IT JUST ISN'T WORTH IT

One of my all-time favourite children's books is *Hope for the Flowers* by Trina Paulus.[4] The book tells the tale of a caterpillar named Stripe who finds himself clambering his way to the top of a huge pile of caterpillars. All of Stripe's fellow climbers are equally determined and desperate to reach the pinnacle of the huge, squirming caterpillar pillar – despite none on them actually knowing what is at the top. After the initial shock of all the pushing and kicking inside the caterpillar pillar, Stripe quickly learns what he must do to succeed – he must 'climb or be climbed'. This single-mindedness serves Stripe well. He becomes single-minded and his fellow caterpillars 'become only threats and obstacles' – which Stripe turns into 'steps and opportunities'. One day Stripe accidentally finds himself talking to another caterpillar named Yellow. This is very inconvenient because after their conversation Stripe notices that he has lost his single-mindedness. Stripe climbs on, avoiding Yellow as much as possible until the day Stripe encounters Yellow again, blocking his only way up. The three lines that describe what Stripe does next are incredibly poignant:

> *'Well, I guess it's you or me,' he said, and he stepped squarely on her head.*
>
> *Something in the way Yellow looked at him made him feel just awful about himself.*
>
> *Like: no matter what is up there – it just isn't worth it.*[5]

When I first read this last line it pierced my heart – because, just like Stripe, there have been many moments in my working life when I have felt that the individualist 'climb or be climbed' ways of working I was unwillingly participating in just wasn't worth it.

The great irony of the lone wolf mentality is that unless we work together there is no way we can pull off the scale and speed of innovation that enables sustained performance and the ongoing delivery of great employee and customer experiences. The belief that we need to go it alone not only goes against the grain of our true nature, it also makes it impossible for us to innovate and therefore thrive as collectives.

Letting go: I have to go it alone

Understanding to uplift

Does the belief 'I have to go it alone' influence your choices and actions?

BURNING QUESTIONS

How might letting go of this belief uplift your working life?

How might letting go uplift others in your life?

Is there something you need to give yourself permission for, in order to let it go?

What might shift in your working life if you were to *respond* from connectedness, instead of *reacting* from imagined aloneness?

What new possibilities might emerge if you no longer believed the thought 'I have to go it alone?'

What might you choose to *think* and *believe* instead?

BREAKING FREE OF OTHER BELIEFS

The beliefs I speak about in this book are by no means a complete list. We can use the following exercise to uncover and let go of other limiting beliefs that are operating below our level of conscious awareness.

Uncover

Write a list of 50 things you believe to be true about yourself in the context of your work.

Review the list and classify each belief as either: uplifting, neutral or limiting.

Identify your most limiting belief.

Reflect

How might letting go of this belief uplift your working life?

How might letting go of this belief uplift others in your life?

Reframe

Write down five alternative beliefs.

Select *one* alternative belief that feels both uplifting and within your reach. Choose an alternative belief that is more positive, but do not choose a belief that feels completely unbelievable to you. Over time you can choose incrementally more and more uplifting beliefs.

Is there something you need to give yourself permission to feel or experience in order to engage with this new uplifting belief?

Uplift

Every time you notice thoughts associated with your old limiting belief, play with doing a mental 'edit replace' with a different thought associated with your alternative belief and see what happens. You might notice over time that your replacement thoughts become more and more uplifting.

She let go.
She let go. Without a thought or a word, she let go.
She let go of the fear.
She let go of the judgments.
She let go of the confluence of opinions swarming around her head.
She let go of the committee of indecision within her.
She let go of all the 'right' reasons.
Wholly and completely, without hesitation or worry, she just let go.
She didn't ask anyone for advice.
She didn't read a book on how to let go.
She didn't search the scriptures.
She just let go.

...

No one was around when it happened.
There was no applause or congratulations.
No one thanked her or praised her.
No one noticed a thing.
Like a leaf falling from a tree, she just let go.
There was no effort.
There was no struggle.
It wasn't good and it wasn't bad.
It was what it was, and it is just that.
In the space of letting go, she let it all be.
A small smile came over her face.
A light breeze blew through her.
And the sun and the moon shone forevermore...

Safire Rose[6]

LETTING IN

You must be the one to do or undo whatever it takes you to activate your own furiously prolific heart.

Brooke McNamara[1]

Feelings

Although many of us think of ourselves
as thinking creatures that feel, biologically
we are feeling creatures that think.

Jill Bolte Taylor[1]

Most days at work we will ask a colleague, 'How are you doing?' In Australia we tend to ask, 'How are you going?' Unfortunately, the sad reality is that we are generally not at all interested in the answer to this question nor are we prepared to respond to an honest answer. Perhaps this is the reason we rarely ask ourselves the very same question.

The practice of letting in our feelings is about increasing our awareness and acceptance of both our emotions and the physical feelings in our bodies. By learning to better tune into our own feelings, we grow our capacity for true presence.

We are all quick to blame the actions of others for being miserable. We conclude that we have had a terrible day because of the passive aggressive email we received from a colleague, the look of disapproval from the CEO or the way our boss dismissed our idea in a meeting. It is easy to blame others as the cause of our suffering and unhappiness. The truth is that our bodies react to our external world and then our minds quickly attach meaning to that reaction – and this is what causes our suffering. As Yuval Noah Harari said, 'I never react to the outside world; I always react to the sensations in my own body.'[2] At work, we often place all our emphasis on thinking – not feeling.

At work our feelings typically don't really count all that much. Not only are our emotions casualties of the legacy work paradigm that worships cognition – so are our tired, sick, polluted bodies.

Learning how to work with our feelings is a super-power. It starts by becoming more aware of physical sensations in our bodies as well as our interpretations, stories, assumptions and beliefs. From this place of awareness and presence, we can learn to reduce our emotional and psychological suffering and reactivity and reconnect with our essential nature. This opens up a pathway to liberation and freedom. The best part? We can tap into a sustainable source of inner peace and vitality that is immune to even the most incompetent or narcissistic bosses. We learn how to remain open-hearted at work. As Pema Chodron teaches us, 'As we become more conscious of our thoughts and emotions and look at them with kind-hearted interest and curiosity, we begin to see how we armor ourselves against pain.'[3]

OUR THREE BRAINS

More and more, science is beginning to come to grips with the complex relationships and interdependencies that exist within our bodies. In 2019 *Forbes* magazine published an article that said:

> *Neuroscience now tells us that we each have three brains. The one we most often think about and pay attention to is the "head" or cephalic brain. We also have a heart (cardiac) and a gut (enteric) brain. Each has sensory neurons, motor neurons, ganglia, and neurotransmitters. They are able to take in information, process it, store it and access it when needed.*[4]

Another particularly interesting emerging area is the field of *neuro-cardiology* that explores the brain-heart connection. We now understand that our heart has a complex neural network that is sufficiently extensive to be characterised as 'a brain on the heart'.[5] Our *heart-brain is* an intricate network of ganglia, neurotransmitters, proteins and support cells. Historically science focused on understanding how our heart responds to the command of our brain. We now understand that communication between the heart and brain is a dynamic, continuous, two-way dialogue, with each organ continuously influencing the functioning of the other. Research is also now showing that our heart sends our brain far more messages than our brain sends our heart.

Research into the roles of our heart brains and gut brains is still in its infancy. I can't see any downside in rounding our decision-making process to intentionally harness our heart brain for compassion, our head for creativity and our gut brain for courage. The simple three-step process would look something like this:

1. Checking with our hearts to ensure that the decision we have just made feels congruent with our values.
2. Using our heads to make new connections and discover creative ways to move forwards.
3. Harnessing the courage from our gut to take action.

RECONNECTING WITH OUR BODIES

We spend much of our working hours in our heads. One of my yoga teachers is particularly fond of exclaiming 'most people are just heads on sticks!' If our body sends us a signal that something is not quite right, we are quick to dull it back into compliance so that we can valiantly soldier on. Many of us punish or starve our body in order to squeeze it into a narrow definition of attractiveness. We may deprive ourselves of essential sleep and then jack ourselves up with sugar and caffeine. We resist the urging of a full bladder as long as possible just to get through a few more emails. Perhaps we arrive home gagging for a drink to take the edge off our stress. Maybe we go to bed buzzing with so much pent-up frustration and anxiety we have to sedate our bodies into submission so that we get just enough sleep to do it all again tomorrow. We may even find ourselves bragging about how little nourishment we are surviving on as a badge of honour that symbolises how busy and important we are. I realise that this is a bleak picture and it is also true that more and more leaders are waking up to the reality that a strong, flexible mind starts with a strong, vital, flexible body. However, generally speaking in workplaces around the world we still have a long way to go to truly connect and honour our bodies and the thousands of messages they are sending us every day while we are at work.

BECOMING MORE AWARE OF OUR EMOTIONS

By practising checking in with our bodies throughout the working day we can also become more familiar with our emotional states. A powerful habit is to ask ourselves several times throughout the day, 'What's going on inside of me right now?' Our body will always give us a truthful response if we know how to listen to it. In the words of Eckhart Tolle:

> *If you really want to know your mind, the body will always give you a truthful reflection, so look at the emotion, or rather* feel *it in your body. If there is an apparent conflict between them, the thought will be the lie, the emotion will be the truth. Not the ultimate truth of who you are, but the relative truth of your state of mind at the time.*[6]

In the same way we can become more attuned with the physical sensations in our bodies, we can learn to get better at being with our emotions.

Asking 'are my feelings important or justified?' is similar to asking 'do I have a right to be hungry?' We all have a right to every emotion we feel and our emotions carry important messages. The key to the embodying of our essence is giving ourselves permission to feel and learn to work with our emotions – without amplifying them. In the words of Professor Marc Brackett:

> *Feelings are a form of information. They're like a news report from inside our psyches, sending messages about what's going on*

> *inside the unique person that is each of us in response to whatever internal or external event we're experiencing. We need to access that information and then figure out what it's telling us. That way we can make the most informed decisions.*[7]

In the book *My Stroke of Insight*, brain scientist Jill Bolte Taylor explains that the physical experience of even our strongest emotion only lasts for ninety seconds.[8] That's around 20 breaths. I would argue that, despite what the voices in our head tell us – we can all withstand even the most painful emotions for 20 breaths.

The problem is that our *actual* experiences of painful emotions – such as shame, anger, frustration – last much longer than just ninety seconds. This is because our minds are triggering that same emotion on loop over and over again. We replay (and probably exaggerate) the experience through replaying it like a movie in our minds. Incredibly, it is possible for the human mind to replay a painful ninety-second emotion on loop for twenty years… or more.

EMOTIONS AS A TOOL FOR CHANGE

The experience of strong emotions at work is to be expected. If we have submitted to unfair circumstances, anger is inevitable. When we feel strong emotions at work, we are conditioned to suck them up so as not to rock the boat. So we keep our feelings to ourselves all day to avoid conflict. We are afraid that if we speak the truth of how we are feeling we would make other people uncomfortable or suffer ramifications of not toeing the party line. We don't realise that the decisions we make every day to suppress and deny our feelings come at a huge cost – not only to our wellbeing but to the wellbeing of our families, who often bear the brunt of the suffering we inflict on ourselves. Over time by directing so much of our energy towards keeping the peace we become less and less familiar with our own inner landscape. We lose touch with our own thoughts, needs, values and wants. As the pressure builds, we desperate try to keep a lid on things but eventually we erupt. This uncontrolled and usually poorly timed eruption confirms our worst fears – that our feelings are destructive and unhelpful.

Strong emotions can be a tool for positive change at work in that they can challenge us to become more familiar with our own needs and learn how to skilfully and assertively speak up for ourselves. By speaking up, we can repair our sense of personal agency and self-esteem. In the words of Harriet Lerner:

> *Feelings of depression, low self-esteem, self-betrayal, and even self-hatred are inevitable when we fight but continue to submit to unfair circumstances, when we complain but live in a way that betrays our hopes, values and potential.*[9]

We can all learn to harness our emotional energy to clarify our needs and strengthen ourselves and our relationships. Instead of fearing strong emotions or venting our hurt or discharging it on inappropriate targets, we can use our emotional energy to fuel our agency, dignity and growth. With skill and practice we can learn how to reacquaint ourselves with our inner emotional landscape and assertively and calmly communicate what we need to be true to ourselves at work.

CLARIFYING WHERE WE STAND

Developing and practising the ability to calmly engage in conversations about the things that are important and communicate them in a clear non-blaming way will help us avoid a great deal of unnecessary suffering, including:

- feeling that we are powerless and have no choice but to submit to unfair circumstances
- feeling like we have no control over our work
- not being able to address the real issues that are causing us pain
- maintaining the status-quo at the expense of our self

- feeling there is something wrong with us (instead of understanding there is something not working well in our relationships or environments)
- feeling too afraid to speak up in case it makes other people uncomfortable
- betraying ourselves based on a fear that stating our needs will expose differences and leave us standing alone (when it is a pathway to true belonging).

When we are making changes in our behaviour based on a new relationship with our feelings it is wise to start slowly with small changes. Organisations are dynamic systems and changes to the relationships within the system will create ripple effects and feedback loops. It is important to take things slowly and to test, learn and respond. We must just focus on improving ourselves. We cannot change the behaviours or reactions of others, and the cost of trying to can be high. It is our responsibility alone to be clear on our own values and to behave in ways that are congruent with these values. It is not our job to change other people – all we can do is stand with clarity, compassion and integrity in our version of the truth.

Here are a few questions we can use to work with strong emotions and clarify where we stand.

- What emotions are present for me right now?
- What meaning have I attached to my circumstances? What specifically about this situation is making me feel these emotions?
- What is this feeling *really* about?
- What do I hope to accomplish?
- Where does my responsibility for that outcome start and end?
- What, specifically, can I commit to changing in myself?
- What are the things that I *won't* do?

REDUCING ENTANGLEMENT WITH STRONG EMOTIONS

The emotional pain our minds generate is a primary source of physical pain and physical disease.

When we have physical pain, we don't identify with it – for example, we would say, 'I have a headache' not 'I am a headache.' Yet when we experience emotional suffering, we often automatically allow it to consume us. We are quick to declare, 'I am angry.' With practice, we can begin to notice we are separate to our emotions. We can learn to notice the presence of strong emotions, such as anger in our bodies and our minds and instead say, 'I am *feeling* angry.' Put another way – when we say 'I am angry' we are identifying with the weather in our minds. When we say 'I am feeling angry' we are reminding ourselves that we are the sky, not the weather. This is a subtle but important difference. Learning to untangle ourselves and build trust that we can be with strong emotions is essential if we are to clearly see all the options available to us in moments that matter.

Labelling thoughts and emotions can also support us to recognise the presence of strong emotions and to lessen their grip on us. Just labelling emotions as they arise in us can significantly increase our capacity to respond rather than react to the situation. Silently labelling thoughts and emotions as they arise we expand that tiny space that exists 'between stimulus and response'. Pema Chodron suggest that we think about our thoughts as bubbles, and labelling our thoughts as like 'touching a bubble with a feather'.[10]

One of my coaching clients, Bob, came to understand that when he was triggered and in a trance he was often consumed by an experience of being a volcano that was about to explode. Through our conversations, he came to see that there was a stark contrast in how he was showing up as leader when his focus was on 'keep a lid on the volcano' versus when he was showing up in his most resourceful, mindful state. When Bob was at his best, he was calm, empathetic and strongly attuned to what the situation called for. By becoming aware of the thoughts and feelings he was experiencing in the trance-state of being a volcano about to explode, he was able to practise changing his state. Over time, he got much better at recognising the feelings in his body that told him he was in a trance – clenched jaw, tight shoulders, heat in his face. Using this awareness, he could then practise making space for the emotions in play, investigate the stories he was believing in that moment and from this place of curiosity, discern his wisest course of action with acceptance and awareness. Bob learnt how to break his trance and move himself into a state of mindful awareness. He continued to be triggered, however he spent less time being a volcano before he noticed that he had drifted way off-course and needed to take action to get himself back on course and in alignment with his leadership aspirations. By improving his capacity to notice when he was triggered and remember that he could get back behind the helm was the key to overcoming this unhelpful pattern of thinking and behaviour.

Learning to be with all our emotions, both the comfortable and the uncomfortable ones, is essential to the work of self-fidelity. With practice, we can all begin to trust in our capacity to work with all of our emotions – even the tricky emotions like anger and shame. Ultimately this means that our choice to belong to an organisation does not need to come at the expense of having a clear and healthy sense of self.

SOME OF THE THINGS THAT CAN GET IN THE WAY

Now that we have established how it is important that we improve our awareness of our feelings, let's take a look at some of the things that get in the way.

Two of the main barriers to the practice of being with our feelings are the false beliefs that we should be able to control our feelings, and that some feelings are good and some are bad. These beliefs are at the root of a tremendous amount of unnecessary suffering and are huge barriers to being faithful to ourselves for better and for worse, in good times and in bad. They also drive us to numbing. The seeds of these beliefs start when we are children. If we were hurt or upset, we may have been told, 'Oh, you are okay, honey, please don't cry' or worse still, 'Stop your crying or I will give you something to *really* cry about.' If we experienced these sorts of reactions to painful or strong emotions it may have led us to believe that our pain is at best inconvenient, or at worst, completely inappropriate.

Growing up, I decided that my father's work-related stress meant I needed to be very vigilant at restoring the equilibrium at home. This resulted in a belief that my feelings were not important. In my mind, my self-appointed role as family peace-keeper required a deep commitment to becoming a super-low-maintenance high-achieving machine. I really took this commitment very seriously. In fact, my belief that I needed to be low-maintenance even extended to my haircut – as evidenced by this rather tragic school photo. I remember the Saturday morning I decided my long hair was an unnecessary inconvenience to my family (because it required assistance to wash and brush). I marched down to the local barber and firmly instructed him to 'cut it all off and make it short like a boy'. Believing I needed to be a super-low-maintenance high-achieving machine had some benefits, but also came with a huge cost, although my haircuts at the local barber were a real bargain. I was driven to study hard and my grades were good enough to become dux of my school. My idea of having fun was just a tad constrained – as a child I loved pretending to be a very useful and efficient secretary and spent hours honing my typing skills on a typewriter I had requested for my birthday. Also, my first kiss was a long time coming. Later on, there was the small matter of years spent in therapy.

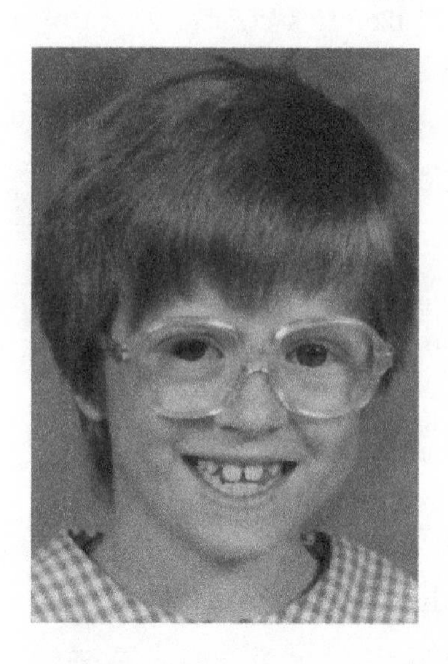

NUMBING

When the voices in our heads convince us that certain emotions are bad or that we can't handle difficult emotions, we turn to numbing. We all numb – it is just a matter of how and how often. We numb ourselves with mindless social media scrolling, binge-watching TV, over-working, over-exercising, comfort eating and alcohol. Staying crazy-busy is another common way we numb ourselves. As Brené Brown says, we are living 'hard and fast' so that 'the truths of our lives can't catch up with us.'[11]

The big problem with numbing is that we can't selectively numb only the feelings we want to avoid. When we allow ourselves to think that we lack the strength to be with difficult emotions for 20 breaths, we also rob ourselves of experiencing nourishing emotions such as gratitude, love, joy and connection. In the words of Khalil Gibran:

> *Some of you say, 'Joy is greater than sorrow,' and others say, 'Nay, sorrow is the greater.' But I say unto you, they are inseparable. Together they come, and when one sits alone with you at your board, remember that the other is asleep upon your bed.*[12]

One of the most common ways we numb ourselves is with alcohol. The 2020 coronavirus pandemic saw significant increases in alcohol sales. During the lockdown period there was a sign outside my local cafe-cum-wine-bar that read 'Coffee keeps me busy until it's time to drink wine'. In Australia, Hello Sunday Morning (an organisation that aims at changing people's relationship with alcohol) reported a 45 per cent increase in searches seeking help with daily drinking at the height of the pandemic.[13] Glennon Doyle said this about her decision to end her unhealthy relationship with alcohol:

> *Since I got sober, I have never been fine again. Not for a single moment. I have been exhausted and terrified and angry. I have been overwhelmed and underwhelmed, depressed and anxious. I have been amazed and awed and delighted and overjoyed. I have been reminded constantly that the ache will pass.*[14]

Now, I am certainly not opposed to drinking alcohol. In fact, I believe that enjoying a good glass of wine with a good meal and good friends is one of life's great pleasures. But I do believe that it is important to have a wide-awake awareness of the nature of our relationship with alcohol. There is an enormous difference between savouring and celebrating the good things in life – and wanting to dull or escape from the reality of life. The insidious disease of alcoholism has nothing to do with how much someone drinks, when they drink, what they drink or how often they drink. Alcoholism is an unhealthy relationship with alcohol. An alcoholic is someone whose primary relationship is with alcohol and the disease causes them to prioritise this relationship above all others – leading to dire consequences.

Many of us also numb through over-working and social media. This form of numbing as a coping strategy can lead to tremendous suffering and addiction to our devices. As Cal Newport says, 'the urge to check Twitter becomes a nervous twitch that shatters uninterrupted time into shards too small to support the presence of an intentional life.'[15] Device addiction is also extremely insidious. It is so easy to suddenly find ourselves attempting to do meaningful work and live our lives in 'tiny shards of time'. This way of living makes it impossible to grow into the fullest expression of ourselves.

Many people sleep with their phones next to their beds and their device is the first thing and the last thing they see every evening and morning. Researchers from Harvard and the University of Virginia conducted an experiment in which they gave people a choice to either spend time alone in a room, without anything (including no devices) or get an electric shock. The vast majority of them chose the electric shock.[16] It is now commonplace to take our phones to the toilet with us. Have you ever found yourself waiting in a long line to use a toilet at a venue and noticed how so many people emerging from the stalls are in the act of putting their phones back into their bags or pockets?

Whether we are an exhausted, distracted numbing junkie who is desperate to stop the ride and get off, or just someone who wants to get a bit better at maintaining our peak levels of focus for longer stretches of time – we can all take steps to reduce our dependency on numbing and distractions. It starts by becoming aware both of the ways in which we numb ourselves and the real cost of these behaviours.

We can all develop greater self-awareness and greater self-regulation of our feelings. Over time we can build our confidence in our ability to navigate hard things – at work and in life. This is an essential element of the practices of self-fidelity.

Learning how to be with our feelings is also of the utmost importance in our pursuit of discovering our own answer to the 'big kahuna question' – If I am the sky and not the weather… then what is my true nature? The answer to this question will never come from thinking or cognition – the answers to this question will only ever emerge in the realm of feeling.

Letting in: **Feelings**

Understanding to uplift

INSIGHTS

The practice of letting in our feelings
is about increasing our awareness and acceptance of
both our emotions and the physical feelings in our bodies.

By learning to better tune into our own feelings,
we grow our capacity for true presence.

BURNING QUESTIONS

How might being more aware of your feelings and emotions
uplift your working life?

How might it uplift others in your life?

Is there something you need to give yourself permission for,
in order to let in your feelings?

**What new possibilities might emerge
if you were more aware of your feelings,
and less likely to numb them
or become entangled with them?**

PLAY

What practices will you play with
to grow your awareness of your feelings and emotions?

How might you play with soaking in positive emotions using RAIN?
(Recognise, Amplify, Investigate, Nourish)

Vitality

There is a vitality, a life force, a quickening that is translated through you into action, and because there is only one of you in all time, this expression is unique.

Martha Graham[1]

My late grandmother Jean Warne was a woman who epitomised life-long vitality. I have no doubt that she is the genetic source of my zest and my commitment to never lose touch with the thrill of living. My favourite memories of her come from her final years. I still chuckle when I think back to the Christmas lunch when she laughed so hard at the corny joke in the Christmas cracker that her false teeth fell out of her mouth and into her lunch. (Why did the bald man put a rabbit on his head? Because from a distance, it looked like a hare!) I also have a memory from my last visit with her in the nursing home where she lived. Over a cuppa, I asked her if she was participating in any of the group activities that were on offer in the community room. Upon hearing my question, she lowered her tea-cup and turned to me slowly, eyes wide with horror. 'Have you *been* in that room? It is full of old people!' She was in her mid-90s at the time. Oh, how I hope to embody such pluck in my twilight years.

Vitality is best described as our life force. It is the sum total of our physical, emotional, mental and spiritual energy. Without vitality there is just no way we can fully embody our essential nature because we are in survival mode. Without vitality we cannot be caring, courageous, creative or playful. Without vitality we are too busy struggling to stay afloat to be any of these things.

The foundation of our vitality is created by engaging in meaningful work with people whom we respect and feel respected by. We also maintain a good base level of vitality by choosing to rest, move our bodies and get enough sleep. We can also be discerning about the food, drink, substances and content we imbibe – as well as the people and environments we expose ourselves to.

GETTING CLEAR ON OUR NON-NEGOTIABLES

We all know what we need to do to nourish our minds, bodies and spirits – the problem is that we often choose to do things that deplete and harm us. To increase buoyancy, we can become more intentional about *letting in* the things that will inspire, nourish and embolden us on our pilgrimage – our non-negotiables.

Non-negotiables are the things we need to prioritise in order to nourish, protect and rest our mind, body and soul. No two people have the same needs when it comes to the specific things we need to fill our cups. A great way to take action towards greater vitality is to get really clear on our non-negotiables and much better at honouring them.

Perhaps you know you are a much better leader when you have done a short run in the morning, if you are able to get home in time for dinner with the kids, or if you finish early once a week to play a sport, take a class or spend time in your garden. Whatever it is, it is your job alone to figure out what you need and how you plan to honour those things every week. Once you have figured this out, share your plan with your colleagues and family, explain how honouring these things make you a better person to be around. You might even like to ask them to hold you accountable. It would be wise to also explain how you plan to honour your non-negotiables with them while also honouring your other commitments. Understanding the non-negotiables for your family members and supporting each other to honour them is also a wonderful way to create a thriving home.

In my role as Global Director for Employee Experience at a leading healthcare company, we set an expectation for all people leaders across the organisation to discuss non-negotiables as part of their standard one-on-ones with their direct reports. This small change had significant positive impacts and moved us closer to the creation of a genuinely caring and inclusive culture. I remember feeling so pleased to see three members of my team heading out for a run at about 10am one work day – knowing that they would all do better work together because of it.

When I was working in a particularly challenging environment earlier in my corporate career, my 6:30am Bikram Yoga class was my primary sanity strategy. I vividly recall telling one of my team members who had suggested an 8am meeting that it would be a really, really bad idea for everyone if I were to skip my yoga for a meeting that could easily happen later in the day.

I have been a dedicated morning exerciser for over twenty years now. When moving my body my monkey mind quietens, so I have the capacity to be more creative, bold and playful in my thinking. I know for sure my best thinking happens when I move my body. When that alarm clock goes off, my morning mantra is 'get up and get moving – because half-arsed is better than no-arsed'. I have never, ever regretted moving my body in some way to start a busy work day.

Another significant benefit of building physical strength is the positive impact it can have on your mind. As they say, strong body, strong mind. I do not consider myself to be athletic, but I have really pushed my body to the very edges of its capability. In doing so, I have uncovered sources of inner strength I did not know I possessed. The physical experiences that have most significantly contributed to my emotional growth include skydiving, bungee-jumping, running a full marathon and competing in sprint triathlons. All of these experiences have contributed in significant and lasting ways to make me the person I am today.

Without vitality we cannot be caring, courageous, creative or playful. Without vitality we are too busy struggling to stay afloat to be any of these things.

WORK FRIENDSHIPS

Friendships with colleagues is an important way we feel connected and engaged at work. Research has found that those of us who have a best friend at work are far more likely to be engaged and more productive. Recent research from Gallup in the US found that a mere two out of ten employees had a best friend at work and by moving that ratio to six in ten, organisations could expect to realise 36% fewer safety incidents, 7% more engaged customers and 12% higher profits.[2]

Friendships at work are a vital source of nourishment for us – the select people with whom we can share the (often embarrassing) realities of our struggles with work and with life without fear of judgement or betrayal of trust. I love Maria Popova's description of a friend:

> *A person before whom we can strip our ideal self in order to reveal the real self, vulnerable and imperfect, and yet trust that it wouldn't diminish the friend's admiration and sincere affection for the whole self, comprising both the ideal and the real.*[3]

Having just a few people in our lives who can see both the ideal and the real in us can greatly enhance our working lives. Over my career I have been fortunate enough to have had relationships with kindred spirits at work who have proven worthy of being part of this most trusted inner circle of support. Allowing myself to be seen and therefore be held by these friendships was the equivalent of wearing a lifejacket after falling overboard in a strong swell. In addition to having good friendships, having a mentor can also be greatly beneficial. Bob Proctor describes a mentor as 'someone who sees more talent and ability within you, than you see in yourself, and helps bring it out of you.'[4] I have a circle of people in my life that I think of as 'frientors' – good friends who are also good mentors. They are people who I feel a genuine connection to and whose perspectives I deeply respect. These are the people who help me to see my goodness and my potential when I have lost sight of it.

As part of her teaching, Tara Brach invites us to remind ourselves of our interconnectivity as humans by silently repeating, 'We are friends. We are friends,'[5] whenever we interact with people we don't really know or even those with whom we may have a difficult relationship. This simple reflection is described as a form of 'stealth metta' – where metta means lovingkindness. It's a simple way of reconnecting with others that opens our hearts to the plight of others.

It is also helpful to understand that nourishing moments of real connections are not limited to the interactions we have with people we already know. Research shows that short and temporary interactions we have with strangers and acquaintances – micro-connections – can nourish us in significant ways. These small moments of connection with people we don't know can be just as influential on our mood as the deeper interactions we have with our closest friends and family members.

BEING ABLE TO SAY SORRY

Given the importance of our relationships and the reality that much of what we are practising in the pursuit of self-fidelity may be new to us, being able to say sorry is also essential. A genuine and heartfelt apology can repair damage that has been done to our connections with colleagues, friends and family members.

There have been many moments over my career when I have come to see that my ways of thinking or behaving had been hurtful to others, and have extended heartfelt apologies to colleagues. Many times, people have told me how rare it was to experience a senior leader recognising that their actions had inflicted hurt and taking responsibility for their actions.

A good apology is all about the feelings that arise in ourselves and the hurt party – not about the words that are spoken. Harriet Lerner has created a fantastic resource on how to say sorry in her book, *Why Won't You Apologize? Healing Big Betrayals and Everyday Hurts.* Here is how Harriet describes the importance of a good apology:

> *It's not the words 'I'm sorry' that soothes the other person and allow them to feel safe in the relationship again. More than anything, the hurt party wants us to listen carefully to their feelings, to validate their reality, to feel genuine regret and remorse, to carry some of the pain we've caused, and to make reparations as needed. They want us to really 'get it' and to make sure there will be no repeat performance.*[6]

Regardless of how we grow our vitality – getting clear on what we need to thrive and committing to hardwiring those things into every working week is an essential element of a self-fidelity practice.

Letting in: **Vitality**

Understanding to uplift

INSIGHTS

Vitality is our life force – the sum total of our physical, emotional, mental and spiritual energy.

Without vitality we can't embody our essential nature because we are in survival mode.

Without vitality we cannot be courageous, caring, creative or playful.

BURNING QUESTIONS

How might prioritising your vitality uplift your working life?

How might it uplift others in your life?

Is there something you need to give yourself permission for, in order to prioritise your vitality?

What new possibilities might emerge if your vitality was non-negotiable?

PLAY

What practices will you play with to protect and nourish your vitality?

Linking

Most of us need more linking and
less ranking in our lives

Elaine N. Aron[1]

When we boil down all the inter-personal dynamics we experience in work and in life, there are two fundamental ways we can relate with another human being – we can either be linking or ranking.

Linking is our innate tendency to be drawn to others, to want to help, connect and care. When we are linking, we are connecting human-to-human, heart-to-heart. Linking sits at the heart of our capacity to help and be of service to others, to gratefully and graciously accept help and support from others. When we are linking, we are able to experience what the Buddhist philosophy refers to as 'altruistic joy' – genuine happiness for others' experiences of happiness and success. If we are stuck in ranking, the success of others can instead lead to feelings of envy, resentment or self-loathing to emerge within us. Love is the strongest form of linking that emerges through a shared experience of positive emotional resonance.

One of the things I am most proud of over my leadership career to date is my ability to build engaged, high-performing teams. The employee engagement scores for the teams I have led have far exceeded the organisational average. I believe that my track record can be primarily attributed to one thing – my awareness of my conditioned ranking tendencies and my practice of staying true to my natural linking tendency. By setting a strong intention to link with my team members, managers and colleagues, I was able to cultivate trust, respect and connection. Intentional linking supports all of us to bring the best of ourselves to the table to do our best work – together. Our real power and potential is activated through our relationships. The strength of our relationships is our most critical success factor and our ability to form them is our most valuable leadership attribute.

WHY WE RANK

Often, when we are ranking, our conditioning has overridden our natural tendency to link. When we rank, we sever our connection with another person by mentally placing ourselves above or below them, based on some logic or criteria that we deem to be relevant or important in that moment. We compare and rank ourselves versus others based on perceived status, hierarchical power, appearances, education level, social class, religious beliefs – just to name a few. We are social animals and ranking has played an important role in our development as a species. So ranking is not inherently bad or wrong. Ranking can, however, be problematic when it happens often and below our level of conscious awareness. When we are in a trance and in the deep habitual grooves of ranking, we perpetuate disconnection, unnatural separateness and suffering. Linking fosters connection, ranking destroys connection through competition and comparison. In the workplace, chronic ranking can lead to people exerting power over others, hoarding of information and a highly contagious dog-eat-dog mindset that leads to a pandemic of fear and mistrust.

In the world of psychology, ranking is often referred to as social comparison. While there are occasionally legitimate reasons to rank ourselves, we tend to do it constantly. Habitual ranking is generally accepted to be bad for us. Research confirms that linking reduces workplace stress and increases wellbeing and even longevity.[2]

Social media amplifies the prevalence and potency of ranking. As Susan David explains:

> *Social media presents itself as a tool for human connection, but for many of us, it's an engine of self-doubt. The research is clear: Too much social media is bad for your mental health. Frequent users experience myriad problems including increased feelings of sadness, isolation, and envy, and a decrease in overall well-being. On top of it all, these platforms are addictive, meaning that the issues they cause quickly become self-perpetuating. [Social Media Platforms] encourage social comparison on a scale that humanity has never experienced, and psychologists have long agreed that social comparison is toxic.*[3]

Of course, ranking was problematic long before the advent of wide-scale social media addiction. During WWI, forced ranking was used systematically by the military to identify the top candidates for promotion in the military. Forced performance ranking systems and mindsets persist today in many organisations as part of this dehumanising legacy. Our propensity towards ranking at work is further amplified by the competitive, hierarchical and individualistic forces at play in many workplaces. Ranking is encouraged in schools and in sport.

Historically, anyone who held a management job was automatically ranked by organisational systems as being better, smarter and more knowledgeable than people who occupied the rungs below them in the organisational hierarchy. Some organisations still use the term 'superiors' to describe people who hold more hierarchical power. I have been in many organisations where crucial decisions were poorly made, ill-informed by the 'HiPPO-effect' (the Highest-Paid-Person's Opinion). I have also experienced ugly ego ping-pong matches involving two people who are stuck in ranking, both desperately trying to prove and assert themselves. There have been times at work when I have been witness to a full-blown 'pissing contest' between two senior males. At the other end of the spectrum, I have also seen many examples of people being co-conspirators in the diminishment of their own potential by ranking themselves (and their ideas and perspectives) so far below those of others, that they don't dare to speak up or speak their truth.

More and more organisations are awakening to a new paradigm of leadership that is grounded in serving and supporting the folks closest to customers. The leaders who successfully inspire and enable organisational growth understand that their job is to dissolve friction and clear roadblocks for the people who serve customers. Progressive organisations are letting go of the notion that addition of the word 'chief' to someone's job title means they are entitled to exert power over others and provide all the answers. More and more we are coming to see that – in the words of Simon Sinek – 'a leader is not someone who is in charge, a leader is someone who takes care of those in their charge'.[4]

LINKING AND SELF-WORTH

Healthy linking with another person becomes possible when neither individual sacrifices, silences or betrays themselves and there are no attempts to change, convince, out-rank or fix the other person. When we are with another person and holding a linking intention, we honour our shared worthiness and our connectedness. Those of us who struggle with low self-worth are prone to perceiving ourselves as lesser than others, mentally placing other people at a higher rank relative to us. Sometimes these feelings of low self-worth can also cause us to rank ourselves above others in an attempt to create a sense of value in the world. This attachment of our self-worth to external criteria in this way is a hollow and destructive substitute for authentic feelings of worthiness.

LINKING AND EVOLUTION

In the book *The Undervalued Self* Elaine N Aron says:

> *Linking is far more than a technique to feel better about yourself. Linking, coming together is central to life itself. One-celled organisms linked to become simple animals. Simple animals linked to form complex ones: and many of these animals formed groups to help each other. In all cases they were attracted to, needed to understand, and helped one another – my definition of love. Now some of us aim to link with every other being in peace and goodwill. Surely linking will evolve us into stronger and stronger forms.*[5]

It is ludicrous to think we rank our way to the embodiment of our essence. Awakening to the power of linking is about noticing when we have slipped into ranking mode and being committed to the practice of intentionally replacing ranking with linking whenever we can. Being committed to an ongoing practice of intentional linking is a vitally important element of being true to ourselves at work.

Letting in: **Linking**

Understanding to uplift

INSIGHTS

Linking is our innate tendency to be drawn to others,
to want to help, connect and care.

When we are linking,
we are connecting human-to-human, heart-to-heart.

Linking sits at the heart of our capacity to help,
to be of service and to accept support from others.

BURNING QUESTIONS

How might more intentional linking uplift your working life?

How might it uplift others in your life?

Is there something you need to give yourself permission for,
in order to be in linking-mode more often?

**What new possibilities might emerge
if you were to engage in more linking and less ranking?**

PLAY

What practices will you play with
to replace ranking with linking, where possible?

Values

Open your arms to change,
but don't let go of your values.

Dalai Lama[1]

Often we experience a subtle pressure within the workplace to forego our own personal values in favour of the values espoused by our organisation – or in favour of the unspoken value-system that worships profit and performance above all else. Over the years, through a great many trials and tribulations, I have learnt the importance of remaining connected with my own core values at work.

CORE VALUES

According to two decades of research conducted by Patricia Faison Hewlin, around one in three of us feel pressure to suppress our personal values at work. The irony for many of us is that when we betray our own values in order to try to fit in at work, we erode our engagement in our work. As Patricia explains:

> *When we put up this facade, it creates a sense of dissonance, and we experience higher symptoms of depression. We end up less engaged and less committed to our organisation, with more intentions to leave. That's the irony of it all: Because we're pretending to fit in, we eventually decide we don't want to.*[2]

So how can we create greater clarity around our core values? The key identifying features of our core values are:

- **They meet our innate needs** – Our core values guide us to meet our innate needs as humans – to feel connected to others, to trust in our worthiness and belonging, to see our own goodness and value, to feel like we are making a difference and to cultivate a sense of mastery and autonomy.
- **They guide us towards greater fulfillment** – when we are being guided by core values, we experience a deeper, more enduring sense of inner peace and fulfillment.

I have found John DeMartini's book *The Values Factor* to be helpful in gaining greater clarity on my core values.[3] John offers a series of questions to help to reveal your highest values. The questions include:

- What objects fill your space?
- How do you spend your time?
- How do you spend your money?
- Where are you most organised and reliable?
- What dominates your thoughts?
- What inspires you?

When you answer these questions, common themes quickly emerge. In the context of our self-fidelity practice it is helpful to identify one or two core values. This is because research has shown that those of us most willing to inhabit our vulnerability and practise courage connect our behaviours with just one or two core values.[4] My two core values are growth and wellbeing.

JUNK VALUES

I first discovered the term 'junk values' when I discovered Johann Hari's book *Lost Connections.* While the term was new to me, the concept was all too familiar. Johann describes junk values as a form of 'internalised oppression' that tricks us into believing that we can find happiness 'in all the wrong places'.[5] Unlike our core values, junk values are values that have been imposed on us. They are often materialistic or associated with perceived status. Once we allow junk values to attach themselves to us, they pollute our minds in much the same way junk food pollutes our bodies.

Perhaps the most important thing to understand about junk values is that they are corrosive to our core values – because what we focus on grows. Psychologist Tim Kasser suggests that we think about our combined values as a finite pie. Each value – junk or core – takes up a slice of that pie.[6] This means that the more we focus our energy on the behaviours, thoughts and activities associated with junk values, the more they expand. This reduces the energy and time we have for living our nourishing, genuine core values. Tim explains it this way – 'it is not that materialistic people don't care about their kids [but] as the materialistic values get bigger, other values are necessarily going to be crowded out.'[7] By increasing our awareness and focus on our core values, we displace junk values.

Over my two-decade career, I have had experiences of workplace bullying at the hands of leaders who were so blinded by junk values of power, status, greed and control that they had completely abandoned their core values. The twist of the knife in my personal experiences of workplace bullying was that the perpetrators were always female.

Junk values lead us to worship at the altar of the false gods of consumerism and comparison and their insatiable taunts of 'you don't have enough stuff' or 'you are not doing enough.' They trick us into believing that if we amass enough nice clothes, get enough 'likes', have enough pairs of fabulous shoes, fit into our jeans, pack healthy lunchboxes, have quiet, smart obedient kids and a good marriage, that we will finally be happy. That we will finally be enough. When we are under the spell of junk values we may experience urgent cravings that cause behaviours of compulsive doing, striving and proving. We may feel that these behaviours are out of our control.

There are a few identifying features of junk values:

- **They are outside of ourselves** – Junk values cause us to attach our sense of self-worth and happiness to something that is outside of ourselves and often materialistic in nature such as our achievements, our possessions, how we appear to others, our status, our salary, our job title or how smart and well-behaved our kids are.
- **They are insatiable** – Any satisfaction we experience from the fulfillment of junk values is generally short-lived and we experience an ongoing sense of deficiency and danger that comes from being susceptible to the commercial and political manipulations that reinforce these messages of fear and scarcity.
- **They may make us feel like we are not fully in control** – When we strive to live according to junk values, we may feel we are being propelled by forces outside of our awareness and control, we may even be aware that we hate the way we are behaving but feel powerless to change course.
- **They rely on external references** – In order to judge whether we are doing a good job at our junk values we need to compare ourselves to others or imagine how we are perceived by others.

The importance of learning how to recognise when we are being led astray by junk values and using our aspirations and core values to guide us back on course cannot be overstated.

Letting in: **Values**

Understanding to uplift

INSIGHTS

Our core values meet our innate needs
and guide us towards greater fulfillment.

Junk values are a form of 'internalised oppression' that trick
us into believing that we can find happiness
'in all the wrong places'.

Junk values are corrosive to our core values.

BURNING QUESTIONS

How might getting clearer on your core values uplift your working life?

How might it uplift others in your life?

Is there something you need to give yourself permission for,
in order to let go of junk values and re-orient to your core values?

**What new possibilities might emerge
if you were to live in full integrity with your core values?**

PLAY

What practices will you play with
to begin to re-orient to your core values?

Aspirations

Return to your longing. It will teach you everything.

Sue Monk Kidd[1]

I was recently in Tokyo, Japan facilitating a workshop for Thrive Global and was fortunate to have a free afternoon before my evening flight back to Melbourne. I decided to brave the Tokyo Subway system and visit the Meiji Shrine. It was well worth the effort. In the inner precinct of the shrine there is a place where visitors write wishes on wooden plates called 'ema' and hang them on a large wooden structure in the hope that they come true. Here is a photo of the hanging wishes on the day of my visit.

Reading those wishes from visitors from all over the world was the highlight of my trip to Japan. It became clear to me that afternoon that the highest aspirations we hold for our lives transcend cultural differences.

Here are a few of the wishes that I found to be particularly touching.

> *I am grateful for everything that has happened in my life and for everything that is yet to come. I am grateful for everyone in my life. I pray for happiness and success and good health to my family and loved ones. I pray that I get into medical school to become a doctor so I can help heal the world. And lastly, I promise to always love myself.*
>
> *To live my whole life with my wife by my side.*
>
> *I pray for my father's health. His spirit, strength and wellness.*
>
> *I hope to have a future full of love, health, success, happiness, passion and laughter. I pray to find passion in all that I do, and one day to fulfill the role of wife and mother.*
>
> *I pray for good health, great and fun experiences and a long and happy life for me and my family. Also, I really want to make music but don't want to do it on my own – I want to start a band!*
>
> *I wish for love and peace.*
>
> *I am thankful for the ability to take care of others and for the many gifts of my life. I hope to find love.*

BEING GUIDED BY OUR ASPIRATIONS

The word *aspiration* comes from the root 'to breathe.' Our aspirations are our most fundamental desires. An aspiration has the power to both ground and inspire us. An aspiration is not the same as a purpose or passion – it is not only focused on what we want to achieve or do. Instead, an aspiration reflects a highest intention we hold for our lives. Aspirations are not constrained or defined by goals or plans and are not subject to disappointment. When we are guided by our aspirations, we can let go of failures and hold onto lessons and learnings – all the time gaining more clarity. Aspirations can

Our longings are the soft but persistent nudging of our most heartfelt aspirations for our lives.

support us to live and work with passion, while also being at peace with whatever happens.

The practice of self-fidelity invites us to get clear on our aspirations. When we are being guided by our aspirations, we can be courageous. Our aspirations can guide us towards the creation of a working life that is aligned with the truth of who we are. And, in times of disorientation, our aspirations serve as our North Star.

LONGINGS

Our longings are the soft but persistent nudging of our most heartfelt aspirations for our lives. Much of the time we tend to block our longings. They can feel like an inconvenience. We may feel that we are too tired and overwhelmed to pay them any heed. Perhaps we cram every waking hour in order to vigilantly maintain a hum of busyness just loud enough to drown out our longings.

In *The Book of Longings*, Sue Monk Kidd writes the following beautiful lines:

> *All my life, longings lived inside me, rising up like nocturnes to wail and sing through the night. Bless the largeness inside me, no matter how I fear it… When I am dust, sing these words over my bones: she was a voice.*[2]

Our longings are a reliable inner-guidance-system. They guide us towards our aspirations and alert us when we are off track. They tell us whether the life we are living is the life we really yearn for. Longings may take the form of re-occurring symbols or dreams. Perhaps our longings communicate with us in the form of goosebumps. Whatever form they take, if we ignore our longings, our aspirations will continue to elude us.

The practice of letting in invites us to return to our longings and to use them as guideposts towards a working life that can be well lived.

Letting in: **Aspirations**

Understanding to uplift

INSIGHTS

Our aspirations are the most fundamental longings we hold for our lives.

An aspiration has the power to both ground and inspire us.

Aspirations are not constrained or defined by goals or plans and are not subject to disappointment.

Aspirations support us to serve and to live and work with passion, while also being at peace with whatever happens.

BURNING QUESTIONS

How might getting clearer on your aspirations uplift your working life?

How might it uplift others in your life?

Is there something you need to give yourself permission for, in order to orient towards your aspirations?

What new possibilities might emerge if you were to find the courage to return to your longings?

PLAY

What practices will you play with to orient towards your highest aspirations?

Love

I have noticed recently how little we are
speaking of what is joyous to us and instead we are
recycling the hurt of the world – we have
forgotten to feed ourselves with love.

Sarah Blondin[1]

Most people are sceptical about the relevance of love at work. Perhaps in some workplaces the topic of love is taboo. Love may suffer from an unfortunate association with old stories of inappropriate, scandalous behaviour.

I believe that when we are at our best, our work becomes an expression of our love. Work is our love made visible, valuable and relevant. The world desperately needs more leaders to 'see the light' and who are brave enough to work in a way that is grounded in love. My hope is that in time we can talk openly in workplaces around the world about our fundamental need for love in the same way as we talk about our fundamental need for fresh air and water – without a single raised eyebrow or eye roll.

There are many people who believe that our essential nature as human beings is love and that the meaning of life is to remember and return to this essential nature. If the idea of our essential nature being love is a step too far for us, perhaps the idea that love is a powerful source of inspiration and growth is more palatable. Maya Angelou said, 'Love recognizes no barriers. It jumps hurdles, leaps fences, penetrates walls to arrive at its destination full of hope.'[2]

Science tells us that positive emotions such as love trigger growth and support us to become better versions of ourselves. Dr Barbara Fredrickson's ground-breaking work explores the potential-activating power of love. In her book *Love 2.0: How Our Supreme Emotion Affects Everything We Feel, Think, Do, and Become* Dr Fredrickson shares her findings that love, and its absence, fundamentally alters the biochemicals in our bodies which in turn can alter the way our DNA is expressed in our cells. Dr Fredrickson's upgraded 2.0 definition of love describes love as micro-moments of 'positivity resonance' where there is the presence of three factors – shared positive emotions, biobehavioural synchronicity and a motive of mutual care. This means that love is actually a fleeting but completely renewable emotion that can 'blossom anytime two or more people – even strangers – connect over a shared positive emotion'.[3]

Dr Fredrickson's research provides a radically new concept of what love is and why it matters, and created a hugely compelling case for more fully embracing this 'supreme emotion' in our lives and workplaces. She explains:

> *Love nourishes your body the way the right balance of sunlight, nutrient-rich soil, and water nourishes plants and allows them to flourish. The more you experience it, the more you open up and grow, becoming wiser, and more attuned, more resilient and effective, happier and healthier.*[4]

A young child once described their experience of being with someone who is being loving towards them: 'When someone loves you, the way they say your name is different. You just know your name is safe in their mouth.'[5] The late Dr Wayne Dyer offers us practical guidance on what it means to embody lovingness:

> *Notice when you're inclined to judge yourself or others as though you or they are unworthy of love. This means suspending your need to be right in favour of being kind toward yourself and others, and deliberately extending kindness everywhere. This*

> *means giving love to yourself and others rather than demanding love. This means your loving gesture of kindness is heartfelt because you feel love flowing from within – not because you want something in return. A tall order? Not really, unless you believe that it's going to be difficult.*[6]

GRIEF IS LOVE THAT DOES NOT HAVE THE NORMAL PLACE TO GO

I once heard Sharon Salzberg describe grief as 'love that does not have the normal place to go'.[7] When I have worked in environments where the unwritten rules required me to suppress my essential caring, loving nature in my interactions with my colleagues, I experienced a sort of constant, low-level grief.

Being in the presence of another human being and feeling like we have to protect ourselves or prove ourselves is extremely draining. Feeling safe and free to be both warm-hearted and open-hearted and experiencing a heartfelt connection with another living being is deeply nourishing. Imagine the new possibilities that would emerge in workplaces across the world if our hearts were open and connected instead of closed and protected.

In the book *Belonging – Remembering Ourselves Home* Tako-pa Turner speaks beautifully to our search for belonging and a home of love:

> *This is the great irony of belonging: that in all your searching for a home of love, it was yours to give away all along. And the real reward of your quest is to fling your doors open and let your life become a shelter of belonging for others.*[8]

Of course, opening our tender, long-shielded hearts to the slings and arrows of the world is not easy. Letting in love takes courage but the rewards are immense when we can trust that we are strong and that we can do hard things.

Love connects us and ignites powerful forces within us, making us more flexible, creative, wise, attuned to others, and over time, more resourceful. The act of letting in love is arguably the most powerful potential-activating practice we can engage in. By learning to let more love into our working lives, we deeply nourish ourselves. Love has the power to transform our working lives. As Rick Hanson says 'love is the multivitamin, the universal medicine'.[9]

Letting in: Love

Understanding to uplift

INSIGHTS

Love is a micro-moment of 'positivity resonance' –
the presence of shared positive emotions,
synchronicity and a motive of mutual care.

Love connects us and ignites powerful forces within us,
making us more flexible, creative, wise, attuned to others,
and over time, more resourceful.

Love has the power to transform our working lives.

The world desperately needs more leaders
who are brave enough to work in a way that is grounded in love.

BURNING QUESTIONS

How might being more open
the presence of love uplift your working life?

How might it uplift others in your life?

Is there something you need to give yourself permission for,
in order to be open to experiencing
micro-moments of 'positivity resonance' at work?

What new possibilities might emerge
if you were to find the courage to return to your longings?

PLAY

What practices would you play with
if you were to be more open to the presence of love at work?

Intuition

Intuition, not intellect, is the 'open sesame' of yourself.

Albert Einstein[1]

In the 1946 book *Autobiography of a Yogi*, Paramahansa Yogananda said, 'Intuition is soul guidance, appearing naturally in man during those instants when his mind is calm.'[2] Steve Jobs asked for Paramahansa's autobiography to be given out at his memorial. Steve was a leader who understood the power of intuition, having spent time in India observing that 'the people in the Indian countryside don't use their intelligence like we do, they use their intuition instead, and their intuition is far more developed than the rest of the world.'[3] Steve spoke very openly about the role his intuition played in creative processes. Sadly, for many leaders today, conversations about intuition are still seen as woo-woo taboo.

Intuitive messages emanate from a deeper wisdom – one that transcends the voices in our heads. Nearly everyone has had the experience of an inexplicable correct intuitive hunch. More and more, science is beginning to confirm the importance of our intuition. Psychologists Martin Seligman and Michael Kahana explain, 'It has long been realised that many important decisions are not arrived at by linear reasoning, but by intuition.'[4] They describe intuition-based decisions as those 'made rapidly, generally with a high level of confidence and in a way that is not conscious and not easily articulated afterwards.'[5]

A great example of an intuitive-based decision can be found in Malcolm Gladwell's book *Blink* where he shares the story of art historian Thomas Hoving experiencing instant 'intuitive repulsion'[6] upon seeing an ancient Greek statue acquired by the J Paul Getty Museum in Los Angeles. After extensive testing, the statue was found to be a very, very good fake.

It is so easy lose touch with our intuition. Perhaps we have spent long periods ignoring or suppressing it. I know that has been the case for me. I have been especially prone to ignoring intuitive messages that have told me that something 'is not quite right' in the context of entering into a new relationship. I have found that I am much better at heeding my intuition when it comes to decisions regarding my children.

Perhaps we have convinced ourselves that we are far too busy to stop and experience the moments of inner quiet that support the emergence of intuitive wisdom. In the book *Thrive* Arianna Huffington says:

> *It's never been harder to tap into our inner wisdom, because in order to do so, we have to disconnect from all our omnipresent devices – our gadgets, or screens, our social media – and reconnect with ourselves... If our intuitive voice had the same strength-of-signal bars as our phones, we'd often see that we are out of range of our wisdom.*[7]

So, how do we stay in range of our intuitive wisdom? In addition to ensuring we are getting enough sleep (which is the foundation of not only our wellbeing but also our capacity to hear our inner wisdom) we can also get into the habit of paying closer attention to moments of intuition.

INTUITION RETROS

I am still learning how to discern between the voices in my head and my intuition. When I am successful in hearing and acting on my intuition, I like to do a quick 'retro'. A retro is shorthand for an Agile ritual called a retrospective where you take a few minutes to reflect on what has recently happened in order to glean learnings.

From my intuition retros I have been able to understand that my intuitive messages meet a few criteria. Firstly, they are effortless and spontaneous – they drop into my awareness with no warning, out of nowhere and with no effort. Secondly, they don't always make logical sense – I can't explain them with my rational mind.

I had a recent experience of intuitive wisdom guiding me in a small way one morning when I was leaving the house for a run with my friend Carolyn. Next to the front door, there was a large canvas painting that I had done years ago that I was planning to drop to our local charity shop. Out of nowhere the message came – offer the painting to Carolyn. The voices in my head quickly attempted to overrule the message by telling me that my friend would be offended by a suggestion that she take my junk. However, at the end of the run I said, 'Hey, I don't suppose you would have any use for a large canvas painting?' Carolyn's face lit up and she said, 'Oh yes, my partner creates large abstract art' (something I did not know) 'and just yesterday he said he really needed a big canvas.' While this is a small example that many people would call a simple coincidence, as we put the canvas in Carolyn's car, I knew that I had just experienced a moment of listening to my intuition.

If you feel out of touch with your intuition, a good place to start is to pay attention to when your intuition may be guiding you in small ways.

For me, moments of intuition feel like brief openings of the portal into an aspect of my intelligence that science and I don't yet fully understand. My inner wisdom exists deep inside me, beneath all the 'shoulds', underneath all the conditioning. It's an ever-present knowing that waits patiently for my attention.

Jean Houston said 'our bodies and minds are coded with an extraordinary array of possibilities and potentials. The bad news is that we learn to use very few of them. It is as if we were a musical instrument with a million keys, but we tootle and hoot on only some twenty of them'.[8] Learning to connect with our intuition plays an important role in learning how to be true to ourselves. Nurturing our intuition and growing our awareness of our deeper wisdom offers a pathway to enrich and deepen our self-fidelity practice. Intuition is available to all of us, when we choose to believe in it.

Letting in: Intuition

Understanding to uplift

INSIGHTS

Intuitive messages emanate from a deeper wisdom
– one that transcends the voices in our heads.

Intuition-based decisions are those
'made rapidly, generally with a high level of confidence and
in a way that is not conscious and not easily articulated afterwards.'

Learning to connect with our intuition plays an important role
in learning how to be true to ourselves.

Intuition is available to all of us, when we choose to believe in it.

BURNING QUESTIONS

How might being more aware
of your intuition uplift your working life?

How might it uplift others in your life?

Is there something you need to give yourself permission for,
in order to be open to your intuitive wisdom?

**What new possibilities might emerge
if you were to harness the power of your intuitive wisdom?**

PLAY

What practices will you play with
to connect with your intuition?

Gently,
allow your heart to hand you
every last piece
of who you truly are.

This is the food you've been hungry for.
This is the water that will quench.

Brooke McNamara[9]

Remembering

Each time a person stands up for an idea, or acts to
improve the lot of others, or strikes out against injustice,
he sends forth a tiny ripple of hope, and crossing each other
from a million different centres of energy and daring,
those ripples build a current that can sweep down
the mightiest walls of oppression and resistance.

Robert F Kennedy[1]

While this book does not pretend to provide a total solution to the challenges we each face in our working lives, the practices we have covered can support us to uplift our working lives in powerful ways.

We have discovered how to:

- understand and trust in our essential nature
- grow the things that make us unique
- remember that our worthiness is unquestionable
- be intentional about what we give our attention to
- meet the moments that matter with presence
- break free of the beliefs that weigh us down
- strengthen and embolden ourselves to meet the challenges ahead.

INTEGRATION

There are many different ways we can integrate and embed all we have discovered through our practice. Figuring out the best way to do this requires ongoing playful experimentation and imagination. There is no one size fits all. I have played with many different ways to creatively imagine and visualise all of the practices that cultivate self-fidelity. I encourage all of us to do the same.

To deepen our self-fidelity practice, we may find it helpful to focus on one element at a time. Perhaps we just want to grow a stronger awareness of our capacity to care or be creative at work. Perhaps we might focus on becoming more aware of our heaviest limiting beliefs and how they are holding us back.

Whatever area of focus feels right for us, start by setting a clear intention. Be clear about the shifts we hope to experience through the deliberate, sustained, playful focus on a specific element and be sure to think about what this shift will feel like and how it will show up in our working life.

To help us remember the four core practices of self-fidelity, if we are visual, we might like to bring this to mind:

W!LLL

For me, bringing to mind the above string of characters serves as a reliable prompt to **W**ake up! **L**et be, **L**et go and **L**et in. I like how together these symbols resemble the word 'will'. So, bringing this image to mind also reminds me of the opportunity I have in every moment to wake up and exercise my free will.

If we want to play with a powerful breathing practice that integrates all the elements we have covered, we can record ourselves reading the following passage – or a personalised version of it. This recording will be a tool that we can use to experience an uplift any time we need it. All we need to do is find a quiet place and press play.

Integrated breathing practice

Waking up – I remember! I am NOT the voices in my head.

Coming back to presence, back into my breathing body,
I close my eyes and become aware that I am right here, right now.

I can feel my feet on the floor, the clothes on my skin
and the coolness of the air as it enters my body.

Focusing my attention on my breath
I inhale slowly through my nose,
and fill my throat, chest and belly.
I feel my life force expand and uplift me.

Now, moving my attention to my exhaling breath,
with each slow, long exhale, I allow my body to soften and let go.
Letting any heaviness, holding or tension
just gently fall away.

In the stillness at the top of each inhale
and at the bottom of each exhale,
I can welcome whatever is here, and make space for it.

As the chatter in my head recedes,
I can relax and become aware of the weather of my mind.

Observing my thoughts with curiosity and openness,
I watch my thoughts as they arise, stay for a moment
and then dissolve away.

And notice the alternative truths that naturally emerge.

Lingering in this state of open awareness
for a few more breaths, I remember
I am unique and I am worthy
I am open-hearted and I am caring
I am creative and I am playful
I am free and I belong
I am potential and I am peace.

And whenever I feel ready, I gently open my eyes.

My inner wisdom exists deep inside me, beneath all the 'shoulds', underneath all the conditioning. It's an ever-present knowing that waits patiently for my attention.

ACTIVATING OUR PARTICULAR TYPE OF GENIUS

> We are among the most important people to have ever lived.
> We will determine whether humankind will grow or die,
> evolve or perish.
> We will need a gathering of the potentials of the
> whole human race and the particular genius in every
> culture if we are going to survive our time.
>
> Jean Houston[2]

Through the practice of self-fidelity we discover that we are not helpless victims of our circumstances. And that the small cages we have locked ourselves in for so long were always merely figments of our conditioning. We discover that true belonging awaits us when we stop betraying ourselves to fit in and believe in our own worthiness.

Being true to ourselves does not require us to quit our jobs and to start working for ourselves. For many of us, our best path of service exists within the context of an organisation. This is a noble and important path of service and one that generates prosperity for many. Our organisations are lucky to have us – and only the leaders who rejoice in their people feeling free will retain them. Only the organisations that are comprised of brilliant, wide-awake humans who choose to be there will thrive.

Great leaders understand their precious people are captains of their own ships and that those ships are merely temporary members of the fleet. Employees who are captains of their own ship trust in their own individual agency while understanding the power of being part of a collective. Ideally, whenever or however the moment arrives, when it is time to part ways, both the organisation and the employee should leave enhanced by the leg of the pilgrimage they charted together.

The liberation of our worthiness, open-heartedness, warm-heartedness, playfulness, and creativity will never come about by working harder. The hidden jewels buried deep within us cannot be coerced through even the most elaborate and lucrative system of incentives and rewards. There is no single lever we can pull within individuals or organisations to activate human potential and brilliance at work.

Only through courageous, humble, thoughtful conversations will we expand the frontiers of our understanding and discover entirely new ways of thinking about ourselves, each other and the work we do together. Through these conversations we will uncover yet another layer of paradox – that our desire to uplift comes coupled with a deep fear of what that might mean.

The pilgrimage of being true to ourselves at work is one that navigates the churning intersection of what we most resist and most desire. Self-fidelity is a commitment to figuring out what fulfillment, vitality, freedom and belonging *really* mean to us and how these desires best harmonise with the organisations we work within, the people we love and the world we occupy.

Many years ago during a meeting with my manager, I expressed my outrage that a high-performing member of my team had left a recent meeting with our executive team feeling utterly downtrodden and humiliated. I will never forget what my manager said to me. He said, 'Cassie, I don't know what sort of utopian organisation you dream about in that head of yours, but it does not exist. If you think that this place is bad, go and work for one of the banks. They will crush you like a fly.'

Perhaps he was right. Perhaps the utopian world of work I dream of – one that treats people with kindness and respect and lifts them up – does not exist yet. But that does not mean we should not try to create it. As Kristina Karlsson said, 'Every human achievement begins as someone's dream.'[3]

We must keep on moving onwards and upwards together, towards our guiding aspirations to transform our working lives and express the truth of who we are. As our working lives begin to harmonise with our essential nature, we uplift the human spirit, soothe our souls and regenerate life. Unimaginable possibilities will begin to emerge as our work begins to flow from a place of togetherness, presence and love. We may discover that everything we have been searching for has been patiently waiting inside of us all along.

By being true to ourselves at work we discover how best to serve our troubled world with love – and fling open the windows of our own particular type of genius.

Being true to ourselves might just be our salvation.

EASING INTO A BIGGER CONVERSATION

This is the end of the book, but I sincerely hope that it is not the end of our conversation. If the ideas I have shared in *Self-Fidelity* resonate with you, I invite you to help shape the conversation about how being true to ourselves at work has the potential to uplift life. Visit **self-fidelity.com** to learn more.

You will also find me on LinkedIn spreading the good word about self-fidelity. I would also love to connect with you on that platform. Find me here: **linkedin.com/in/cassandra-goodman**.

It doesn't interest me what you do for a living.
I want to know what you ache for,
and if you dare to dream of meeting your heart's longing.

...

It doesn't interest me where or
what or with whom you have studied.
I want to know what sustains you
from the inside out when all else falls away.

I want to know if you can be alone with yourself,
and if you truly like the company you keep in the
empty moments.

Oriah[4]

Postscript

Our genius is to understand, and stand beneath
the set of stars present at our birth, and from that place
to seek the hidden, single star, over the night horizon,
we did not know we were following.

David Whyte[5]

The day I spontaneously and fully committed to being true to myself at work started off not unlike any other day. It was a warm Saturday morning. The smell of jasmine was in the air and I was in my standard weekend active wear. It had been a particularly challenging week at work. The environment I was working in was heavy with fear and greed-fuelled politics and I could feel myself drifting out of alignment with my values and aspirations.

I was walking to my car from the supermarket, arms laden with groceries, when I saw it – a small ornate sign on the footpath that said in curly red letters – Tattoo Parlour, Walk-Ins Welcome.

Suddenly, something crystallised inside me.

Within seconds I was standing inside a portal to another world. A humming, buzzing world filled with dark, beautiful things. A world inhabited by people who make big, lasting commitments. People who boldly embody the message: This is who I am.

'Um, hello…how much does a tattoo cost…and how long does it take?' The rapid-fire answer was '$120. We'll have you out of here in 40 minutes.' Clearly, I was not the first slightly desperate-looking middle-aged mum to be pulled through their doors like a moth to a flame.

'Okay! Just give me a minute.'

I stepped back outside into the bright sunlight and dug up my phone from the bottom of my bag. The telephone conversation with my husband went something like this:

Me: Hi honey, I'm going to be a bit late getting home with the groceries.

Him: Okay, everything all right?

Me: Yeah, um…I am just going to get a tattoo.

Silence.

Him: What?

Me: Don't worry, it's just a small one, a little star on my wrist.

Him: Ah, okay…

Me: I just need a reminder, something visible, so I don't keep forgetting to follow my North Star, I really think it will help me.

Him: Okay then, if you are really sure… But you are going to have to deal with the kids when they tell us that they want a tattoo.

Honestly, I was not really sure if I was doing the right thing – even though I would never have admitted that to my husband at the time. Despite the distinct possibility that I had finally lost my marbles, I decided to have faith in my own knowing. I decided that getting a symbol of a star permanently etched into my left wrist was somehow my next best step.

And I am so glad I did.

I love my little North Star tattoo and the commitment, non-conformity and spontaneous activism it symbolises. I have since learnt that the Latin root of the word desire is *de sidere*, meaning *of the stars.* My tattoo is a permanent reminder to stay true to my highest aspirations.

My kids are still young enough to think that my tattoo is cool, and so far, they have not asked when they can get one. My hope is that they will never need one. My hope is that they grow up with an unbroken line of sight to their uniqueness, their worthiness and their right to do good work with good people. That they have an unwavering awareness of their brilliance and their vast potential.

If this were to happen, perhaps they might be part of a liberated generation that renders the mid-life crisis redundant. Perhaps, they might even be part of the generation that saves our world.

Now, that would be *really* cool.

Help Spread the Word

My dream is to inspire 5 million people
to uplift their working lives by 2025.

Because changing the way we work
has the potential to uplift all life.

I need your help to bring this dream to life.

If you enjoyed *Self-Fidelity*,
please help others to discover this book.

Here are some of the ways you can help:

Post a photo of yourself reading *Self-Fidelity* and #selffidelity
Tell a friend about the book and why it resonated with you
Buy *Self-Fidelity* as a gift for someone you know
Pass this copy onto someone else who may enjoy it

Visit self-fidelity.com/social to learn more about how you can help
spread the word about the power of being true to ourselves.

Thank you!

Gratitude

There are so many people who have supported me during the messy three-year process of creating this book – far too many to list. I am deeply grateful to each and every person who generously offered their encouragement, guidance and support. You have all helped me to hold the course and to trust I had something worth sharing here. This book has been deeply enriched by the many open-hearted conversations I have had the privilege of being part of.

Dr Stuart Brown, thank you for generous support and encouragement and for inspiring me to keep playing. Thank you, Dr Rick Hanson, for the wisdom of your teachings and your words of encouragement in 2018 – 'If you feel that you have a book in you, then write the book!' Thank you also for giving me the language to describe three of the core practices of self-fidelity – Letting go, Letting be and Letting in. Thank you Allan Sparkes for showing me that great leadership is about finding the courage to care. Kelly Irving, thank you for guiding me through the many trials and tribulations of book-writing. Michael Hanrahan, Karen Comer and the team at Publish Central, thank you for your amazing support and patience.

Thank you, Denise Orloff and the fabulous team at YogaLyfe for creating a beautiful space for me to connect with my breath, heart and body with joy and laughter. Lisa Ball, thank you for so generously sharing your sparkling intellect and wholehearted wisdom with the world. Michele Troughear, thank you for supporting me to deepen my meditation practice and for your kindness, patience and generosity. Thank you, Meaghan Smith, for helping me to create a style that reflects the real me. Thank you Fi Mims for helping me to create an authentic brand. Gemma Sykes, thank you for your 'fierce love'. Carolyn Howard, thank you for your friendship your honesty and for all those wonderful running conversations. Sam De Mel, thank you for your love and friendship, for sharing your incredible gifts with me and for walking beside me every step of the way.

Thank you to my mum and dad for your love and for all you have done to support me over the years. Thank you to my Aunty Jill for your love and for preserving and sharing the stories of our family. Thank you to my two gorgeous boys, Elliot and Zachary, for supporting my desire to contribute to the creation of workplaces where people 'can unfurl like beautiful flowers'. Thank you to my gorgeous husband Andrew, for grounding my yang with your yin and for all that you do to support and organise our rambunctious family, including doing a tremendous job at crisis home-schooling during global pandemics.

Finally, I want to say a very special thanks to the following people for their kindness, generosity, wisdom and encouragement: Jasmine Malki, Andi Pert, Rachel Audige, Debra Tagg, Ingrid D'Lima, Richard Brisebois, Richard Hodge, Bill Sheffield, Blair Newman, Alex Blakemore, Mei Ouw, Ainsley Jeffery, Fiona McUtchen, Andrew McUtchen, Elise Morris, Alex Christou, Cath Andrew, Gemma Saunders, Alana Bennett, Kalina Krawczyk, Melissa Buckingham, Emma Kovac, Sophie Hart, Claire Jones, Oscar Trimboli, Tina Patterson, Mia Elliott, Marianne Roux, Rebecca Hopkins, Louise Weine, Ash Buchanan, Renata Bernarde, Lisa Leong, Sophie Veale, Michelle Crawford, Michelle Mason, Fiona Cull and Anthea Spark. Thanks also to the crew at Jack the Geezer for fuelling me with hundreds of delicious almond lattes.

SUPPORTING MY SUPPORT CREW

I wanted to do my little bit to support my support crew – all of whom are very good people doing very good work in the world.

Michele Troughear micheletroughear.com

Michele Troughear is my meditation coach, and friend. Michele brings an abiding love, fascination and respect for the practice of meditation into every session she leads, with the goal of helping others train their own minds to greater happiness and clarity.

Lisa Ball lisajulieball.com

Lisa is my yoga teacher, and friend. Lisa has been joyfully dedicated to the path of yoga and meditation for over 15 years. Lisa teaches yoga and meditation, and also facilitates workshops, retreats and yoga teacher training programs.

Carolyn Howard pilates2gether.com

Carolyn is my Pilates and chi running coach, and friend. Carolyn teaches Pilates, Chi Running and Chi Walking as tools to experience joy and satisfaction, to breathe deeper and to stand stronger in life – physically and emotionally.

Fi Mims fimimsphotography.com.au

Fi is my brand coach, go-to photographer extraordinaire, and friend. Fi works with inspirational thought-leaders, entrepreneurs and business owners to amplify their personal brand and inspire others to work with them.

Endnotes

PROLOGUE

1. A A Milne, www.goodreads.com/quotes/601136-always-remember-yo-are-braver-than-you-believe-stronger-than
2. D Whyte, *Everything is waiting for you*, Many Rivers Press, 2003.

INTRODUCTION

1. J Mellencamp, 'Jack & Diane', *American fool*, produced by John Mellencamp & Don Gehman.
2. B Brown, *The gifts of imperfection*, Center City, United States: Hazelden Information & Educational Services, 2010.

What is self-fidelity?

1. William Shakespeare, *Hamlet* (Polonius, act 1, scene 3).
2. A Schweitzer, (prof), *The philosophy of civilization: Part 1, The decay and the restoration of civilization; Part 2, Civilization and ethics*, Whitefish MT, United States: Kessinger Publishing, 2010.
3. M W Martin, *Albert Schweitzer's reverence for life: Ethical idealism and self-realization*, Hampshire, England: Ashgate Publishing Limited, 2007.
4. J Campbell, *A Joseph Campbell companion*, New York, United States: HarperCollins Publishers Inc, 1992.
5. C Dweck, (Dr), *Mindset: Changing the way you think to fulfil your potential*, London, United Kingdom: Little, Brown Book Group, 2012.
6. A Buchanan, *Benefit mindset schools guide*, Melbourne: Cohere, 2020.
7. M A Singer, *The untethered soul: The journey beyond yourself*, Oakland, CA, United States: New Harbinger Publications, 2007.

Elements of the practice

1. D Whyte, *Crossing the unknown sea: Work as a pilgrimage of identity*, United States: Penguin Putnam Inc, Riverhead Books, 2002.

2. B Brown, *The gifts of imperfection*, Center City, United States: Hazelden Information & Educational Services, 2010.

The challenges we are navigating

1. S Elworthy, *Pioneering The Possible: Awakened Leadership for a World That Works*, Berkeley, United States, North Atlantic Books, United States, 2014.
2. J Hari, *Lost connections: Why you're depressed and how to find hope*, London, United Kingdom: Bloomsbury Publishing PLC, 2019.

Why I care so deeply

1. D Whyte, *Crossing the unknown sea: Work as a pilgrimage of identity*, United States: Penguin Putnam Inc, Riverhead Books, 2002.
2. T Morrison, 'Toni Morrison, The art of fiction', *The Paris Review*, No. 134, 1993.

How to use this book

1. C Sanford, *The regenerative business: Redesign work, cultivate human potential, achieve extraordinary outcomes*, London, United Kingdom: John Murray Press, 2017.
2. D Whyte, 'The conversational nature of reality', *On being with Krista Tippett*, 2016.
3. G Doyle, *Untamed: Stop pleasing, start living*, London, United Kingdom: Ebury Publishing, 2020.
4. D Whyte, 'The conversational nature of reality', *On being with Krista Tippett*, 2016.

Supporting ourselves

1. M Wheatley & D Frieze, 'Using emergence to take social innovation to scale', www.margaretwheatley.com/articles/emergence, 2006.

FOUNDATIONS

1. B Dylan, 'Forever young', New York, 1973.

Understanding our essential nature

1. H Thurman, *Living wisdom of Howard Thurman: A visionary for our time*, United States: Sounds True, 2010.
2. E Easwaran, *The Bhagavad Gita*, United States: Nilgiri Press, 2007.

3. C Sanford, www.carolsanford.com/essence-discovery/ www.carolsanfordinstitute.com/what-is-regeneration-principle-4-singularity/

Connecting to our essential nature

1. 2020 Embodiment Conference, Compassionate Inquiry with Dr. Gabor Maté, www.theembodimentconference.org

Redefining work and success

1. M Angelou, www.businessinsider.com.au/maya-angelou-quotes-2014
2. B D Rosso, K H Dekas & A Wrzesniewski, 'On the meaning of work: A theoretical integration and review', *ScienceDirect*, 2010.
3. A Smith, *An inquiry into the nature and causes of the wealth of nations*, London: Great Britain: W. Strahan and T. Cadell, London, 1776.
4. F W Taylor, *The principles of scientific management*, Harper & Brothers, 1911.
5. B D Rosso, K H Dekas & A Wrzesniewski, 'On the meaning of work: A theoretical integration and review', *ScienceDirect*, 2010.
6. D Kelley, 'A Philosophy for the 21st Century', www.atlassociety.org/post/a-philosophy-for-the-21st-century, April 5, 2011.
7. E Seppala and K Cameron, 'Proof that positive work environments are more productive', *Harvard Business Review*, December 1, 2015.
8. K Gibran, *The prophet*, United States: Alfred A. Knopf, 1923.
9. ibid.

How work shapes us

1. B Schwartz, *Why we work*, London, United Kingdom: Simon & Schuster Ltd, 2015.
2. D Frieze, 'How I became a localist', TEDx Talks, Jamaica Plain.
3. H D Thoreau, *Walden: Or, life in the woods*, New York, United States: Dover Publications Inc., 1995.
4. C Taylor, *Walking the talk: Building a culture for success*, London, United Kingdom: Cornerstone, 2015.
5. M Hechter & K-D Opp, *Social Norms*, Russell Sage Foundation.
6. C Taylor, *Walking the talk: Building a culture for success*, London, United Kingdom: Cornerstone, 2015.
7. C Sanford, 'Language as clue – Part 1, The effect of paradigms on creating systemic change in business', www.medium.com, July 6, 2019.

8. B Schwartz, *Why we work*, London, United Kingdom: Simon & Schuster Ltd, 2015.
9. C Sanford & B Haggard, 'The regenerative economic shaper perspective paper –Part 3, A framework for architecting the next economy', www.medium.com, June 11.
10. D Frieze, 'How I became a localist', TEDx Talks, Jamaica Plain.
11. C Sanford & B Haggard, 'The regenerative economic shaper perspective paper –Part 3, A framework for architecting the next economy', www.medium.com, June 11.
12. O Scharmer & K Kaufer, *Leading from the Emerging Future: From ego-system to eco-system economies*, San Francisco, United States: Berrett-Koehler, 2013.
13. T Duggan, *Cult status*, Seaforth, NSW, Australia: Pantera Press, 2020.
14. A Keys, *More myself: A journey*, London, United Kingdom: Pan MacMillan, 2020.
15. L P Frankel, *Nice girls don't get the corner office: Unconscious mistakes women make that sabotage their careers*, Little, Brown & Company, 2014.
16. M Buckingham, *Nine lies about work, A freethinking leader's guide to the real world*, United States: Harvard Business Review Press, 2020.
17. J Hatmaker, *Fierce, free, and full of fire: The guide to being glorious you*, Grand Haven, United States: Brilliance Corporation, 2020.
18. M Oliver, The best liberal quotes ever, William P. Martin, 2004.

Growing our inner resources

1. M Angelou, www.goodreads.com/quotes/11877-my-mission-in-life-is-not-merely-to-survive-but
2. R Hanson, *Hardwiring happiness: How to reshape your brain and your life*, London, United Kingdom: Ebury Publishing, 2015.
3. ibid.

Transforming our mindset

1. C Sanford, *The regenerative life: Transform any organization, our society, and your destiny*, United Kingdom: John Murray Press, 2020.
2. S R Cook-Greuter, 'Making the case for a developmental perspective', *Industrial and Commercial Training*, vol. 36, no. 7, Emerald Group Publishing Limited, 2004.

3. C Dweck, (Dr), *Mindset: Changing the way you think to fulfil your potential*, London, United Kingdom: Little, Brown Book Group, 2012.
4. A Buchanan, *Benefit Mindset Schools Guide*, Melbourne: Cohere, 2020.
5. ibid.

Embracing paradox

1. D Whyte, 'The conversational nature of reality', *On being with Krista Tippett*, 2016.
2. G Norris, 'Paradox of noise', www.awakin.org, May 24, 2011.
3. ibid.
4. A Schweitzer, (prof), *The philosophy of civilization: Part 1, the decay and the restoration of civilization; Part 2, civilization and ethics*, Whitefish MT, United States: Kessinger Publishing, 2010.
5. H Lerner, *The dance of anger: A woman's guide to changing the patterns of intimate relationships*, New York: William Morrow & Company, 2014.
6. B Brown, *The gifts of imperfection*, Center City, United States: Hazelden Information & Educational Services, 2010.
7. I Claremont De Castillejo, quoted in *The heart aroused*, David Whyte.

Why self-fidelity matters

1. T Brach, *Radical compassion: Learning to love yourself and your world with the practice of RAIN*, London, United Kingdom: Ebury Publishing, 2020.
2. S Turkel, *Working: People talk about what they do all day and how they feel about what they do*, New York: The New Press, 1997.
3. B Wigert, Ph.D. & J Harter, Ph.D., 'Re-engineering performance management', Gallup, 2017.
4. 'State of the global workplace report', Gallup, 2017.
5. B Wigert, Ph.D. & J Harter, Ph.D., 'Re-engineering performance management', Gallup, 2017.
6. 'Employee burnout: causes and cures', Gallup, 2020.
7. M J Wheatley, *So far from home: Lost and found in our brave new world*, San Francisco, United States: Berrett-Koehler, 2012.
8. Y N Harari, *21 Lessons for the 21st century*, London, United Kingdom: Vintage Publishing, 2019.

9. A Edmans, 'The link between job satisfaction and firm value, with implications for corporate social responsibility, 2012.
10. P Faison Hewlin, Ph.D, 'How To Be More Authentic At Work', *Greater Good Magazine*, Greater Good Science Center, UC Berkeley, 2020.
11. W Harman, 'Why a world business academy?' World Business Academy website, originally published 1987.
12. J Houston, *A passion for the possible*, San Francisco, United States: HarperCollins Publishers Inc, 1999.
13. P Coelho, www.paulocoelhoblog.com
14. H Lerner, *The dance of anger: A woman's guide to changing the patterns of intimate relationships*, New York: William Morrow & Company, 2014.
15. S Godin, *Linchpin: Are you indispensable? How to drive your career and create a remarkable future*, London, United Kingdom: Little, Brown Book Group, 2018.

From understanding to uplift

1. J Clear, *Atomic habits*, London, United Kingdom: Random House Business Books, 2018.
2. D Whyte, 'Sometimes', *Everything Is Waiting for You*, Many Rivers Press, 2003.
3. ibid.
4. A Lushwala, *Who You Are*, Vimeo, Pachamama Alliance, 2019.
5. J Clear, *Atomic habits*, London, United Kingdom: Random House Business Books, 2018.
6. J Hreha, 'Why our conscious minds are suckers for novelty', www.thebehavioralscientist.com
7. J Clear, *Atomic habits, London, United Kingdom: Random House Business Books*, 2018.
8. ibid.
9. K McGonigal, *The willpower instinct: How self-control works, why it matters, and what you can do to get more of it*, Wayne, United States: Avery Publishing Group, 2013.
10. Y N Harari, *21 Lessons for the 21st century, London*, United Kingdom: Vintage Publishing, 2019.
11. ibid.
12. P Chodron, www.goodreads.com/quotes/506874-you-are-the-sky-everything-else-it-s-just-the

13. R Hanson, *Hardwiring happiness: How to reshape your brain and your life*, London, United Kingdom: Ebury Publishing, 2015.
14. ibid.
15. T Brach, *Radical compassion: Learning to love yourself and your world with the practice of RAIN*, London, United Kingdom: Ebury Publishing, 2020.
16. Thich Nhat Hanh, *Stepping into Freedom*, Berkeley, United States, Parallax Press, 2001.
17. J Nestor, *Breath: The new science of a lost art*, Penguin Books Ltd, 2020.
18. Bhante Henepola Gunaratana, 'Breathing', *On practice*, 1995.
19. J Nestor, *Breath: The new science of a lost art*, Penguin Books Ltd, 2020.
20. C André, 'Proper breathing brings better health, *Scientific American*,2019.
21. C O Scharmer, *Theory U: Leading from the future as it emerges*, Berrett-Koehler, 2016.
22. Thich Nhat Hanh, *Heart of the Buddha's teaching*, Berkeley, United States: Parallax Press, 1999.
23. C Logue, www.goodreads.com/quotes/580799-come-to-the-edge-he-said-we-are-afraid-they

WAKING UP

1. Z Salbi, *Freedom is an inside job: Owning our darkness and our light to heal ourselves and the world*, Sounds True Inc, 2018.

Being present

1. S Harris, *Waking up: Searching for spirituality without religion*, Transworld Publishers Ltd, 2015.
2. C Jung, www.goodreads.com/quotes/44379-until-you-make-the-unconscious-conscious-it-will-direct-your
3. T Brach, *Radical compassion: Learning to love yourself and your world with the practice of RAIN*, London, United Kingdom: Ebury Publishing, 2020.
4. P Chodron, *Living beautifully: With uncertainty and change*, Boston, United States: 2019.
5. G Doyle, *Untamed: Stop pleasing, start living*, London, United Kingdom: Ebury Publishing, 2020.

6. J Hari, *Lost connections: Why you're depressed and how to find hope*, London, United Kingdom: Bloomsbury Publishing PLC, 2019.
7. R Hanson, (Dr), 'Key points of awareness – Part I', www.dev.rickhanson.net/key-points-awareness-part/
8. Ram Dass's Mindfulness Meditation, Insight Timer, www.insighttimer.com/ramdass/guided-meditations/mindfulness-meditation-6
9. R Harris, *The happiness trap: Stop struggling, start living*, London, United Kingdom: Little, Brown Book Group, 2008.
10. ibid.
11. S Tsabary, (Dr), Oprah's SuperSoul Conversations Podcast, 'Dr. Shefali Tsabary: The awakened life', 2019.
12. V Frankl, *Man's search for meaning: The classic tribute to hope from the Holocaust*, London, United Kingdom, Ebury Publishing, 2008.
13. ibid.
14. C. Otto Scharmer & Katrin Kaufer, *Leading from the emerging future: From ego-system to eco-system economies*, San Francisco, United States: Berrett-Koehler, 2013.
15. J Kabat-Zinn & O Winfrey, *The path made clear: Discovering your life's direction and purpose*, London, United Kingdom: Pan MacMillan, 2019.
16. F Ostaseski, *The five invitations*, New York: Flatiron Books, 2019.
17. N Armstrong, www.goodreads.com/quotes/82469-it-suddenly-struck-me-that-that-tiny-pea-pretty-and
18. M Michalewicz, *Life in half a second*, United Kingdom: Credibility Corporation Pty Ltd, 2013.
19. S Jobs, Steve Jobs' 2005 Stanford Commencement Address, YouTube
20. T Henry, *Die empty – Unleash your best work every day*, New York, United States: Penguin Putnam Inc, 2015.
21. ibid.
22. S Pressfield, *The war of art: Break through the blocks and win your inner creative battles*, New York, United States: Black Irish Entertainment LLC, 2012.
23. M Oliver, 'The summer day', *House of light*, Beacon Press, 2018.

Attachments

1. Celtic Prayer of Approach, quoted by G Doyle in *Untamed: Stop pleasing, start living*, London, United Kingdom: Ebury Publishing, 2020.

2. A Lamott, *Crooked little heart*, New York, United States: Bantam Doubleday Dell Publishing Group Inc, 1999.

Beliefs

1. B H Lipton, *The biology of belief*, London, United Kingdom: Hay House UK Ltd, 2015.
2. Rumi, *A community of the spirit Rumi: The big red book: The great masterpiece celebrating mystical love and friendship*, New York, United States: HarperCollins Publishers Inc, 2011.
3. E Langer, (prof), 'Ellen Langer: Science of mindlessness and mindfulness', *On Being with Krista Tippett*, 2016.
4. J Hari, *Lost connections: Why you're depressed and how to find hope*, London, United Kingdom: Bloomsbury Publishing PLC, 2019.
5. ibid.
6. ibid.
7. ibid.
8. O Winfrey, *The path made clear: Discovering your life's direction and purpose*, London, United Kingdom: Pan MacMillan, 2019.
9. M Gladwell, *Blink: The power of thinking without thinking*, London, United Kingdom, Penguin Books Ltd, 2006.

The voices in our heads

1. D Harris, *10% Happier: How I tamed the voice in my head, reduced stress without losing my edge, and found self-help that actually works – A true story*, London, United Kingdom: Hodder & Stoughton, 2017.
2. M A Singer, *The untethered soul: The journey beyond yourself*, Oakland, CA, United States: New Harbinger Publications, 2007.
3. M C Hammer, 'You can't touch this', cowritten, produced and performed by MC Hammer, *Please Hammer, Don't Hurt 'Em*, 1990.
4. E Tolle, www.thework.com/

Connecting to our essential nature

1. A Nin, *The Diary of Anais Nin 1931–1934*, United Kingdom, Mariner Books, 1977.
2. K Patel, Spacious, www.wisdominwaves.com

LETTING BE

1. R W Emerson, www.goodreads.com/quotes/876-to-be-yourself-in-a-world-that-is-constantly-trying

Being worthy

1. W Dyer, 'Words With Wayne Dyer', Interview with Karl Saliter, www.elephantjournal.com, May 4, 2014.
2. M Williamson, *A return to love*, New York, United States: HarperCollins Publishers Inc, 2011.
3. M Dooley, *The complete notes from the Universe*, Hillsboro, Oregon, United States Beyond Words Publishing, 2020.
4. C G Jung, *The undiscovered self*, New York, United States: Penguin Putnam Inc, 2007.
5. D Ford, *The dark side of the light chasers*, London, United Kingdom: Hodder & Stoughton, 2001.
6. L Messenger, *Daring & disruptive: Unleashing the entrepreneur*, The Messenger Group, 2015.
7. R Powell, *Wabi sabi simple: Create beauty, value imperfection, live deeply*, Holbrook, MA, United States: Adams Media Corporation, 2004.
8. L Cohen, 'Anthem' lyrics, Sony/ATV Music Publishing LLC.
9. T Real, www.terryreal.com, quoted in Esther Perel's blog, 'Letters from Esther, the myth of self-love, www.estherperel.com/blog/letters-from-esther-8

Being vulnerable

1. T Turner, *Belonging – Remembering ourselves home*, Her Own Room Press, 2017.
2. D Whtye, *Consolations: The solace, nourishment and underlying meaning of everyday words*, Many Rivers Press, 2015.
3. B Brown, *Daring greatly*, London, United Kingdom: Penguin Books Ltd, 2016.
4. M Angelou, Senior Convocation Address, Schoellkopf Stadium, 2008.
5. C Jung, www.goodreads.com/quotes/347602-shame-is-a-soul-eating-emotion
6. B Brown, *The gifts of imperfection*, Center City, United States: Hazelden Information & Educational Services, 2010.
7. Z Salbi, *Freedom is an inside job: Owning our darkness and our light to heal ourselves and the world*, Sounds True Inc, 2018.
8. B Brown, *The gifts of imperfection*, Center City, United States: Hazelden Information & Educational Services, 2010.

9. M L Slepian, N P Camp & E J Masicampo, 'Exploring the secrecy burden: Secrets, preoccupation, and perceptual judgments', *Journal of Experimental Psychology*, 2015.
10. M L Slepian, 'Why the secrets you keep are hurting you', *Scientific American*, February 5, 2019, www.scientificamerican.com/article/why-the-secrets-you-keep-are-hurting-you/
11. Z Salbi, *Freedom is an inside job: Owning our darkness and our light to heal ourselves and the world*, Sounds True Inc, 2018.
12. H Stone (PhD) & S Stone (PhD), *Embracing your inner critic*, HarperCollins Publishers Inc, 2011.
13. S Elworthy, 2020, www.spiritual-wildfire-summit.com/scilla-elworthy
14. E Gilbert, *Big magic: How to live a creative life, and let go of your fear*, London, United Kingdom: Bloomsbury Publishing PLC, 2016.
15. B Brown, *I thought it was just me (But it isn't)*, New York, United States: Gotham Books, 2008.
16. C Chanel, www.goodreads.com/quotes/75485-the-most-courageous-act-is-still-to-think-for-yourself

Being caring

1. Brother D Steindl-Rast, quoted in *Crossing the unknown sea: Work as a pilgrimage of identity*, D Whyte, United States, Penguin Putnam Inc, Riverhead Books, 2002.
2. R Goffee and G Jones, 'Why would anyone be led by you?' Harvard Business School, 2000.
3. 'Leading with inner agility', *McKinsey Quarterly*, McKinsey & Co, March 29 2018.
4. P Drucker, www.goodreads.com/quotes/375321-your-first-and-foremost-job-as-a-leader-is-to
5. F Frei, Harvard Business School Professor, quoted by S Sandberg, 'Fortune favors the bold', *Time Magazine*, 2015.
6. B Brown, *Dare to lead*, London, United Kingdom, Ebury Publishing, 2018.
7. 'Wangari Maathai: Marching with trees', *On Being with Krista Tippett*, 2019.
8. M Wheatley, *Who do we choose to be?'* Oakland, United States: Berrett-Koehler Publishers, 2017.
9. ibid.
10. ibid.

11. A Huffington, *Thrive: The third metric to redefining success and creating a happier life*, London, United Kingdom, Ebury Publishing, 2015.
12. V H Murthy, *Together: Loneliness, health and what happens when we find connection*, London, United Kingdom: Profile Books Ltd, 2020.
13. H Lerner, *The dance of anger: A woman's guide to changing the patterns of intimate relationships*, New York: William Morrow & Company, 2014.
14. ibid.
15. ibid.
16. D Keltner, *Born to be good: The science of a meaningful life*, New York, United States: WW Norton & Co, 2009.
17. K Neff, *Self compassion*, London, United Kingdom: Hodder & Stoughton, 2011.

Being creative

1. D Kelley & T Kelley, *Creative Confidence: Unleashing the creative potential within us all*, London, United Kingdom: HarperCollins Publishers, 2015.
2. ibid.
3. R J Sternberg, *Wisdom, intelligence, and creativity synthesized*, Cambridge University Press, 2003.
4. D Kelley & T Kelley, *Creative Confidence: Unleashing the creative potential within us all*, London, United Kingdom: HarperCollins Publishers, 2015.
5. ibid.
6. S Godin, 'Out on a limb', www.seths.blog/2013/01/out-on-a-limb/ January 5, 2013.
7. TEDxTucson, G Land, 'The failure of success, Adobe State of Create Survey, 2016, www.blogs.adobe.com/creative/adobe-max-unlocks-creative-potential/
8. Adobe State of Create Survey, 2016, www.adobe.com
9. V Van Gogh, www.goodreads.com/quotes/33575-if-you-hear-a-voice-within-you-say-you-cannot
10. B Marley, 'Zion Train', Uprising, Bob Marley & The Wailers album.
11. W E Henley, *Invictus, A book of verses*, Read Books, 2014.
12. O Wilde, www.goodreads.com/quotes/314567-in-your-soul-are-infinitely-precious-things-that-cannot-be
13. D Whyte, *The heart aroused*, New York, United States: Bantam Doubleday Dell Publishing Group Inc, 1998.

Being playful

1. S Brown, (Dr), *Play: How it shapes the brain, opens the imagination and invigorates the soul*, New York: United States: Penguin Putnam Inc, 2010.
2. B Sutton-Smith, as quoted in *Psychology Today*, 'What's the opposite of play?', April 05, 2016, www.psychologytoday.com/au/blog/conceptual-revolution/201604/what-s-the-opposite-play
3. S Brown, (Dr), *Play: How it shapes the brain, opens the imagination and invigorates the soul*, New York: United States: Penguin Putnam Inc, 2010.
4. ibid.
5. E Goodenough, *Secret spaces of childhood*, Ann Arbor, United States: The University of Michigan Press, 2003.
6. G Roth, www.greatthoughtstreasury.com/author/gabrielle-roth
7. www.goodreads.com/quotes/2846-and-the-day-came-when-the-risk-to-remain-tight

LETTING GO

1. Shantanand Saraswati, *Good Company*, London, United Kingdom, The Society for the Study of Normal Psychology, 2004.

I am not enough

1. M Angelou, www.goodreads.com/quotes/120991-you-alone-are-enough-you-have-nothing-to-prove-to

I can't handle this

1. G Addair, www.goodreads.com/quotes/1216350-everything-you-ve-ever-wanted-is-on-the-other-side-of

I need to shield my heart

1. P Chodron, *When things fall apart: Heart advice for difficult times*, Boston, United States: Shambhala Publications Inc, 2016.

Work is the opposite of play

1. D Keaton, 'You pay for privilege: Why Diane Keaton's enviable life has come at some cost', *The Sydney Morning Herald*, Sunday Life, August 8, 2020.

Self-care is selfish

1. Buddha, as quoted in J Kornfield, *Buddha's little instruction book*, New York, United States: Bantam Doubleday Dell Publishing Group Inc, 1994.
2. A Huffington, *Thrive: The third metric to redefining success and creating a happier life*, London, United Kingdom, Ebury Publishing, 2015.
3. The School of Life, *The Sorrows of Work*, United Kingdom: The School of Life Press, 2019.

I don't have enough time

1. T Ferriss, *Tools of Titans*, London, United Kingdom: Ebury Publishing, 2016.
2. www.barrettstudio.com/project/sanctuary-of-humanity www.facebook.com/saltmonument
3. S R Covey, *The 7 habits of highly effective people: Powerful lessons in personal change*, New York, United States: Simon & Schuster, 2013.
4. G Mark, D Gudith & U Klocke, *The cost of interrupted work: More speed and stress*, University of California, Irvine, www.ics.uci.edu
5. J Stanley, 'Why that smart watch is not such a clever idea, especially during COVID-19', *Sydney Morning Herald*, April 18, 2020.

I have to go it alone

1. Statement from The Elders, of the Hopi Nation, Arizona, June 8, 2000.
2. ibid.
3. ibid.
4. T Paulus, *Hope for the flowers*, Mahwah, United States: Paulist Press International, 1986.
5. ibid.
6. S Rose, 'She let go', www.safire-rose.com/books-and-media/poetry/she-let-go

LETTING IN

1. B McNamara, Reunion, www.brookemcnamara.com/reunion/

Feelings

1. J Bolte Taylor, *My stroke of insight*, London, United Kingdom: Hodder & Stoughton, 2009.
2. Y N Harari, *21 Lessons for the 21st century, London*, United Kingdom: Vintage Publishing, 2019.

3. P Chodron, *Living beautifully: With uncertainty and change*, Boston, United States: 2019.
4. B Gorman, 'Change leadership: Why your head, heart and gut are critical to listen to', *Forbes*, Mar 4, 2019.
5. www.heartmath.com/
6. E Tolle, *The Power of now*, Novato, CA, United States: New World Library, 2004.
7. M Brackett, *Permission to feel*, London, United Kingdom: Quercus Publishing, 2019.
8. J Bolte Taylor, *My stroke of insight*, London, United Kingdom: Hodder & Stoughton, 2009.
9. H Lerner, *The dance of anger: A woman's guide to changing the patterns of intimate relationships*, New York: William Morrow & Company, 2014.
10. P Chodron, *Living beautifully: With uncertainty and change*, Boston, United States: 2019.
11. B Brown, *Rising strong, London*, United Kingdom: Ebury Publishing, 2015.
12. K Gibran, 'On joy and sorrow', Academy of American Poets, Poem-a-Day on February 10, 2019.
13. News.com.au, Hello Sunday Morning report, 'Rise in Australians drinking 'every day'', July 22, 2020.
14. G Doyle, *Untamed: Stop pleasing, start living*, London, United Kingdom: Ebury Publishing, 2020.
15. C Newport, *Digital minimalism: Choosing a focused life in a noisy world*, London, United Kingdom: Penguin Books Ltd, 2019.
16. A Huffington, *Thrive: The third metric to redefining success and creating a happier life*, London, United Kingdom: Ebury Publishing, 2015.

Vitality

1. M Graham, www.goodreads.com/quotes/13539-there-is-a-vitality-a-life-force-an-energy-a
2. Gallup, 'Why we need best friends at work', 2018.
3. M Popova, 'Reclaiming friendship: A visual taxonomy of platonic relationships to counter the commodification of the word "friend"', www.brainpickings.org/2016/08/16/friendship/
4. B Proctor, www.goodreads.com/quotes/4473069-a-mentor-is-someone-who-sees-more-talent-and-ability

5. T Brach, 'Radical compassion (Part 3): The awakening & realization of belonging', Insight Timer Blog, wwwinsighttimer.com/blog/radical-compassion-sense-of-belonging/
6. H Lerner, *Why won't you apologize?: Healing big betrayals and everyday hurts*, United Kingdom: Prelude, 2018.

Linking

1. E A Aron, *The undervalued self,* New York, United States: Little Brown and Company, 2010.
2. ibid.
3. S David, Emotional agility blog, 'The social comparison trap', July 15th 2020.
4. S Sinek, *Together is better: A little book of inspiration,* London, United Kingdom: Penguin Books Ltd, 2018.
5. E A Aron, *The undervalued self,* New York, United States: Little Brown and Company, 2010.

Values

1. Dalai Lama XIV, www.goodreads.com/quotes/209035-open-your-arms-to-change-but-don-t-let-go-of
2. P Faison Hewlin, (Ph.D) 'How to be more authentic at work', *Greater Good Magazine*, Greater Good Science Center, UC Berkeley, 2020.
3. J DeMartini, *Values factor: The secret to creating an inspired and fulfilling life*, New York, United States, Penguin Putnam Inc, 2013.
4. B Brown, *Dare to lead: Brave work. Tough conversations. Whole hearts,* London, United Kingdom: Ebury Publishing, 2018.
5. J Hari, *Lost connections: Why you're depressed and how to find hope*, London, United Kingdom, Bloomsbury Publishing PLC, 2019.
6. ibid.
7. ibid.

Aspirations

1. S Monk Kidd, *The book of longings,* LCC, United States: Penguin, 2020.
2. ibid.

Love

1. S Blondin, Live Awake Podcast, 'Feeding the heart and caring for goodness', 9 April 2020.

2. Maya Angelou, www.goodreads.com/quotes/126888-love-recognizes-no-barriers-it-jumps-hurdles-leaps-fences-penetrates
3. B L Fredrickson, *Love 2.0: How our supreme emotion affects everything we feel, think, do, and become*, New York, United States: J P Tarcher, US/Perigee Bks., US., 2014.
4. ibid.
5. W Dyer, (Dr), *Being in balance*, London, United Kingdom: Hay House, UK Ltd, 2016.
6. ibid.
7. S Salzberg, R Hanson, (Dr), Being well podcast, S3:EP111, 'Real change with Sharon Salzberg'.
8. T Turner, *Belonging – Remembering ourselves home*, Her Own Room Press, 2017.
9. R Hanson, *Resilient: 12 Tools for transforming everyday experiences into lasting happiness* London, United Kingdom: Ebury Publishing, 2018.

Intuition

1. A Einstein, www.goodreads.com/quotes/7606666-intuition-not-intellect-is-the-open-sesame-of-yourself
2. P Yogananda, *Autobiography of a Yogi book*, Los Angeles, United States: Self-Realization Fellowship, US., 2004.
3. W Isaacson, *Steve Jobs*, New York, United States: Simon & Schuster, 2011.
4. M Seligman & Kahana, 'Unpacking intuition', *Perspectives on Psychological Science*, July 1, 2009.
5. ibid.
6. M Gladwell, *Blink: The power of thinking without thinking*, London, United Kingdom: Penguin Books Ltd, 2006.
7. A Huffington, *Thrive: The third metric to redefining success and creating a happier life*, London, United Kingdom: Ebury Publishing, 2015.
8. J Houston, *A passion for the possible*, San Francisco, United States: HarperCollins Publishers Inc 1999.
9. B McNamara, *Feed your vow, thirteen poems to amplify presence & aliveness* www.brookemcnamara.com/

REMEMBERING

1. R F Kennedy, 'Ripple of Hope' speech, University of Cape Town, 1966.

Activating our particular type of genius

1. J Houston, A *passion for the possible*, San Francisco, United States: HarperCollins Publishers Inc 1999.
2. K Karlsson, *Your dream life starts here: Essential and simple steps to creating the life of your dreams*, kikki.K, Australia, 2019.
3. Oriah, *The invitation*, New York, United States: HarperCollins Publishers Inc, 2006.
4. D Whtye, *Consolations: The solace, nourishment and underlying meaning of everyday words*, Many Rivers Press, 2015.